M000189160

Publisher's Notice: **London office telephone access code change***
For the avoidance of error, Edward Harle Limited have published the updated
telephone code and number which takes effect from 22nd April 2000, in this book.
Prior to 22nd April 2000, the old Inner London code and numbers will have applied.
They are: Telephone: **+44 [0]171-222 2635**. Fax: **+44 [0]171-233 0185**.

With effect from 22nd April 2000, the code for access to Inner London telephone numbers
changed from 0171 to **020** with a **7** prefixed to the first three digits of the number.
The London number is amended to: **[020]-7222 2635**. Fax: **[020]-7233 0185**.
*Calls from **within** the United Kingdom:* Dial **[020]-7222 2635**. Fax: **[020]-7233 0185**.
*Calls from **outside** the United Kingdom:* Dial **+44 [0]20-7222 2635**. Fax: **+44 [0]20-7233 0185**.

24-hour North American/global telephone and fax order lines:
The New York telephone and fax numbers, which access the New York and London
offices simultaneously, remain unchanged. Telephone: **212-447 5111**. Fax: **212-679 1094**.

* These changes were officially confirmed on 4th March 1999, midway through production of this book.

RED COCAINE

THE DRUGGING OF AMERICA AND THE WEST

An exposé of long-term Russian
and Chinese intelligence operations aimed at
achieving the demoralisation and ultimate control
of the West through drugs, as a dimension of the
continuing Leninist World Revolution.

JOSEPH D. DOUGLASS, JR.
Introduction by Dr Ray S. Cline
Former Deputy Director for Intelligence,
Central Intelligence Agency

EDWARD HARLE
London & New York

About the Author:

Joseph D. Douglass Jr. PhD

Dr Joseph Douglass is a national security analyst and author with expertise in defence policy, threat assessment, deception, intelligence and political warfare, nuclear strategy, terrorism, advanced chemical and biological warfare agents and applications, and international narcotics trafficking. Since the mid-1980s, his primary focus has been research into various dimensions of cultural warfare and notably into the illegal drugs plague, with emphasis on its origins, support structures, marketing – and the question: 'What can be done?'

Dr Douglass received his PhD in electrical engineering from Cornell University in 1962 and has taught at Cornell, the Navy Postgraduate School at Monterey, and Johns Hopkins School of Advanced International Relations in Washington, D.C.. He has worked in and for the national laboratories (Sandia Corporation), the US Government, where he was Deputy and Acting Director, Tactical Technology Office, Advanced Research Projects Agency – and with various defence contractors, such as the Institute for Defense Analyses and System Planning Corporation. He is a former member of the Weapons Systems Evaluation Group, US Army Science Board, and a former consultant to the Arms Control and Disarmament Agency and Senate Foreign Relations Committee. He currently directs The Redwood Institute, which was formed to address the internal problems America faces – such as illegal drugs, crime and impoverished education – and to identify root causes, evaluate national policy and devise alternative policy options.

The Author has been a pioneering analyst and is perhaps best known for his groundbreaking studies of nuclear weapons policy, the impact of precision-guided munitions, the nature of the Soviet nuclear threat, the risks arising from chemical and biological warfare agents, and intelligence aspects of international narcotics trafficking.

His unclassified books include *The Theater Nuclear Offensive* [1976, reprinted ten times]; *Soviet Strategy for War in Europe* [Pergamon Press, 1980, also translated into and published in German]; *Soviet Strategy for Nuclear War* [Hoover Institute Press, 1979: numerous printings, translated into and published in Japanese]; *CBW: The Poor man's Atomic Bomb* [Institute for Foreign Policy Analysis, 1984]; *Why the Soviet Union Violates Arms Control Treaties* [Pergamon-Brassey's, 1988]; *Conventional War and Escalation* [The National Strategy Information Center, 1981]; *The Superpowers and Strategic War Termination* [co-editor, Pergamon-Brassey's, 1989]; and the present work, originally entitled: *Red Cocaine: The Drugging of America* [1990]. This new edition has been prepared with a view to meeting continuing demand for the work, in both the United States and elsewhere, following the strategic adjustment completed in 1991 when the Communist strategists switched to pursuing their manic World Revolutionary objectives through covert Communism and a 'new form' of reversible 'state-controlled capitalism' – working, as Lenin taught his 'illuminated' followers, 'by other means'. ∎

Dedicated to

**All who have lost a friend
or a loved one
to the evil scourge of drugs.**

It is high time to fight back.

Cover design: C. L. Story

RED COCAINE

This revised Second Edition published in Great Britain
and the United States in 1999 by:

Edward Harle Limited
108 Horseferry Road
Westminster
London SW1P 2EF
United Kingdom
Telephone: +44 [0]20-7222 2635
Facsimile: +44 [0]20-7233 0185

Edward Harle Limited
Suite 1209
280 Madison Avenue
New York NY 10016-0802
United States
Telephone: **212-447 5111†**
Facsimile: **212-679 1094†**

† **Orders may be phoned or faxed, as appropriate, to these New York
numbers, which access the London and New York offices simultaneously.**

Copyright © 1990, 1999 by **Dr Joseph D. Douglass, Jr.**

First published in the United States, 1990, by Clarion House, Atlanta, GA.
The present text is extensively revised and Chapter 12 is entirely new.

ISBN 1-899798-04-8

Library of Congress Catalog Card Number 90-82064

All rights reserved. No part of this publication may be reproduced
or transmitted in any form or by any means, electronic or mechanical, including
photocopying, recording, or any information storage and retrieval system, without either prior permission in writing from the publishers or a licence permitting
restricted copying. In the United Kingdom such licences are issued by the
Copyright Licensing Agency, 90 Tottenham Court Road, London W1P 9HE.
Brief quotations in reviews or articles are hereby permitted.

The right of Dr Joseph D. Douglass Jr. to be identified as the Author
of this work has been asserted by him in accordance with the
United Kingdom Copyright, Designs and Patents Act 1988.

British Library Cataloguing in Publication Data.
A catalogue record for this book is available
from the British Library.

Also published by **Edward Harle Limited**
and available from the above addresses:

'The Perestroika Deception': The World's Slide towards
The 'Second October Revolution' [*'Weltoktober'*] **ISBN-899798-03-X**
By **Anatoliy Golitsyn**, the famous genuine Soviet defector and Author
of the equally prophetic work *'New Lies for Old'* [1984].

DESIGNED BY CHRISTOPHER STORY FRSA
Typeset in Palatino, Frutiger and Univers by:
Lithofax Limited, 108 Horseferry Road, Westminster, London SW1P 2EF, United Kingdom.
Printed in Great Britain by:
Lithofax Limited, 108 Horseferry Road, Westminster, London SW1P 2EF, United Kingdom.

CONTENTS

ACKNOWLEDGMENTS

In developing this book, I have received invaluable criticism and encouragement from numerous colleagues and friends. I would especially like to thank Ray Sleeper, Ray Raehn, John Lenczowski, Robert Wilson, Scott Miler, Marianne Hall, Dan Bagley, and George Kowals, for their encouragement and assistance. Above all, I would like to acknowledge the patience and special efforts extended by the late **General Jan Sejna** in recreating his personal experiences with Soviet and Chinese drug intelligence operations. Without his generous assistance, this book could certainly never have been written. I also wish to express my gratitude to several publications which have helped to bring parts of this material to the public's attention. The essence of the message first appeared in the *Journal of Defense and Diplomacy*; in *America the Vulnerable* and *Soviet Strategic Deception*, Lexington Books; in *Global Affairs*; and in *Washington Inquirer*.

Finally, I want to thank Ellen Levenseller and Terri Lukach for their painstaking assistance in reviewing and editing the manuscript, and James Whelan and W.W. 'Chip' Wood for their many thoughtful suggestions and help in developing the final manuscript of the original edition [1990]. The Second Edition [1999] has been reorganised, edited and prepared by Christopher Story, of Edward Harle Limited. Chapter 12 is entirely new. ∎

ABOUT EDWARD HARLE LIMITED

Edward Harle Limited was established in 1995 by **Christopher Story**, the Editor and Publisher of *Soviet Analyst*, An Intelligence Commentary, for the specific purpose of publishing (and making available over the long term) books of impeccable provenance and quality on global strategy and intelligence-related affairs, including the subversion of morality and received religion, with a special focus on the continuing revolutionary offensive against Western civilisation. The drug scourge is a product of this offensive, which is directed by intelligence services reporting to covert Communist strategists in Moscow and Peking. The first title published by Edward Harle Limited was *'The Perestroika Deception'* by **Anatoliy Golitsyn** [1995 and 1998], a work which illuminates and explains the strategy and world revolutionary objectives of the continuing collective of Leninists, for whom there has been no discontinuity since 1917, let alone since 1991. Further volumes in this series are in preparation. ∎

INTRODUCTION TO THE
SECOND EDITION

The *Communist Manual of Instructions on Psychopolitical Warfare*[1], the text of which survives in the public domain in part because it was used in underground schools such as the Eugene Debs Labor School at 113 E. Wells Street, Milwaukee, Wisconsin, in the 1930s and subsequently, contains explicit statements concerning the intended use of drugs against targeted populations for revolutionary purposes. In an address to American students attending the Lenin University prior to 1936, Lavrentii Beria, one of the most evil men ever to have lived, urged the students of 'psychopolitics'†, which Beria called 'a division of geopolitics', to study special revolutionary techniques designed 'to produce a maximum of chaos in the culture of the enemy…. **You must labour'**, he urged in his remarks, which have remained in the public domain along with the *Communist Manual* text itself, **'until we have dominion over the minds and bodies of every important person in your nation'**.

Chapter 9 of the *Communist Manual* reveals that the Freudian school had *already* been hijacked by the Leninist revolutionaries. 'Vienna', it states, 'has been carefully maintained as the home of psychopolitics, since it was the home of psychoanalysis…. our activities have long since dispersed any of the gains made by Freudian groups, a*nd have taken over these groups*'. Now consider the following advice contained in Chapter 3 of the *Communist Manual*: 'The rich, the skilled in finance, the well informed in government are particular and individual targets for the psychopolitician…. Every rich man, every statesman, every person well informed and capable in government, must have brought to his side as a trusted confidant, a psychopolitical operator'.

The best-known recent product of the diabolical 'success' of such a psychopolitician, posing as a 'healer' – a false 'psychiatrist' ill-received among professional psychiatrists in London – is the late Princess Diana, whose mind was 'turned', deconstructed and then filled with 'garbage values' in the final years of her tragic life. Her case fits precisely with this instruction from the *Manual*:

'The families of these persons ('from the top strata of society', the *Manual* explained) are often deranged from idleness… and this fact must be played upon. The normal health and wildness of a rich man's son must be twisted and perverted and… turned into criminality or insanity. This brings at once someone in "mental healing" into confidential contact with the family…. [By this means] there could be

---

†'Psychopolitics', as explained in the *Communist Manual*, is the (satanic) art and science of asserting and maintaining dominion over the thoughts and loyalties of individuals, officers, bureaus, and masses, and the effecting of the conquest of enemy nations through subversive and instrumental 'mental healing'.

placed at the side of every rich or influential man a psychopolitical operator'.

While Beria and his successors sought primarily to attack and derange influential people and policymakers in the West, as a short cut to destabilising policy 'to embroil or upset the economic policies of the [targeted] country', they also had in mind the use of drugs *as a means of degrading society generally*. Thus **'the masses' in whose name the Communists purported to agitate** were *themselves* to be the *direct* victims of a global narcotics offensive.

The *youth* of society, in particular, were to be targeted – since they would in due course assume positions of influence, with their values and loyalties corroded and 'changed' to the irreversible benefit of the revolution.

The self-evidently satanic nature of this programme should come as no surprise: after all, Marx became a satanist in his late teens[2]; Lenin is known to have attended at least one satanic event ('black mass') on the island of Capri; and Stalin (and of course the 'national' socialist, Hitler) were preoccupied almost exclusively with the agenda of the inhabitants of 'the bottomless pit' – death.

Thus the *Communist Manual* directed Lenin University students as follows:

'By making readily available drugs of various kinds, by giving the teenager alcohol, by praising his wildness, by stimulating him with sex literature and advertising to him or her practices as taught at the Sexpol[3], the psychopolitical operator can create the necessary attitude of chaos, idleness and worthlessness…. He can, from his position as an authority on the mind, advise all manner of destructive measures. [As an educationist] he can teach the lack of control of this child at home. He can instruct, in an optimum situation, the entire nation in how to handle children – and instruct them so that the children, given no control, given no real home, can run wildly about with no responsibility for their nation or themselves. The misalignment of the loyalty of youth to a [non-Communist] nation sets the proper stage for a realignment of their loyalties with Communism. **Creating a greed for drugs, sexual misbehaviour and uncontrolled freedom and presenting this to them as a benefit… will with ease bring about our realignment** [of loyalties]'.

The Sunday Telegraph, of London, published a report on 5th February 1995[4] entitled: 'The new Switzerland: junkies, prostitutes and street killings'. The author, Patricia Morgan, revealed that 'since prostitution was legalised last December [1994], brothels have thrust themselves into the limelight, advertising their wares in graphic detail. The same may be said of the 1994 Christmas stamp, a shameless travesty of the religious season, which displayed not the Virgin and Child but a phallus surrounded by stars. A motto was stamped above the design: Stop AIDS'.

A 'traumatic collision' was 'under way between the old order and a new nihilism…. After sex, **drugs**. It is discarded syringes, not snow, that lie on the ground around Zürich Kornhaus Bridge. *Scarcely anything like the Letten district drugs scene exists anywhere:* what looks like a high security prison, patrolled by guards, is in fact the local junior school. The perimeter wire keeps out the addicts and prostitutes'. Cross the bridge into Toronto from the US side of the Canadian border, and with what is the visitor greeted? The most oppressive and disgusting display that the 'entertainment' subculture has to offer anywhere in the world.

In the United Kingdom each weekend, an estimated 1.5 million young people spend Friday or Saturday night at 'raves', high on a synthetic drug called 'ecstasy' imported illegally from Holland, the mecca of permissiveness these past two decades; many deaths from this lethal concoction have been reported, and the long-term damage being inflicted is unquantified. At gymnasiums and night-clubs, a new 'designer-drug' known as 'liquid ecstasy' was being extensively marketed in early 1999, after 'test-runs' in various parts of the country and among the homosexual communities in big cities. If this substance – gammahy-droxybutyrate, or GHB – is mixed with alcohol, lethal effects can quickly follow. Following the death of 27-year-old Ian Hignett, who expired suddenly after ingesting this substance at some UK nightclub without knowing what he was taking, Detective Chief Inspector Colin Matthews, of Merseyside Police, told *The Daily Telegraph*[5] that 'people taking this liquid are dicing with death'. They are indeed, since it possesses the delightful characteristic of being liable to depress the central nervous system.

Does the worthy Merseyside Detective Chief Inspector know that this evil substance is almost certainly a byproduct of the continuing Soviet/ Russian chemical and biological weapons programme? If not, why has MI5/MI6 not advised him of this strong probability?

Will the intelligence contained in *Red Cocaine* come as 'news' to those, such as the admirable Colin Matthews, who labour conscientiously at the 'sharp end' of the drug scourge, and see its devastating consequences for British youth at first hand, in the course of going about their duties?

Why has Western civilisation been degraded since the 1960s, and *who is behind this phenomenon?* The answer, in brief, is that the West has been the unknowing victim, for the past several decades, of long-term Soviet-Chinese strategic intelligence operations using drugs as a means of procuring the progres-sive demoralisation of Western society and a concomitant degradation of the gene pool – with youth the prime target of this satanic offensive.

Communism, a form of devilish collectivist mania which, consistently with all forms of mental aberration, knows no rest – going 'round and round in circles' (hence 'revolution') – *cannot succeed on its own terms.* From the outset of Lenin's World Revolution, therefore, the Comintern sought 'special' (secret) ways of undermining society – using a methodology taught by Lenin and elaborated later by the founder of the Italian Communist Party, **Antonio Gramsci.**

Gramsci argued that 'power is best attained in developed countries through a gradual process of radicalisation of the cultural institutions – a process that would in turn transform the values and morals of the society. Gramsci believed that as society's morals were softened, so its political and economic foundation would be more easily smashed and reconstructed. [Hence it was necessary] to infiltrate autonomous institutions – schools, media, churches, public interest groups – so as to transform the culture, which determines the environment for political and econ-omic policies'[6].

Red Cocaine, which definitively eliminates all doubt that the global drugs scourge has been hijacked, developed and co-opted by foreign intelligence opera-

tives and has become a primary dimension of the continuing Leninist World Revolution, is a classic work which the Establishment in the United States preferred
to ignore. Self-evidently, its message is applicable not just in the United States, but
also throughout the West, where governments are grappling, largely blindly, with
a phenomenon whose origins they do not understand.

Red Cocaine confirms that Lavrentii Beria's determination that narcotics
should be deployed in the interests of the Revolution, has been consummated
since his liquidation at the hands of his satanic masters. It further confirms that
the use of drugs to degrade targeted Western societies is an integral component
of what can be called 'the Gramsci dimension' of the continuing World Revolution which has engulfed the West. Interestingly, contemporary revolutionaries
carefully omit this fact from their open discussions of 'the Gramsci dimension' –
suggesting that they may fear **exposure** of this diabolical element of their
demented activities. For instance, in a 1996 summary of the progress made in
winning 'the Gramscian war of position', which he fervently supported, Michael
Walzer[7] listed as 'positive gains' of the contemporary revolution virtually everything *except* the debilitating drugs epidemic: the legalisation of abortion; the
extension of environmental, safety and public health regulations; the destruction
('transformation') of family life; the acceptance of cultural pluralism; gay rights
politics; affirmative action; feminism; wholesale secularisation and infiltration of
the churches; and the colossally wasteful escalation of public expenditure on welfare provision (needed to address, in part, the consequences of the narcotics offensive waged covertly by the revolutionaries against society). How curious that the
global drugs plague released in order to poison our children was *omitted* from that
perverse list of the continuing World Revolution's hidden 'achievements'.

The appearance of this revised and updated edition of Dr Douglass's classic
work happened to coincide with that of a learned book on the same subject, in
which it is stated that 'corruption has been rampant in Russia and Eastern European countries since the collapse of the Soviet Union, making them easy marks
for the marketing and money-laundering activities of the drug syndicates'[8].

This statement alone contains *three* diversionary themes. *First*, it implies that
the 'drug syndicates' are 'stand-alone' phenomena, from which it would easily
follow (as is intended) that their primary motivation is the familiar one of greed.
Dr Douglass shows conclusively in Red Cocaine that this is the very opposite of the
truth – the primary motivation being strategic (demoralisation). *Secondly*, it is
implied that drugs are a **new** experience for the 'former' USSR. But in the 'former' Soviet Bloc, as today (under 'covert Communism'), *all* activities were and
are 'licensed': for instance, the (fake) 'political parties' in Russia are splintered
from the Communist Party and are supervised and controlled by it to this day[9].
The 'mafia' exists and operates *by licence of the intelligence services*, serving their
agenda of 'criminalism' (the exploitation of organised crime *in the interests of strategy*). Under MVD General Eduard Shevardnadze's Georgian S.S.R., drugs were
employed strategically for social and political engineering purposes [10].

Thirdly, the statement obliterates the reality – which is that **Soviet/Russian
and Chinese intelligence are the primary *originators* of the drugs offensive,**

since the criminalist agenda is of the *essence* of the World Revolution in its current advanced phase. Indeed, **THE FUTURE IS GLOBAL CRIMINALITY**, as Dr Douglass explains in Chapter 12. Or *it will be*, if Western policymakers remain asleep for a further decade, while the remaining Western institutions are irretrievably corrupted – as an alarmingly sizeable proportion of the international banking community has been already. Indeed, *Red Cocaine* reveals that, *from the outset* (in the 1960s), elements of the Western banking community collaborated with the Soviets and Czechs to perfect secret arrangements for laundering the proceeds of the Soviet drug offensive against the West.

Studies of the drugs scourge (however learned and well-meaning) which sidestep, obfuscate or ignore the facts revealed in *Red Cocaine* – the original edition of which, after all, has been in the public domain for a decade – add to the confusion surrounding this issue. They also do the work of the offensive intelligence organisations' disinformation apparatus, which is preoccupied with ensuring that attention remains permanently diverted away from the true 'seat of the fire'.

Unfortunately, because the West's response to this low-level warfare has been ineffective to date, the international banking system has been severely compromised, so that the corruption of the banks makes it difficult to find an adequate response. Even so, the message of *Red Cocaine* remains as relevant today as a decade ago – so that it has become more irresponsible and amoral than ever, to leave one's head buried in the sand.

In his work *'What is to be Done?'*, Lenin answered his own question by prescribing the global revolution which has engulfed the world – and which proceeds towards its objective of World Control while, as his lieutenant Dimitri Manuilski predicted, 'the bourgeoisie sleeps'. Dr Douglass answers Lenin's question with the only effective response possible: **exposure**. For this is the **one** response the political perpetrators of the global drug offensive cannot stomach. ∎

CHRISTOPHER STORY, London, January 1999.

References:

1. *Communist Manual of Instructions on Psychopolitical Warfare*, with an address by Lavrentii Beria, Stalin's Interior Ministry Chief, to American students at the Lenin University, cited in *'Brainwashing, A Synthesis of the Russian Textbook on Psychopolitics'*, Kenneth Goff, a Communist who attended lectures based on the *Communist Manual* between May 2nd, 1936 and October 10th, 1939.

2. See *'Was Marx a Satanist?'* Rev. Richard Wurmbrand, Diane Books Publishing Co., Glendale, CA, 1976-77.

3. The Sexpol, a Leninist School of Sexual Politics, from which contemporary feminism and other Gramscian aberrations are derived. That feminism (a means of dividing the sexes), like the drug offensive, is an instrument of the revolution, was confirmed by the radical reformist Betty Friedan in her book *'The Second Stage'* [Summit Books, 1981], summarised by Ellen Willis in *The Nation*, USA, 14th November 1981, pages 494-495:

'Feminism is not just an issue or group of issues; **it is the cutting edge of a revolution in cultural and moral values**.... The objective result of every feminist reform, from legal abortion... to child-care programs, is **to undermine traditional family values and increase women's personal and sexual freedom**'.

4. Patricia Morgan, *The Sunday Telegraph*, 5th February 1995.

5. 'Mother's plea as son is killed by new 'party drug'. Nigel Bunyan, *The Daily Telegraph*, London, January 14, 1999, page 13.

6. Antonio Gramsci's *Selections from the Prison Notebooks*, ed. Q. Hoare and G. Nowell Smith (London, 1971), cited by Dr S. Stephen Powell, *Covert Cadre*, Green Hill Publishing, Ottawa, IL, 1987, pages 160, 359-360.

7. *What's Going On?* [cf. Lenin's *'What is To be Done?'*] by Michael Walzer, *Dissent*, Winter 1996, New York, pages 6-7.

8. *Hard Target: the United States' War Against International Drug Trafficking, 1982-1997*, Ron Chepesiuk, McFarland & Company, Inc., Jefferson, NC, 1999.

9. See Footnote, page 180, for details of the documentary basis for this statement.

10. See James A Inciardi, 'Drug Abuse in the Georgian S.S.R.', *Journal of Psycho-Active Drugs*, October-December 1987.

WHAT THEY SAID ABOUT *RED COCAINE*

• A powerful and well-documented case of a deliberate policy decision, first by the authorities in Beijing and then in Moscow, to contribute to the decay of American society…. *Red Cocaine* puts the facts on record. We ignore the message it reveals at our own peril •.
DR RAY S. CLINE , former Deputy Director for Intelligence, CIA.

• *Red Cocaine* at last blows the lid off the most explosive aspect of drug trafficking, the Soviet connection. Here is the shocking story of the drugging of America by international Communism •.
ROBIN MOORE, Author of *The French Connection.*

• This eye-opening book proves the insidious involvement of the Soviet intelligence services in the deliberate spread of the drug menace in the United States •. **CHAPMAN PINCHER**, Author of *Secret Offensive* etc.

• *Red Cocaine* is a seminal work which is essential reading for all serious students of the continuing Leninist World Revolution today (1999). A *sine qua non* for understanding why Western civilisation is under such relentless and ruthless attack is to be aware of the history of the long-term drug offensive against the West by Russian and Chinese intelligence, as a key element of the ongoing assault on the structures and institutions of society in order to 'change loyalties' irrevocably for revolutionary purposes •.
CHRISTOPHER STORY, Editor and Publisher, *Soviet Analyst*, 1999.

WHAT THEY SAID ABOUT COCAINE

• We will disarm the capitalists with the things they like to taste •.
CHOU EN-LAI , *1958*

• Deception and drugs are our first two strategic echelons in the war… •.
NIKITA KHRUSHCHEV, *1963*

• I was ordered to load up the United States with drugs •.
MARIO ESTEVEZ GONZALEZ, Cuban Intelligence agent, **1981.**

• Drugs are used as political weapons. The target was the youth… •.
ANTONIO FARACH, high-level Nicaraguan official, **1984.**

• Drugs are considered to be the best way to destroy the United States. By undermining the will of American youth, the enemy is destroyed without firing one bullet •. **MAJOR JUAN RODRIGUEZ,** Cuban intelligence officer, citing and invoking **Antonio Gramsci**, **Lavrentii Beria** and **Sun-Tzu** in a single sentence, **1988.** [Sun-Tzu: the ancient Chinese military deception strategist].

• Opium should be regarded as a powerful weapon. It has been employed by imperialists against us, and now we should use it against them •.
[*Fact:* Mao Tse-Tung deployed drugs against Chinese populations – *Ed.*].

OBSERVATIONS ON THE LATE GENERAL JAN SEJNA BY THE U.S. DEFENSE INTELLIGENCE AGENCY [DIA]

❝ … Source has provided reliable information to the US Government for over 20 years ❞. **DIA [POW/MIA]** , 18th April 1992.

❝ … Source has provided reliable information to the US intelligence community for many years …. Source did submit to a polygraph examination during which no deception was detected ❞. **LT. GENERAL CLAPPER**, Director, Defense Intelligence Agency, 27th April 1992.

❝ … has made significant contribution to Defense Intelligence [DI] products addressing various aspects of the political/military affairs of the former Soviet Union and Warsaw Pact [and] provided substantive support to allied intelligence services …. Proven track record as a Defense Intelligence Agency substantive expert… record of excellence in substantive support to Defense Intelligence ❞. **DAVE SISSON**, Senior Analyst, Defense Intelligence Agency, November 5, 1992, Inter-office letter to Alan Young.

ABOUT THE SECOND EDITION
Where the context allows, no attempt has been made to amend the dates, timeframe and thus, the tenses, used in the text. However wherever the Editor felt that the interests of clarity would be served, tenses *have* been amended. *Red Cocaine* first appeared in **1990**, and the text reflects this context. The situation is now *far worse* than described in the book, and nothing in *Red Cocaine* has become irrelevant in the intervening years. The reader will find it helpful to bear in mind, though, that there has been *no discontinuity* since the events of 1989-91, when the world imagined that the 'Cold War' had ended. Rather, the Leninist revolutionaries have been working, to cite Lenin, 'by other means'. ■

NOTE ON THE USE OF BRITISH ENGLISH
In conformity with the publisher's usual practice, spelling and the structure of sentences has been converted to British English, except of course where the context dictates otherwise. The first edition of *Red Cocaine* was written, naturally, in American English. It is the policy of Edward Harle Limited to use British English, as a general rule. In 'translation', the Author's meaning and intentions have been followed throughout. Exceptions to the use of British English forms here include the retention of the American format for dates (e.g., January 1, 2000), and of course the use of American spelling in quotations or wherever else the context so demands. There are also certain difficulties with words like 'program', for which the American usage has been retained in most contexts. ■

WARNING

This book has been known to generate strong emotional responses. *Red Cocaine* is a case study of evil: of the governments and people responsible for flooding the United States with drugs; of American public officials who have suppressed intelligence and looked the other way to favour 'special interests' and also to advance secret political agendas.

The information presented in *Red Cocaine* explains why the so-called war on drugs in the United States has been so ineffective. It challenges the erroneous belief that the drug problem is 'home-grown', the result of America's otherwise unexplained 'thirst' for drugs. This erroneous belief, carefully nurtured by politicians and drug traffickers, stands between America and the waging of an effective war on drugs for a very simple reason: a nation simply cannot wage war on its own people. This belief that *Americans themselves are the cause* is used by public officials to justify their poor results – and doing nothing about the nefarious activities of governments, politicians, intelligence services and the banks.

Red Cocaine was written to explode this belief, to expose *the real forces* behind the illegal drug trade, and to reveal the political protection that enables drug trafficking to survive and grow. Nothing has emerged since this book was published nearly a decade ago to contradict **any** of the information contained herein. On the contrary, the evidence is even more overwhelming that the analysis cannot be refuted. Indeed, it is highly significant that *no refutation has been attempted* – for the obvious reason that none is possible.

Although *Red Cocaine* primarily addresses the drugs offensive directed by Soviet and Chinese intelligence against the United States, *all* Western countries are targeted, as part of the World Revolution's relentless, manic struggle to remodel the world according to what is clearly a diabolical model. In order for the drug scourge to be addressed constructively in *any* country, the information contained in *Red Cocaine* should be absorbed first.

One purpose of republishing and updating *Red Cocaine*, therefore, is to make the work readily available to the concerned general reader, and to professionals and policy-makers not only in the United States – where demand for the book has remained intact over the years – but also in key targeted countries around the world. Furthermore, the publisher pledges that this classic book will *remain* in print – since the central mission of Edward Harle Limited is to ensure the continuing availability of works which will assist all those who have to struggle against the Leninist World Revolution being waged against us in its new, more insidious and 'invisible' manifestations. ∎

PREFACE

At dawn on July 14, 1989, Cuba's General Arnaldo Ochoa Sanchez was executed by firing squad, along with three other Cuban officers. Ochoa was one of Cuba's most popular Army officers. A recipient of the Hero of the Republic medal, his career dated back 31 years to the revolution, when he was a member of the famed Camilo Cienfuegos brigade. More recently, he had commanded the Cuban forces in Ethiopia, the Cuban advisory group in Nicaragua, and the 50,000 Cuban troops in Angola.

General Ochoa was found guilty of helping Colombia's Medellín drug cartel smuggle cocaine into the United States. His trial, which was conducted in secret, began on Sunday, June 26, 1989. The star witness was General Raúl Castro, the Minister of Defence and Fidel Castro's brother, deputy, and expected successor. Raúl Castro denounced Ochoa and called for exemplary punishment. All members of the military tribunal also denounced General Ochoa. The military prosecutor, General Juan Escalona, said in his conclusion that General Ochoa 'betrayed his people, his fatherland and Fidel... and cast a slur on the prestige and credibility of the revolution'.

The trial and sentencing were conducted with despatch. Along with Ochoa, thirteen other officers were charged. Four, including Ochoa, were sentenced to death, the rest receiving long prison terms. No one offered any defence. All of the accused pleaded guilty. At one point, as reported by the Cuban News Ministry, Ochoa answered 'No' when asked if Raúl Castro had known of his activity. But, no less than a dozen defectors from Cuban intelligence and its Ministry of Interior, which is responsible for internal security, as well as from Nicaraguan intelligence and its Ministry of Interior, diplomats from Nicaragua, and assorted drug traffickers, have stated unequivocally that both Fidel and Raúl Castro knew about Cuba's involvement in drug trafficking, approved it, and *profited* from it. Which is the true story? Was Fidel involved or not?

Luís Carlos Galan was a Colombian Presidential candidate. He was a prominent senator who had campaigned against the drug lords. It bought him a casket.

On August 18, 1989, he was shot down by assassins believed to be working for the drug cartels. His murder followed similar slayings of four other officials who were acting against the interests of the drug lords – one, two days earlier, and three only a few hours before Galan's murder. In response, President Virgilio Barco ordered the arrest of all suspects. Overnight, 11,000 people believed to have been connected to the drug cartels were arrested. None of the top drug dealers were among those apprehended, and most of those arrested were released within a day or two.

Immediately following the mass arrests announced in Bogotà, President Bush announced a $65 million military equipment-assistance program for Colombia. More was to be included in the forthcoming drug strategy program, not only for Colombia, but for other beleaguered nations such as Peru, Bolivia and Mexico. However, a former Bogotà City Council member, Clara Lopez Obregòn, raised a serious issue concerning the utility of such assistance: 'You can't enforce the law if within the law enforcement agencies you have people from the other side'.

As an indication of the scale of the problem here, when Cuba and Czechoslovakia first established drug operations in Colombia in the early 1960s, all recruited personnel were first subjected to intense background security investigations. One was performed by the Communist Party of Colombia and the other by a Communist agent who was a high official in Colombia's Ministry of Interior.

Are those in the United States who are responsible for planning military assistance for Colombia aware of such complications? How do they assess the threat in Colombia?

Following the mass arrests in Colombia, there were a series of bombings, as the government and the cartels declared war on each other. The very next week, more than 500 people were arrested for violating a curfew that had been imposed in Medellín, home of the infamous Medellín drug cartel. Among those arrested were 27 Cubans carrying forged Costa Rican passports. What were they doing there? Clearly, they could not, by any stretch of the imagination, have been tourists or businessmen.

Several defectors had previously reported strong ties between Cuba and the cartels. The principal go-between was said to be Cuban Ambassador Fernando Ravelo Renedo, who works for Manuel Pineiro Losada, head of the Cuban Communists' 'Americas Department', which has special responsibility for sabotage and subversion throughout the Western hemisphere. Pineiro was previously the head of Cuban intelligence. Cuba is also the main sponsor of Colombia's M-19 guerrilla revolutionaries and the military/terrorist arm of Colombia's Communist Party, the Revolutionary Armed Forces of Colombia (FARC), both of which are also heavily involved in narcotics production and trafficking.

In late 1985, an almost unknown form of cocaine, 'crack', was introduced to the US market – just in time for the Christmas holidays. By mid-January, it was reported in eight States; by June 1986, it had spread across the nation and had become recognised as a severe challenge.

By 1989, the use of crack had become epidemic. It is now believed to be the main cause of drug use increase in recent years, the main cause of escalating crime and violence in American cities, and the main cause of escalating child abuse, hospital emergency room overload, and babies born with addiction and learning disabilities.

The US Drug Enforcement Administration published a study on crack entitled *Crack Cocaine Overview 1989*. A similar report had been published in 1988. Both reports concluded: 'Large-scale, interstate trafficking networks controlled by Jamaicans, Haitians and Black street gangs dominate the manufacture and distribution of crack'. Their primary targets are also identified: the inner-city minorities, mainly Black people and Hispanics, although crack is also making its way into rural and suburban areas. The principal suppliers mentioned in the study are two: Cubans and Colombians. A US Justice Department study revealed, also in 1989, that women are now as likely to be hard-core drug users as men. Another study showed that AIDS cases among drug addicts were expected to surpass those among homosexuals within one or two years. The focus of the AIDS epidemic is shifting to the poor, drug-ridden urban neighbourhoods. More than 40 percent of reported AIDS cases have occurred among Black people and Hispanics, although these two groups only constitute about 20 percent of the US population. Again, the responsible drug is crack.

The speed with which crack has spread, its focused distribution, and its sales price and marketing, which is designed to capture the young and ignorant with only a few dollars to spend, all suggest a trained professional organisation. William Bennett, the director of the Office of National Drug Control Policy, referred to this phenomenon as 'an *innovation* in cocaine retailing'. Where did the crack come from? Is what we are seeing the result of a planned operation? If so, who is responsible?

In 1988, ABC-TV presented a moving account of the drug scourge entitled *'Drugs: A Plague Upon the Land'*, narrated by Peter Jennings. Jennings concluded the news special with a thought-provoking observation:

'If this is a war on drugs – and everyone from the President on down calls it that – shouldn't it be fought like a war?'
'If we could prove that the drug problem in the United States was directed by Communist power, what do you think would happen then? Wouldn't the government be mobilised? Wouldn't the best minds in the country be enlisted to plan strategy? There'd certainly be no limit to the amount of money available to fight the war. Every institution in the country would be involved. No one would say, "It doesn't affect me"[1].

Clearly, Jennings was not suggesting that there was a Communist power behind the drug trade. He was only using the example to raise an important question: namely, why was the United States not fighting a serious war on drugs? Nevertheless, in using this example, Jennings had indirectly raised what might be an even more serious question: namely, that if there *were* a Communist power behind the drug trade – the Soviet Union, for example – *who would believe it*?

My anxieties concerning the origins of drug trafficking date back to 1984, when I read an article that described the linkages between the trafficking and revolutionary terrorists in Latin America. The author described the manner in which Cuba assisted the smugglers to move drugs into the United States and, as part of the same operation, provided arms to terrorists and revolutionaries. Evidence on this activity had been collected by the US Attorney's office in Miami and had resulted in the indictment of four high-level Cuban officials by a Federal grand jury in November 1982.

But the story seemed incomplete to me. Court testimony linked the trafficking operation to Cuba's intelligence service, the *Dirección General de Inteligencía*, or DGI, and to the top Cuban leadership, Fidel and Raúl Castro.

But , I wondered, how could Cuba, and especially the DGI, be involved, if the Soviet Union were not behind the operation? The DGI had been under the direct control of Soviet intelligence since the late 1960s. Thus, it seemed extremely unlikely for a DGI operation of this significance to have been conducted without Soviet approval and direction.

As I delved more deeply into the subject, it became apparent that Cuba was not an isolated example. There was also extensive data linking the People's Republic of China to international drug trafficking. Additionally, there was evidence that Nicaragua, Bulgaria, Hungary, [the former] East Germany and North Korea were also involved in trafficking as a matter of official state policy. But, while it seemed inconceivable that these countries could be involved without the Soviet Union also being involved, I still had no direct data on Soviet involvement.

All this was to change radically one day in 1985 when I was having lunch with Jan Sejna, a former high-level Czechoslovak military-political official who had defected to the United States in 1968. General Sejna remains, to my knowledge, the highest positioned Soviet Bloc official ever to seek political asylum in the West, and the only such official who was actually a member of the decision-making hierarchy. It was during the luncheon conversation that I first asked General Sejna if he had any direct knowledge of Soviet involvement in international narcotics trafficking. For the next hour or two, he provided extensive details on Soviet narcotics trafficking operations, including their use of satellite countries, the dates of the key decisions, and most importantly, the basic Soviet strategy.

The information was alarming. Clearly, Sejna's knowledge was of extreme importance, or so I thought. I also suspected that none of the US agencies involved in fighting the drug trade was aware of this information, which turned out to be correct. It was clear to me that Sejna's knowledge was so extensive that a thorough debriefing would require a substantial effort and considerable time. I went to work soliciting support for the task. In the process, my excitement turned to dismay as I began to recognise that none of the US agencies with responsibilities in the drug war were interested in obtaining Sejna's knowledge.

In retrospect, this should have come as no surprise. I have had the unique opportunity to work with General Sejna over the past ten years. This was not the first time that I had encountered a disinterest within the US Government on subjects of strategic importance where Sejna had extensive expertise. Strategic deception; the Soviet long-range plan; Soviet political and military strategy; coordinated Soviet Bloc intelligence operations; Soviet decision making; Soviet Bloc training of international terrorists; and, Soviet Bloc intelligence penetration of organised crime, are just a few examples.

It is quite clear that the national security and policy communities do not like what Sejna has to say, and hence do not pursue his knowledge. *Why* is more difficult to explain. The problem is not credibility. Sejna's testimony has been confirmed over and over again. It is consistent with his background and with other sensitive information. Sejna is acknowledged to be an excellent source at the highest levels in the intelligence community. No, the problem is not one of evaluating and then rejecting data; it is one of not wanting to know in the first place.

In a very real sense, the problem is similar to the challenge faced by government officials when informed that an entire region in the Soviet Union was being systematically starved to death; or, that a régime with which government and business leaders were consorting had just killed 60 million of its own citizens; or, that our partner in *détente* was systematically violating each of the new arms control treaties while destabilising numerous independent governments around the globe, also in direct violation of numerous treaties, international agreements, and personal assurances. no-one wants to hear the news.

But the news is important and needs to be broadcast, because the possible consequences are so serious. How is it possible to fight an effective war on drugs if the accepted image of that war is deficient, or if the primary forces and players are not recognised? The logical answer is that it is not possible.

How then is it possible to bring about a change? This is a question which everyone who is concerned about the drug crisis is bound to consider and take seriously.

In examining the problems associated with drug trafficking, my personal concern is that the situation is far more serious than any of us realise precisely *because* of the political warfare that is being waged; the extensive Communist involvement; the deliberately planned undermining of the health of our youth and our system of values; the corruption prevalent within circles of power and influence; the breakdown in law and order (at home as well as abroad) and associated deliberate political destabilisation; the power of experimental drugs that have not yet been introduced to the marketplace; and the misguided, self-imposed policies and private interests that prevent us from understanding the true nature of what is happening. These 'missing factors' are the focus of this book. The situation is especially serious *because* of these factors, and because they are not part of the 'accepted image'. Nor is this likely to change unless and until people demand a change.

While there has been a great temptation for me to expand this study and to delve into many related and parallel dimensions of Soviet intelligence strategy directed against the United States, our friends and allies, I decided to focus strictly on the drug-trafficking dimension in order to keep the message as simple as possible. Only material believed sufficient to present a credible case focused on the Latin American-United States drug-trafficking situation is included. No attempt has been made to include complementary details on Chinese or Soviet Bloc drug-related intelligence and political influence operations in Africa, Europe, the Middle East, South Asia, Australia, the Far East, or Southeast Asia, except for operations during the Vietnam War, which is discussed in Chapter 6. However Chapter 12 is entirely new, having been completed in December 1998.

It is hoped that the material presented here, which raises serious cause for concern that the drug challenge is not as simple as many authorities would have us believe, may stimulate interest in directing the appropriate agencies to collect and assemble all pertinent data. From my perspective, this is the first step to waging an effective war on drugs: develop a thorough understanding of what is happening and *who* is involved.

Without such understanding, how can an effective counter-strategy ever be developed and implemented? And without it, how can Western civilisation be preserved? ■

JOSEPH D. DOUGLASS, JR
Falls Church, Virginia

---

1. ABC News Special, *Drugs: A Plague on the Land*, 10th April 1988, New York: Transcript produced by Journal Graphics, Inc., 1988, page 13.

INTRODUCTION

This book will come as a shock to most people. For many years, the conventional wisdom has been that the drug problem is strictly of our own making. Without our demand there would be no supply. drug-traffickers are in it only for profit. Furthermore, as a high-level State Department official assured Congress in 1985, there is no evidence of a Communist conspiracy to weaken the American social fabric by promoting the use of drugs.

Red Cocaine presents unpleasant facts contradicting these views. Dr Joseph Douglass, the author of this book, is not selling a theory but instead calling attention to evidence. He has marshalled his facts carefully, presents them responsibly and cautiously, and offers a wealth of soberly documented data. That data describes in detail the efforts of China, the Soviet Union, and its many surrogates, to use drugs over many decades as weapons designed to damage and weaken – if not destroy – the stability of Free World countries. The top target is and always has been, of course, the United States.

Nobody would suggest that the entire drug problem is the result of a Communist plot. There is some truth in the conventional wisdom about our own responsibilities. What you will find in this book, however, is a powerful and well-documented case of a deliberate policy decision, first by authorities in Beijing and then in Moscow, to contribute to the decay of American society. This case cries out for close and serious inspection, by ordinary citizens, as well as at the very highest levels of the US Government. What is history must be reckoned with in predicting the future. Americans deserve full and frank examination of just how deeply Moscow and Beijing have been involved in creating and masterminding the worldwide drug crisis.

This book offers persuasive evidence that the Communist rôle was large, very large. This book shows, with a wealth of documentation, that command and control of that worldwide drug network emanated from the very top leadership levels of the Communist dictatorships. At the very minimum, the US Government ought to provide a full accounting of *Red Cocaine's* thesis that much of today's drug scourge is the direct result of coordinated and cynical Soviet Bloc and Chinese intelligence operations around the world, especially in the Western hemisphere.

If we are serious about winning this war on drugs, we must know, too, to what extent it is true – as this book argues – that top officials in Washington have had access to this evidence for many years, but preferred to hush it up out of concern for what public disclosure would do to US-Sino-Soviet relations.

Clearly, the war on drugs cannot be won unless we know how and where the problem began, unless we know who and where our enemies in that war are. Even as many

Communist states are crumbling and experiencing extraordinary changes, we need to know how this drug genie got out of the bottle and how we can get it back under control.

The author of this important book, Dr Joseph Douglass, possesses the experience, the knowledge, and the ability to present such a case. US Federal Government officials, including those of our intelligence agencies, if not conniving in a cover-up, seem to have lent themselves to what appears to be singular carelessness in dealing with long-available evidence of systematic Communist involvement in the drug trade.

Those of us who have spent the better part of our lives in the intelligence profession are, alas, all too familiar with how and why this can and does happen. It happens because the fact-finding and analysis process is subordinated to supposedly larger geopolitical or strategic considerations determined at the policy level. In the process, the information passed on to our nation's leaders is often brushed aside.

The man who is the principal source of information for *Red Cocaine* was, in a very real sense, a victim of bad timing. His name is Jan Sejna†, and he chose to defect from his native Czechoslovakia, where he occupied a high and crucial post, in 1968. He could not have picked a worse time. In 1968, official Washington, weary of the Cold War and on the losing end of a shooting war in Vietnam, was on the threshold of a new area of *détente*. So it was that this man Sejna, who brought with him unprecedented knowledge of many of the Communist world's deepest and darkest secrets, was about to become to his American hosts not a hero, to be lionised, but an embarrassment, to be hidden away.

What he knew, what might in a earlier era have become widely known and acted on, became, instead, a casualty of the yearning for *détente*. Data that does not support the politically-desired (or fashionable) goal of managing *détente* between Moscow and Washington has a hard time – a very hard time – surfacing or being heard. Needless to say, throughout the intelligence community, scores of conscientious officers fight against this pernicious process, often to the extent of putting their jobs, reputations, and very careers on the line. But their efforts are more often than not a quixotic struggle; simplistic grand strategies will often prevail where facts cannot.

Experts whose experience predates President Nixon's and President Carter's playing the 'China card' – that stunning initiative to court the previously quarantined Beijing régime – had long been well aware of Chinese drug-trafficking. Later we learned, as well, of Soviet ties to international guerrilla and terrorist operations, and the trading of guns for drugs and *vice versa*. Many of us suspected that there was a connection – of some sort – between increased drug-trafficking and the Soviet Union, especially given the various bits and pieces of intelligence on the drug-trafficking activities of its many surrogate client states. Our suspicions rested on the very sound proposition that those surrogates were too tightly tied to Moscow for the Kremlin to be unaware of what they were doing. Perhaps Moscow did not direct and control the international drug business, but they must have been aware of it and allowed it to spread.

Our awareness and suspicions turned to shock as we watched drug-trafficking and international terrorism become front-page news, while *détente* still seemed to matter more than unpleasant facts about drugs.

† *Editor's Note:* General Sejna died in unexplained circumstances in August 1997. Although he had been under CIA-supervised medication for some years, the manner and timing of his death – not long after having participated in Congressional hearings with Dr Douglass on MIA ('Missing in Action') issues and on the use of drugs on missing Western prisoner-veterans – demands elucidation, which has not been forthcoming.

It was into this political swamp that Jan Sejna leaped. Understanding the reluctance at the policy level to face disagreeable information helps one to understand why the reception he got from Washington's intelligence community – as detailed in Chapter 10 of this book – was considerably less than warm. Understanding this also puts into perspective the rumours propagated about him by both the intelligence and policy community, as well as by our principal strategic adversary, the Soviet Union. One can only suppose that it is a tribute to the importance of what he does know that those aimed at discrediting him persist to the present day.

I was posted in Germany as intelligence advisor to the US Embassy in Bonn at the time General Sejna defected; hence I have no first-hand knowledge of or connection with the decisions made at the time. I have noted over the years the various rumours and have watched with interest as his testimony – far from being discredited – has been confirmed or otherwise proven correct again and again. I am, for example, personally aware of the authenticity of what he had to say on the subjects of the Soviet connection with international terrorism; their training of terrorists; and the signal importance of the Soviet Defence Council in Soviet decision-making.

It was, then, a pleasant surprise for me when Dr Douglass arrived in my office one morning and asked if I would be willing to take a critical look at his manuscript.

So I read *Red Cocaine* with great care. I came away impressed. I was impressed with how professionally and objectively Dr Douglass has assembled and presented his arguments. I came away impressed with how he had strengthened the value of the text through abundant and informative endnotes, representing a whole added dimension of data supporting the basic thesis. At the same time, as he said he would do in the Preface, Dr Douglass concentrates on giving the general, non-professional reader a coherent story and enough information to present a clear picture without unduly burdening him with technical detail.

As befits an analysis of this nature, the best approach is to let the facts speak for themselves – understating, if anything, the argument. Dr Douglass has succeeded admirably. The source material is well-developed and, in my opinion, makes plain that Sejna is an excellent source, who for many years has remained underexploited. As a long-time intelligence professional, I regret that so much of the inner workings – or non-workings – of the intelligence community needed to be examined in public. But I believe the facts must be confronted. That officials even to this day and age are still reluctant to face what the Soviet Union was doing in the 1960s and 1970s is equally alarming. The object of this exercise is to present constructive criticism.

To those who would say that, given the cataclysmic upheavals of 1989 in the Soviet Bloc, this is all ancient history, I would respond: **Not so fast, do not be so sure**. Whatever the ultimate outcome of these upheavals, the fact remains that they have not reduced the military capability of the Soviet armed forces, but have actually improved and modernised the vast array of Soviet strategic intercontinental weapons. They have not yet diminished the levels of military assistance provided by Moscow to countries like Cuba, North Korea and Angola.

Nor have they decreased Soviet Bloc intelligence activities around the world. Furthermore, however kindly we might be inclined to feel today about the 'new' Soviet state, the fact is that we cannot begin to mount a truly effective attack on drugs, much less win the war, without understanding everything there is to be known about the origins and growth of the vast narcotics empire. In that sense alone, what Jan Sejna has to tell us in the pages of this book turns out to be of vital concern to all of us.

The drug problem has become a national disgrace and a significant threat to our national security, as well as to the well-being of our free society. It is also a threat to the security of our friends and allies, to the health and welfare of the nations struggling to become free and self-reliant in the family of modern nations. It is time to open our eyes to all facets of the drug-trafficking problem.

Red Cocaine puts the facts on the record.

We ignore the message it reveals at our own peril. ■

Dr RAY S. CLINE
Chairman, United States Global
Strategy Council, and former
Deputy Director for Intelligence,
Central Intelligence Agency.

THE CHINESE
DRUG OFFENSIVE

In 1928 Mao Tse-tung, the Chinese Communist leader, instructed one of his trusted sub-ordinates, Tan Chen-lin, to begin cultivating opium on a grand scale[1]. Mao had two objectives: obtaining exchange for needed supplies and 'drugging the white region'[2] where 'white' was an ideological, not racist, term that Mao used to refer to his non-Communist opposition. Mao's strategy was simple; **use drugs to soften a target area.** Then, after a captured region had been secured, outlaw the use of all narcotics and impose strict controls to ensure that the poppies remained exclusively an instrument of the state for use against its enemies.

Later, Mao would speak of using opium against the imperialists as only a modern phase in the opium wars that began in the 19th century. Opium was a powerful weapon that had been used by the imperialists against the Chinese and should be used against them in a second Opium War'. It was, Mao explained to Wang Chen in a lecture on his plan for planting opium, 'chemical warfare by indigenous methods'[3]. However, the fact that opium had previously been used against the Chinese was only a convenient excuse, not the real reason. Mao first began using opium as a political weapon against his own people, the Chinese, during his drive to establish Communism throughout China. His use of opium expanded simply because it proved to be a very effective weapon.

As soon as Mao had totally secured mainland China in 1949, opium production was nationalised and trafficking of narcotics, targeted against non-Communist states, became a formal activity of the new Communist state, the People's Republic of China.

The Chinese trafficking operation expanded rapidly. Official targets were Japan, the United States military forces in the Far East, neighbouring countries throughout the Far East, and the United States mainland. The primary organisations involved in the early 1950s were the Chinese Foreign Ministry, the Trade Ministry, and the Intelligence Service. North Korea was also trafficking narcotics[4] in cooperation with China at this time, and was directly connected with the flow of drugs into Japan and into the US military bases in the Far East[5].

The domestic narcotics problem in Japan had become serious by 1949[6]. The Criminal Investigation Division of the American Armed Forces in Japan, together with the Japanese authorities, began constructing a net across the whole of Japan to determine how the drugs were coming into the country[7]. By 1951, the Japanese had officially identified narcotics illegally entering their country and the sources of the trafficking – which were the Chinese and North Korean Communists. This trafficking was not limited to opium and heroin, but included hashish, marijuana, cocaine and dangerous synthetic stimulants such as hiropon and aminobutene group drugs[8]. These particular synthetics were especially dangerous and assessed to have been responsible for serious health problems which first appeared in Japan in the early 1950s.

The United States' experience was similar to that of Japan. New trafficking was first identified in the late 1940s. US narcotics and customs agents set up nets to identify the new sources and in 1951 began seizing large quantities of heroin at such major US ports as New York, San Francisco and Seattle[9]. The heroin was determined to have been manufactured in China and the trafficking managed by the Chinese.

In concert with the emergence of Chinese international narcotics trafficking in 1949-52, China's opium production increased steadily and reached a plateau of 2,000 to 3,000 tons per year. This production held steady until 1958-64, when production increased to roughly 8,000 tons as part of the 'great leap forward'[10]. The dates of these increases are important. As will be discussed in Chapter 11, in examining narcotics usage in the United States, there are two abrupt changes in the growth pattern that stand out. The use of narcotics in the United States declined during the 1930s and 1940s. Then beginning in 1949-52, an abrupt upswing took place simultaneously with the launching of China's narcotics trafficking operation. After 1952, narcotics consumption levelled off. Then, in the late 1950s to early 1960s, a second major upswing began. This second abrupt change in the growth pattern coincides almost precisely with a second expansion in the Chinese narcotics operation and with the entry of the Soviet Union into narcotics trafficking, as will be described later. This correlation is one of the indications that the growth in drug-trafficking and drug use within the United States and elsewhere is not a simple natural evolutionary process, or a phenomenon dominated by 'user demand'. Rather, there are strong *sub-rosa* forces at work stimulating and extending the consumption.

In the case of Chinese trafficking, there is no question that it was an official state activity. Data on the Chinese and North Korean trafficking enterprises were obtained by the Japanese internal security, US Army Intelligence, the US Narcotics Bureau operating with the assistance of undercover Treasury agents, and by CIA covert assets in China[11]. The data clearly identified production sources, manufacturing and packaging facilities, trafficking networks, and even management organisations[12]. As will be discussed later, the Chinese narcotics operation was also penetrated and watched by both Soviet intelligence and Czechoslovak intelligence, as were certain Chinese narcotics operations conducted jointly with the Communists in Korea, Vietnam and Japan.

China's narcotics operations also have been described by several Chinese officials who later left China and were granted political asylum in other countries. One such official who left in the late 1950s described a secret meeting of state officials in 1952, when the Chinese operation was reorganised, and a 20-year plan adopted[13]. At this meeting, decisions were made to standardise grades of narcotics, establish promotion regulations, set pricing schedules designed to encourage aggressive marketing, despatch sales representatives, expand research and production, and reorganise management responsibilities[14]. This information is also confirmed by data collected by Soviet and Czechoslovak intelligence agents, as will be discussed in greater detail in Chapters 4 and 6.

The organisation behind the Chinese narcotics operations was extensive and involved many ministries and agencies from the national down to the local levels. These organisations oversaw the reclamation of lands for production (Ministry of Forestry and

Reclamation); cultivation and research to produce better varieties of poppies (Ministry of Agriculture); development of opiates (Committee for the Review of Austerity); management of storage and preparation for export (Ministry of Commerce); management of external trade organisations (Ministry of Foreign Trade); statistical control and programming (Central Government Production Board); finance (Ministry of Finance); marketing through special representatives and political intrigue (Ministry of Foreign Affairs); and security and covert operations (Ministry of Public Security)[15].

The trafficking tradecraft included classical smuggling; transportation by shipping companies (both knowingly and unknowingly); use of Communists and ethnic Chinese abroad; collaboration with international organised crime syndicates; use of foreign posts of mainland parent entities; abuse of diplomatic privilege; use of normal branded merchandise as a cover; transport by mail; and forgery or packaging with misleading trademarks[16]. As will be seen later, Soviet drugs strategy and tactics employ quite similar techniques, organisation and management, targets, and motivations – albeit in the Soviet Leninist style, and on a greatly magnified scale.

Throughout the 1950s and 1960s, probably the most important official exercising day-to-day control over China's narcotics operations was Chou En-lai. As the chief Soviet ideologist, Mikhail A. Suslov, explained during a major speech on China at a meeting of the Soviet Central Committee in February 1964, Chou En-lai's strategy was 'to disarm the capitalists with the things they like to taste [meaning drugs]'[17].

Professor J. H. Turnbull was head of the Department of Applied Chemistry at the Royal Military College of Science, Shrivenham, United Kingdom, and an expert on narcotics trafficking and its strategic implications. In 1972, following the publicity focused on the massive use of narcotics against US soldiers in Southeast Asia (see Chapter 6), Turnbull prepared a succinct summary of Chinese narcotics trafficking strategy. Chinese trafficking, he wrote, was 'directed broadly at the major industrial sectors of the Free World. In purely commercial terms these offer obvious targets, since they provide both large [and] affluent markets...'[18]. These leading industrial sectors were particularly vulnerable due to the open nature of the underlying society.

The production and distribution of drugs, Turnbull emphasised, was 'a valuable source of national income, and a powerful weapon of subversion'[19]. He then identified three basic objectives of Chinese subversive activities employing drugs: 'To finance subversive activities abroad; to corrupt and weaken the people of the Free World; and to destroy the morale of US servicemen fighting in Southeast Asia'[20].

Turnbull's conclusion was almost identical to that reached twenty years earlier by the US Commissioner of Narcotics, Harry Anslinger. It is equally relevant today. 'The covert dissemination of opium narcotics, in particular the addictive drug heroin, for commercial and subversive purposes, represents one of the gravest threats to the armed services and societies of the Free World. The subversive operation must be recognised as a peculiar form of clandestine chemical warfare, in which the victim voluntarily exposes himself to chemical attack'[21]. ∎

References to Chapter 1:

1. Chang Tse-min, *A Follow-Up Report on Chinese Communist Crimes in Drugging the World* (Taipei: World Anti-Communist League, 1979), page 1.

2. *Ibid.*, page 1; and A. H. Stanton Candlin, *Psycho-Chemical Warfare: The Chinese Communist Drug Offensive Against the West* (New Rochelle, New York: Arlington House, 1973), page 73.

3. 'A Look at the Chinese Communist 'Strategy of Narcotic', unpublished paper by Maj. Gen. (Ret.),

Sing-yu Chu, Society for Strategic Studies, Taipei. Cited in *The Inside Story of Red China's Opium Sales* (Taiwan: Hsueh Hai Press, May 1957).

4. Before and during the Korean War, North Korea was closely connected to Communist China. However, after the war, relations with China soured and North Korea became more closely aligned with the Soviet Union. North Korea provided Soviet intelligence with considerable data on the Chinese drug business.

5. See testimony of a Bureau of Narcotics, Treasury Department undercover agent in US Congress, Senate, *Communist China and Illicit Narcotics Traffic,* Hearings Before the Subcommittee to Investigate the Administration of the Internal Security Act and other Internal Security Laws of the Committee on the Judiciary, March 8, 18-19, and May 13, 1955 (Washington, D.C.: US Government Printing Office, 1955), pages 14-17.

6. J. H. Turnbull, *Chinese Opium Narcotics: A Threat to the Survival of the West* (Richmond, Surrey, England: Foreign Affairs Publishing Company, 1972), page 12.

7. See Harry J. Anslinger and William F. Tompkins, *The Traffic in Narcotics* (New York: Funk & Wagnalls Company, 1953), pages 70-116, and Gerd Hamburger, *The Peking Bomb* (Washington: Robert B. Luce, Inc., 1975), page 54. See also Richard Deacon, *The Chinese Secret Service* (New York: Ballantine Books, 1974), pages 449-450.

8. US Congress, Senate, *Communist China and Illicit Narcotics Traffic,* Hearings Before the Subcommittee to Investigate the Administration of the Internal Security Act and Other Internal Security Laws of the Committee on the Judiciary, March 8,18,1955, May 13,1955, and March 19,1955 (Washington, D.C.: Government Printing Office; 1955), pages 34-91.

9. Victor Lasky, 'Red China's Secret Weapon', in Extension of Remarks of Hon. Norris Poulson, US Congress, House, *Congressional Record – Appendix* (Washington, D.C.: US Government Printing Office, April 23, 1953), page A2176.

10. See Candlin, *Psycho-Chemical Warfare: The Chinese Communist Drug Offensive Against the West , op. cit.,* pages 108-118; Hamburger, *The Peking Bomb, op. cit.,* page 235; and *Communist China and Illicit Narcotics Traffic, op. cit.,* page 16.

11. Deacon, *The Chinese Secret Service, op. cit.,* page 447, reports using as many as 37 separate reports from 26 individuals whom Deacon believed had interviewed as many as 50 to 60 defectors, police officers, secret agents, drug squad officers, and intelligence officers.

12. For extensive details and maps of production areas and trafficking routes, see *Psycho-Chemical Warfare: The Chinese Communist Drug Offensive Against the West , op. cit., The Peking Bomb, op. cit.,* and various reports to the United Nations filed by the US Commissioner on Narcotics, Harry Anslinger.

13. Candlin, *Psycho-Chemical Warfare: The Chinese Communist Drug Offensive Against the West, op. cit.,* page 195; and Hamburger, *The Peking Bomb, op. cit.,* page 59.

14. *Tokyo Shinbun ,* January 8, 1953, cited in Richard L. G. Deverall, *Mao Tse-tung: Stop This Dirty Opium Business!* (Tokyo: Toyoh Printing and Bookbinding Co., 1954), pages 64-66. See also Candlin, *Psycho-Chemical Warfare: The Chinese Communist Drug Offensive Against the West , op. cit.,* pages 195-197, 454-455.

15. Candlin, *Psycho-Chemical Warfare: The Chinese Communist Drug Offensive Against the West , op. cit.,* page 214.

16. *Ibid.,* pages 215-216.

17. Interview with Jan Sejna who was present when Suslov discussed China's narcotics trafficking in detail. This data had been derived from Soviet intelligence.

18. Turnbull, *Chinese Opium Narcotics, op. cit.,* page 15.

19. *Ibid.,* page 15.

20. *Ibid.*

21. *Ibid.,* page 16.

THE SOVIETS DECIDE TO 'COMPETE'

When China began waging war with narcotics and drugs in the late 1940s, its drugs strategy was quickly identified. Shipments of drugs were seized and intelligence was collected which identified the source as the People's Republic of China, together with its trafficking routes, techniques, and eventually even the principal organisations behind production and distribution. In the case of the Soviet Union, intelligence on the operation was not immediately available, perhaps attesting to the care exercised by the Soviets in developing secure, covert marketing techniques before Moscow's own offensive was launched. As will be seen, the Soviet offensive was designed to be far more extensive than the Chinese operation, and once in place, was intensified on almost a yearly basis.

While the dubious distinction of initiating large-scale political war with drugs goes to the Chinese, it is the Soviets who have made trafficking the effective political warfare and intelligence weapon it has become – accomplishing this almost without any recognition in the West of Soviet involvement. Not until 1968 did a source surface in the West who possessed detailed knowledge about the Soviet drug offensive. Not until 1986 was any attention directed to his knowledge. The story that follows is the first comprehensive unveiling of that source's detailed knowledge of Soviet narcotics warfare.

The source in question is Jan Sejna, who defected from Czechoslovakia to the United States in February 1968[1]. General Major Sejna was a member of the Central Committee, the National Assembly, and the Presidium and its Party group. He was also a member of the Main Political Administration, its political bureau, and a member of the Administrative Organs Department[2]. He was First Secretary of the Party at the Ministry of Defence, where he was also Chief of Staff and a member of the Minister's *Kolegium*. His most important position was Secretary of the powerful Defence Council, which was the top decision-making body in matters of defence, intelligence, foreign policy and the economy. Sejna was a top-level, decision-making Party official. He regularly met the highest officials in the Soviet Union and other Communist countries. He was present during the inception, planning and implementation of Soviet narcotics trafficking operations.

The Soviet concept of using drugs and narcotics trafficking as a strategic operation, Sejna explains, emerged during the Korean War. During that conflict, the Chinese and North Koreans used drugs against US military forces to undermine the effectiveness of both officers and enlisted men and to raise revenues in the process[3]. The Soviets were also assisting North Korea in the war, albeit not in so obvious a manner as the Chinese.

The war provided the Soviets with an opportunity to study the effectiveness of US forces and equipment. Czechoslovak intelligence assisted the Soviets. As part of this intelligence mission, Czechoslovakia constructed a hospital in North Korea. Ostensibly built to treat casualties, the real use of the hospital was as a research facility in which Czechoslovak, Soviet and North Korean doctors at the hospital experimented on US and South Korean prisoners of war. The Czechoslovak official in charge of the Czechoslovak operations in North Korea was Colonel Rudolf Bobka, of *Zpravdajska sprava* (Zs), the Military Intelligence Administration of the Czechoslovak General Staff. Colonel Professor Dr Dufek, a heart specialist, was in charge of the hospital. Sejna learned about the hospital and related activities directly from Colonel Bobka, from various reports, and from subsequent briefings that summarised the results of the experiments and used the results in studies of the strategic military potential of drug-trafficking[4].

The experiments were justified as preparations for the next war. American and South Korean POWs were used as guinea pigs in chemical and biological warfare experiments, in physiological and psychological endurance tests, and in testing the effectiveness of various mind-control drugs, which were used to make US servicemen renounce America and speak of the benefits of the Communist system [5].

To learn more about the biological and chemical make-up of American and South Korean soldiers, autopsies were performed on captured bodies and POWs who did not survive the various experiments. During this activity, the Soviet doctors determined that an unusually high percentage of young US soldiers had suffered cardiovascular damage, which they referred to as 'mini heart attacks'.

At the same time, Soviet intelligence, which was studying Chinese drug-trafficking[6], determined that the young US servicemen were also the most prominent users of the harder drugs[7]. The Soviet doctors noticed the correlation and hypothesised that one of the factors that probably contributed to the heart damage was drug abuse[8].

News of the physically debilitating effect of the drugs captured the imagination of the Soviet leader, Nikita Khrushchev. Drug and narcotics trafficking, he reasoned, should be viewed as a strategic operation that would directly weaken the enemy, rather than merely as a financial or intelligence tool. Accordingly, he ordered a joint military-civilian, Soviet-Czechoslovak study to examine the total effects of drug and narcotics trafficking on Western society; this included its effects on labour productivity, education, the military (the ultimate target at that time), and its use in support of Soviet Bloc intelligence operations. Nor was this study approached as a question of tactics or as simply an opportunity for exploitation. The narcotics potential was examined in the context of long-range strategy. Costs and risks, benefits and payoffs, integration and coordination with other operations, were all examined. Even the effects of drugs *over several generations*[9], were analysed by scientists from the Soviet Academy of Sciences.

The conclusions of the study were that trafficking would be extremely effective, that the most vulnerable targets were the United States, Canada, France and West Germany, and that the Soviets should capitalise on the opportunity. The study was approved by the Soviet Defence Council in late 1955 or early 1956. The principal guidance from the Defence Council in approving the action was to direct the planners to speed up the timetable of events, which was possible because of certain operational experience with narcotics that already existed within the Soviet Bloc intelligence services but about which the people who had prepared the basic plan were unaware[10]. This plan was formally approved when the Soviets decided to begin narcotics trafficking against the so-called bourgeoisie, especially against the 'American capitalists' – the 'Main Enemy'.

Moreover the study materialised at a most propitious time for the Communists because, simultaneously, the Soviets under Khrushchev's direction were working hard to modernise the world revolutionary movement. Khrushchev believed the movement had grown stagnant under Stalin, and he wanted it rejuvenated, to take advantage of new world conditions.

Soviet strategy for revolutionary war is **a global strategy**. Soviet narcotics strategy is a sub-component of this global strategy and is best understood in this context. While the primary target of this activity is often thought to be the undeveloped world, this is not the case. Soviet strategy and tactics were developed **for the whole world**, within which the most important sectors were the industrialised nations and the most important target, the United States.

The basic updated revolutionary strategy† took shape in the years 1954 to 1956. As detailed by Sejna, there were five principal thrusts in the modernised strategy. *First* was enhanced training of leaders for the revolutionary movements – the civilian, military and intelligence cadres. The founding of Patrice Lumumba University in Moscow is an example of one of the early measures taken to modernise Soviet revolutionary leadership training.

The *second* step was the actual training of terrorists. Training for international terrorism actually began under cover of the 'fight for liberation', within the context of the Comintern's decolonisation policy*. The term 'national liberation' was coined to replace revolutionary war movement as a two-way deception: to provide a nationalistic cover for what was basically an intelligence operation and to provide a label that was semantically separated from the Communist revolutionary war movement.

The *third* step was international drug and narcotics trafficking. Drugs were incorporated into the strategy for waging revolutionary warfare as a political and intelligence weapon for deployment against 'bourgeois societies' and as a mechanism for recruiting agents of influence around the world.

† *Editor's Note:* General Sejna's summary of the basic global revolutionary strategy developed following the death of Stalin is not inconsistent with the account of the long-range revolutionary deception strategy explained in the two books by the Soviet defector, **Anatoliy Golitsyn** [*New Lies for Old* and *The Perestroika Deception, op. cit.*], which concentrated primarily upon deception theory and its application in the context of preparations for the dismantling of the Stalinist model, realised under Gorbachëv, ahead of the orchestrated proliferation of the Leninist World Revolution on a truly global scale, the critical stage currently being experienced. Recall Gorbachëv's consistent adherence and invocation of Lenin at every opportunity, epitomised by the following statement [*Current Digest of the Soviet Press*, 40, Number 7, 1988, pages 3-4]: **'No, we are not retreating a single step from socialism, from Marxism-Leninism'**. Moreover Soviet drug-trafficking operations began in earnest in 1960, *precisely* when the finishing touches were being put to the long-range deception strategy, ratified at the 81-Party Congress held in Moscow in December 1961 [see both Golitsyn works, *op. cit.*] .

* *Editor's Note:* The Comintern laid down that the colonial empires must be destroyed as a prerequisite for the destruction of capitalism, and immediately set about subverting the colonial powers' foreign policy structures with this objective in mind. This policy was promulgated in the Comintern's *Theses on the National and Colonial Questions* contained in *The Theses and Statutes of the Communist International,* as adopted by the Second World Congress, held between July 17th and August 7th, 1920, in Moscow. It was updated in *The Programme of the Communist International* adopted at the Sixth World Congress on September 1st, 1928, which sought 'to overthrow the rule of foreign imperialism' and stated that 'colonial revolutions and movements for national liberation play an extremely important part in the struggle against imperialism'. In 1986, Eduard Shevardnadze, the former police and Party chief in Soviet Georgia whom President Gorbachëv had elevated to the post of Soviet Foreign Minister, congratulated the world Communist movement upon its success in having almost completed this historic task.

The *fourth* step was to infiltrate organised crime and, further, to establish Soviet Bloc sponsored and controlled organised crime syndicates throughout the world.

The *fifth* step was to plan and prepare for sabotage throughout the whole world. The network for this activity was to be in place by 1972.

Because of the close association between organised crime and narcotics, the Soviet entry into organised crime deserves closer scrutiny. Moscow's decision on organised crime was made in 1955. It, too, was to be a global operation targeted against all countries, not just the United States, although organised crime in the United States, along with France, Great Britain, Germany and Italy, were primary targets.

The main reason for infiltrating organised crime was the Soviet belief that high-quality information – information on political corruption, money and business, international relations, drug-trafficking, and counter-intelligence – was to be found in organised crime. The Soviets reasoned that if they could successfully infiltrate organised crime, they would acquire unusually promising scope for controlling many politicians and would have access to the best information on drugs, money, weapons and corruption of many kinds. A secondary motive was to use organised crime as a covert mechanism for distributing drugs.

As in the case of drug-trafficking, the Soviets put together study groups to analyse organised crime, to identify the main criminal groups, to develop a strategy and tactics for infiltrating the groups, to identify what people could be used to promote infiltration, and to examine the possibility for organising or helping to organise new criminal franchises. In Czechoslovakia, the studies went on for six months. These studies were not taken lightly; on the contrary, they were high-level operations involving top officials from military intelligence, counter-intelligence, civilian intelligence and the Administrative Organs Department of the Central Committee.

The first plan was put into action in 1956. Czechoslovakia was given directions on which operations to undertake as part of the intelligence plan, which was reviewed and approved in the fall of that year. The plan instructed Czechoslovak strategic intelligence to infiltrate seventeen different organised crime groups, as well as the mafia in France, Italy, Austria, Latin America and Germany. The Italian Communist Party was used heavily in the infiltration operation. Twenty percent of the Italian police were members of the Communist Party at that time. These members helped Soviet Bloc intelligence agents to infiltrate the mafia . War criminals, e.g. Germans, were also coerced into assisting the Soviet Bloc agents in this endeavour, especially throughout Latin America.

The Czechoslovak operation was very successful and did not cost much money. Organised criminal activity was developed around information collection and blackmail; it was a two-sided operation. Once inside, the agents remained largely passive; they just collected information. Then, at the right opportunity, information would be released for political reasons – for example, to trigger revolutionary changes, or to create a situation that could be exploited by the Social Democrats. This is why the operation was organised within the unit responsible for strategic intelligence: it was used for *strategic* advantage.

Narcotics, terrorism and organised crime were coordinated and used together in a complementary fashion. *Drugs* were used to destroy society. *Terrorism* was used to destabilise the targeted country and to prepare a revolutionary environment. *Organised crime* was used to control the élite. All three strands were long-range strategic operations and all three had been incorporated into Soviet Bloc planning by 1956.

Before actual narcotics trafficking could begin, several preparatory measures were required, the two most important of which were the development of a strategy for the covert marketing of drugs and narcotics, and the training of intelligence cadres. The Soviets wanted to hide their operation from the Chinese and especially from the West, to avoid upsetting acceptance by the West of the Soviet strategy peaceful coexistence[11]. Because the narcotics strategy was new in most of its particulars, the necessary intelligence skills had to be developed and passed to agents. This training activity involved not only Soviets, but East European intelligence agents as well.

Additionally, during the late 1950s, a research program was undertaken to obtain quantitative data on the actual effects of different drugs on soldiers, which involved the use of *Soviet* soldiers as guinea pigs. As part of this research, an espionage program was initiated to penetrate Western medical and science centres, especially those of a military nature, to determine how much the West knew about the effects of drugs on people – particularly their effects on military combat-effectiveness and decision-making.

In parallel, Soviet Bloc intelligence services were directed to learn how much Western intelligence services knew about the drug business and which drug groups they had infiltrated. One of the important questions addressed in this study was the nature and effectiveness of Western intelligence services' ability to monitor the production and distribution of drugs[12]. Several years later, Sejna was to learn the results of this study directly from the Chief of the Soviet General Staff, Marshal of the Soviet Union Matvey V. Zakharov.

Zakharov said that Soviet intelligence had concluded that US intelligence and counter-intelligence were blind, and that this made the Soviet drug operation much easier. The United States' intelligence operations were concentrated, along with those of the British, on narcotics trafficking through Thailand and Hong Kong, where there was so much drug activity and associated corruption that no useful information on Soviet drug trafficking could be collected. The 'background noise' was simply too great.

During the studies, the use of narcotics and drugs became recognised as a special dimension of chemical warfare. In Czechoslovakia, drugs and narcotics research were formally added to military planning, as a dimension of chemical warfare research. This research included tests on the effects of drugs on military performance – for example, on pilot performance, which was studied at the Health Administration of the Rear Services and at the Health Institutes of the Air Force.

Finally, the basic study on the impact of drugs on the West was expanded to improve identification of groups and regions to be targeted. This further study was the responsibility of the International (Foreign) Department of the Central Committee of the CPSU (Communist Party of the Soviet Union). It was, in effect, a political market analysis and marketing techniques study.

One of the last measures to be initiated before the actual mass trafficking operation began was the establishment of training centres for drug-traffickers. In the case of Czechoslovakia, the training centres were joint Soviet-Czechoslovak operations. There were both civilian intelligence-managed training centres, which were jointly planned by KGB (Soviet) officials and Czechoslovak officials from the Second Administration of the Ministry of Interior (the Second Administration was the Czechoslovak KGB intelligence counterpart)[13]; and military intelligence-managed training centres, which were jointly planned by the GRU (Soviet Military Intelligence) and its Czechoslovak counterpart, Zs.

These plans were developed in 1959, as General Sejna recalls, and the Defence Council's review of the plans and decision to fund them, following instructions from the Soviet Defence Council, took place in 1959 or 1960.

The Zs (military intelligence) training centre was located in a Czechoslovak Zs base at Petrzalka, a suburb of Bratislava, situated on the Austrian border. The Second Administration training centre was located next to Liberec, on the West German border.

Each course consisted of three months of intensive training. While indoctrination in Marxism-Leninism was present, the emphasis was strictly on the drug business. The Soviets provided the Czechoslovaks with a copy of the Soviet schedule and lesson plans, which the Czechoslovaks copied. The course included instruction in:

- The nature of the drug business, types and quality;
- Means of production;
- Organisation of distribution;
- Drug markets and buyers;
- Security;
- Infiltration of existing production networks;
- How to use the experience of intelligence networks;
- Communications within drug organisations;
- How to pass intelligence information; and,
- How to recruit intelligence sources.

At the Zs centres, two different groups were processed for training, and these alternated. The first group was recruited by the military and civilian intelligence services. This group was strictly for drug 'criminals' – the attendees were neither Communists nor ideologically motivated. The word 'criminals' is shown here in quotation marks, because that is what the training was to produce. However, all recruits were carefully screened by military or civilian counter-intelligence to make certain that the recruits were clean; that is, that they did not have criminal records or a background in corruption that rendered them susceptible to blackmail by another party. Often, the recruits were sons or daughters of people in positions of power. These people, and the potential risks that would be associated with their recruitment, were often the subject of specific discussions within the Czechoslovak Defence Council.

The second group were people recommended by the First Secretaries of the various foreign Communist Parties. These were Communists who were considered loyal to the cause. They, too, were carefully screened by military or civilian counter-intelligence before being admitted to the course. Their training was slightly different, because their trafficking was also intended to serve a local political purpose and because they operated and communicated through different special (Party or intelligence) channels. Their drug-trafficking (and training) was heavily oriented to support the First Secretary of the local Communist parties; for example, to compromise opposition leaders.

In addition to Czechoslovak instructors, the Soviets often provided two instructors for each course who had practical experience. Most often these were Latin Americans or others who looked the part and spoke fluent Spanish. These instructors would present seminars dealing with practical problems and real life experiences.

As indicated above, the courses ran for three months. Thus, a total of four groups trained each year. The first group to take the Zs course in Czechoslovakia was small – seven future drug criminals consisting of four Latin Americans, two West Germans, and one Italian or French national, as Sejna recalls. By 1964, the group size had expanded to fourteen, and by the end of the 1960s, full capacity, twenty, was reached. Thus a total of approximately thirty students were trained the first year in the Czechoslovakia Zs centre, and by 1968 the annual output of graduates had reached eighty.

The Second Administration centre was of similar size. Additionally, similar drug-trafficker training centres that Sejna was aware of were established in Bulgaria, East Germany and the Soviet Union. And in 1962-63, Czechoslovakia was directed by the Soviets to assist North Korea, North Vietnam and Cuba to establish training centres. On the unreliable assumption that each training centre was the minimum size, each operated at or near its capacity, and no other centres existed or were added after Sejna left, the number of graduates today would exceed 25,000.

The students who attended the course in the Czechoslovak centres were mainly from Latin America, Western Europe, parts of the Middle East, Canada and the United States. Bulgaria's focus was on the Middle East and Southwest Asia – Turkey, Afghanistan, Pakistan, Lebanon and Syria. East Germany handled West Europeans and Scandinavians, and all countries assisted with nationals from the Far East.

The course was free, all expenses paid. Graduates returned to their respective countries and applied their skills. Some built independent operations, others cooperated with ongoing operations. Those who deviated and attempted to 'change sides' were killed[14]. All returned a percentage of their earnings to the Soviet Union directly, which would then reimburse the intelligence services of the satellites that had performed the training. In the case of Czechoslovakia, their cut was 30% of the fees the Soviets received back[15].

The establishment of these training centres completed the preparations for the drug strategy. These activities – strategy development, training, research, espionage, and market analysis – were the principal activities of the early Soviet drugs offensive in the late 1950s. Where there were intelligence operations involving actual trafficking, these were more in the nature of limited probes, tests and continuations of prior intelligence practices. The real trafficking, from Sejna's perspective, did not begin until 1960, by which time the marketing strategy had been worked out, strategic intelligence agents had been trained, and training schools were turning out indigenous graduate drug-traffickers. ■

References to Chapter 2:
1. Jan Sejna, *We Will Bury You* (London: Sidgwick & Jackson, 1982).

2. The Administrative Organs Department is one of the two or three most important departments of the Central Committee. This department has responsibility for the Ministry of Defence, Ministry of Interior (KGB), and the Ministry of Justice. It is the most important department insofar as defence, intelligence, and deception are concerned.

3. In Congressional testimony and in official reports of the Narcotics Division of the US Treasury Department, the Korean War is described as having 'been financed solely from the sale of illicit narcotics'. Lasky, *Red China's Secret Weapon*, *op.cit.*, page A2176.

4. The most significant briefing, which took place in 1956, included Dr Dufek, Colonel-General Miroslav Hemalla of the Military Health Administration, who later became a general and head of the Military Health Administration, Colonel Dr Plzak, whose specialty was the central nervous system and who practiced at the experimental hospital in North Korea, and several other medical specialists.

There was scattered intelligence on certain of the experiments which had given rise to serious concern within US intelligence and within the US Army. See, for example, John Ranelagh, *The Agency: The Rise and Decline of the CIA* (New York: Simon and Schuster, 1986), page 215, and US Senate, Select Committee to Study Governmental Operations with Respect to Intelligence Activities, *Foreign and Military Intelligence: Book 1* (Washington, D.C.: US Government Printing Office, April 26, 1976), pages 392-393.

5. CIA concern about Soviet, Chinese, and North Korean use of LSD and other drugs in mind-bending experiments became real during the Korean War. The concern was apparently valid and justified but there was a lack of understanding of the dimensions and objectives of the Communist programs. Unfortunately, this concern led to the tragically aberrant experimentation by US intelligence which surfaced during the Congressional hearings of 1975-76. See, for example, US Senate, *Final Report of the Select Committee to Study Governmental Operations with Respect to Intelligence Activities, Foreign Intelligence, Book 1* (Washington, D.C.: US Government Printing Office, 1976), pages 392-420.

6. Soviet interest in the use of drugs goes back to the mid-1930s, when the Soviets were experimenting with drugs as a revolutionary tool. One particularly interesting example of the use of drugs in this respect is reported by A. H. Stanton Candlin. He states that in 1934, the Comintern experimented with the use of marijuana in New York City to stimulate student radicals against the New York police. The behaviour of both drugged and undrugged youths were compared.

'During the mêlée that resulted it was obvious to the observers that the drugged group were far more effective than the undrugged one.The former were insensible to pain and also continued to struggle and resist vigorously after they had been arrested. As soon as they were in the police station, the ACLU [American Civil Liberties Union] appeared on the scene and bailed them out. All rioters were then taken to the Rand School of Social Science (listed as a Communist-run organisation by the Federal Government) where they underwent medical and psychiatric examination .... Two days later a conference was held having as its subject the use of marijuana as a conditioning medium for riots and revolutionary violence. It met at the headquarters of the League for Industrial Democracy.... Leading personalities of the Communist Party... participated'.

The principal speaker, Rosito Carrillo (an alias), explained that Mexico had been the proving ground for a new mental-conditioning technique, using marijuana, which heightened revolutionary spirit. The emotions and states of fear, apprehension, and indecision could be inhibited and the senses partially anaesthetised against pain and even the irritation caused by teargas.

Marijuana, or hashish, could be made concentrated enough, Carrillo said, to bring about unconsciousness and even permanent brain damage. He explained that it was a valued weapon in the Communist arsenal to help undermine and topple the capitalist system. Speakers arose and propounded a long-range campaign to win legal acceptance of marijuana and other similar drugs, using as an argument the right to freedom of individual choice. A. H. Stanton Candlin, *Psycho-Chemical Warfare: The Chinese Communist Drug Offensive Against the West* (New Rochelle, New York: Arlington House, 1973), pages 45-47.

Additionally, the use of drugs to subdue societies in the same sense that the drugs were used by Mao Tse-tung is reported to have been first examined by the Comintern in the mid-1930s. Furthermore, the use of drugs as intelligence weapons by Soviet intelligence services to corrupt and extort foreign officials predates the Korean War.

It seems reasonable to hypothesise that this history of Soviet interest in the use of drugs as weapons and revolutionary tools stimulated the Soviets to watch with considerable care and study the impact of Chinese trafficking on the fighting efficiency of the US and South Korean forces, which then led to the decision that drugs were indeed a valuable weapon the use of which should be exploited.

[The use of drugs by the North Vietnamese and Chinese Communists to intensify the attacking spirit has also been reported in recent years. In an article recapturing personal experiences in Vietnam, two examples are presented: 'The way the teargas didn't affect the NVA at all leads me to believe they were hopped up on drugs'. And: 'Quite a few of the NVA we killed inside our wire were bandaged – that night. It was obvious that they had sent their wounded back up to fight the battle. That scared me – to the point that I could not believe that people who had already been wounded and messed up still wanted to fight. I figured they had a lot more drive than I had. Those people were scary, like they were almost superhuman. We found drugs – syringes and chemicals'. Eric Hammel, 'Khe Sanh: Attack on Hill 861A', *Marine Corps Gazette*, February 1989, pages 48, 49.

Furthermore, on June 4, 1989, a Cable News Network broadcast on the fighting in Beijing in which the Chinese soldiers were especially brutal in their attack on students who were revolting against the Communist régime, reported that the presence of drugs was identified in the blood and urine of soldiers who were hospitalised. The soldiers said they had been given injections or 'vaccinations' prior to engaging the students because Tienanmen Square was dirty. Subsequent reports out of Europe stated, in addition, that the soldiers had been given psychological hate conditioning in conjunction with the administration of drugs prior to their assault on the students.

The first use of synthetic drugs to stimulate attacking soldiers may have been undertaken by the Germans in the Second World War. Consider: 'When the German armies waged the *'blitzkrieg'* or 'Lightning war' through France and the Lowlands in 1940, the Allied forces were no match for their stamina and ferocity. The Germans fought like men possessed, and they were. Their pharmacists had synthesised methedrine, a cheap but powerful energising drug that allowed their soldiers to fight vigorously for weeks at a time with no sleep and little food'. William Glasser, M.D., *Take Effective Control of Your Life* (New York: Harper &: Row, 1984, page 138).

Another related finding is reported by Michael Isikoff in 'Users of Crack Cocaine Link Violence to Drug's Influence', *Washington Post*, March 24, 1989, page A10. Isikoff reports on studies that have clearly linked violent behaviour with crack cocaine. Nearly half of the callers to a cocaine hotline reported that they had perpetrated violent crimes, most while under the influence of the drug. There was no perceptible difference between female and male users].

7. The use of drugs during the Korean War, while serious, was not as widespread as it was during the Vietnam War. Indeed, many people who served in the war were not aware of the problem, which

tended to be more marked in specific locations than in others. For example, one area identified by a former counter-intelligence specialist where the use of hard drugs was especially noticeable was among the stevedore battalions in Pusan.

8. US medical personnel also identified cardiovascular damage among young US servicemen. They attributed the cause to diet. The Soviet doctors, too, recognised the possible contribution of diet, but additionally noted the equally possible contribution of drug usage among the US servicemen. It was this latter possibility that captured Khrushchev's imagination. While reports on the adverse medical effects of drugs appeared in the 1970s in Western medical literature, these effects did not really receive medical attention until the 1980s. Recent research has tied cocaine, heroin, marijuana, and other drugs to both cardiovascular damage and brain damage. See, for example, Louis L. Cregler, M.D. and Herbert Mark, M.D., 'Medical Complications of Cocaine Abuse', *New England Journal of Medicine*, December 4, 1986. In many respects, Soviet science, as it pertains to military and intelligence operations, is far ahead of Western science. Take the crucial issue of the consequence of drug use over successive generations. In 1990, the *Wall Street Journal* reports that 'multi-generation use is one of the great unexplored areas in the war against drugs, in part because the phenomenon is so recent'. David Shribman, 'The '60s Generation, Once High on Drugs, Warns Its Children. *Wall Street Journal*, January 26, 1990, page 1. Soviet scientists were studying this phenomenon in the mid-1950s.

9. How much the Soviets knew about the effects of drugs in the mid-1950s is not known. It does appear that **because of their interest in, for example, mind-control and the use of drugs to stimulate revolutionary activity,** they might well have known much more than was known in the free world. The Soviet identification of the harmful effects of drugs on the cardiovascular system appears to predate similar recognition in the West by many years. The question of the effects of drugs over successive generations has only recently received attention in the United States; note growing concern over the permanent disabilities and reduced mental capacities of children born to women who are on drugs, even on marijuana. See, for example, Michael Abramowitz, 'Pregnant Cocaine Users Reduce Risk by Stopping', *Washington Post*, March 24,1989, page A10.

10. This would probably refer to Soviet experience in using drugs to stimulate and otherwise further revolutionary activity and to the experience of their intelligence services in using drugs to extort and bribe foreign officials. Considerable expertise had also been gained from extensive experimentation with drugs for mind-control purposes. Additionally, the Soviets were experimenting with and promoting the use of drugs such as LSD to create mental incapacities. This work is described in a Communist textbook, *Communist Manual of Instructions of Psychological Warfare*, used in the United States to 'capture the minds of a nation through brain-washing and fake mental health', as described by Kenneth Goff, a former Communist turned anti-Communist crusader [see also the Introduction to this book, the Second Edition of the present work]. The textbook contains an introductory address on psychopolitics by Lavrentiy Beria of the Soviet Ministry of Internal Affairs in which he states that 'Psychopolitics is a solemn charge. With it you can erase our enemies as insects. You can cripple the efficiency of leaders by striking insanity into their families through the use of drugs'. The text itself states that 'by making readily available drugs of various kinds, by giving the teenager alcohol, by praising his wildness, by stimulating him with sex literature and advertising to him or her practices as taught at the Sexpol, the psychopolitical operator can create the necessary attitude of chaos, idleness and worthlessness into which can then be cast the solution which will give the teenager complete freedom everywhere – Communism'. *Brain-Washing: A Synthesis of the Communist Textbook on Psychopolitics*, published by Goff, 1956.

11. A good description of Khrushchev's peaceful coexistence strategy is contained in Sejna, *We Will Bury You, op. cit.*, pages 22-36. See also Raymond S. Sleeper, editor, *Mesmerized by the Bear* (New York: Dodd Mead & Company, 1987), pages 216-219.

12. Since 1973, at the initiative of US Customs and the Bureau of Narcotics and Dangerous Drugs, the United States has been sharing US narcotics trafficking control techniques and intelligence on trafficking organisations with various Soviet Bloc customs (intelligence) agencies. In 1988, the US State Department and the Drug Enforcement Administration reported that they were negotiating to share drug-trafficking intelligence with the Soviet Union, including drug samples possibly keyed to different production and distribution networks. This is discussed in detail in Chapter 9.

13. There was considerable confusion in the West (and in the East, for that matter) about the structure of Soviet Bloc intelligence services. This was only natural, because intelligence is highly classified, and classification includes the structure and organisation of the intelligence services themselves.

In Czechoslovakia, probably the best known component of the intelligence service was the StB or State Security (*Statni Bezpecnost*), which prior to 1967 was known as the StB or State Secret Security (*Statni Tajna Bezpecnost*). Its name was changed in 1967 to remove the 'secret', in an attempt to improve its image. Notwithstanding the publicity attached to the StB, there are few people, even in Czechoslovakia, and even within the Czechoslovak intelligence service, who understood what the StB was, and how it fitted into the overall Czechoslovak intelligence system. Quite often, StB was used generically to describe any activity within the entire civilian intelligence system. But this was incorrect and was where the confusion began. [*The Author further explained, in the first Edition of the present work*]:

The civilian intelligence service is organised within the Ministry of Interior. The Ministry is functionally organised into separate administrations. The First Administration is civilian counter-intelligence. This is the StB. This is the organisation that is responsible for keeping track of Czechoslovak civilians and for rooting out traitors and other enemies of the state. The Second Administration is civilian intelligence (as distinct from military intelligence, which is organised within the Military Intelligence Administration of the General Staff). This is the organisation responsible for intelligence operations outside Czechoslovakia; that is, foreign intelligence operations such as espionage, political sabotage, deception and disinformation, and technology theft.

A prime example of the confusion that exists is an article on the 'dread secret police' published during the upheavals in Eastern Europe [1989-90]. 'The StB has been regarded by Western diplomats as the most ruthless and efficient of all the East European security services .... Internationally, the Soviet Union's KGB has often used the StB as a surrogate for doing its dirty work. The StB's connection to international terrorist organisations – through the manufacture of the deadly plastic explosive Semtex [a plastic explosive favoured by terrorists because it emits few telltale vapours and is very hard to detect] – is another mystery'. Dan Morgan, 'Amateurs Probe Dread Secret Police', *Washington Post*, December 14, 1989, page 41.

Here, the author is mixing up, or combining, the first and Second Administrations. Both are ruthless and efficient. Western diplomats in Czechoslovakia will have more contact with the StB or First Administration than with the Second Administration, although without their knowledge. The First Administration will contact them to learn about spies in Czechoslovakia. The Second Administration will try to recruit them to spy for Czechoslovakia. Outside Czechoslovakia, almost all contact will be by the Second Administration. And while both administrations are used as surrogates by the KGB, internationally it is the Second Administration which is the surrogate for KGB intelligence operations, and it is in the Second Administration and military intelligence where terrorist operations and the support provided for them – such as the production of Semtex – are organised. Also, drug-trafficking is organised within the Second Administration and within military intelligence, not in the StB, although the StB does have a counter-intelligence task, which is shared with the Third Administration, military counter-intelligence.

There is also often a confusion as to the importance and rôle of military intelligence. This is probably due to the preponderant number of sources (defectors) from civilian intelligence and the relative scarcity of military intelligence sources. Most civilian intelligence officials do not know much about military intelligence operations and, accordingly, tend to play down the importance of military intelligence.

Another confusion is the notion that the StB 'operates as a state within a state, uncontrolled by its alleged superiors at the Interior Ministry of the Communist Party Central Committee'. Control is the *essence* of the overt Communist system. Everything and everybody is controlled. It is the First Secretary who wields most control. Beneath him, there are numerous committees and commissions also exerting control, many of which are, in turn, controlled by the First Secretary. Additionally, within the satellites, the Soviet Union has its own control mechanisms. To think that organisations, including the StB, run rampant without control is to overlook one of the most important characteristics of the internal structure of the Communist system.

In addition to civilian intelligence and counter-intelligence, there are a variety of other major subdivisions or administrations within the Ministry of Interior that are important components of the intelligence and security system. These are: military counter-intelligence, public security (police), passport control, investigations, jails, interior troops, border troops, customs service, censorship, support for foreign diplomats and embassies, and finance. In comparing the Czechoslovak and Soviet intelligence services, the Czechoslovak Ministry of Interior is roughly comparable to the Soviet KGB (*Komitet Gosudarstvennoy Bezopasnosti* or Committee for State Security). The principal difference is that the public security (police) in the Soviet Union do not come under the KGB. The Czechoslovak Second Administration is comparable to that portion of the KGB that handles intelligence, as distinct from counter-intelligence, investigations, customs, and so forth.

14. When the intelligence plan was reviewed in 1965 or 1966 by the Czechoslovak Defence Council, one of the members asked how effective the program had been. At that time, the chief of military intelligence explained, only seven graduates had not been successful. Of this number, two had been killed by Czechoslovak intelligence when they had attempted to switch sides.

15. General Sejna was present at a discussion with the First Secretary of the Communist Party of El Salvador, who was told directly that in return for weapons and military supplies, it was his Party's responsibility to help the Czechoslovaks pay for the weapons through drugs. The First Secretary responded that the market in El Salvador was limited, but if it was expanded to include the United States and Canada, none of us would have a money problem. The Czechoslovak official who was in charge then advised him that the United States and Canada were the primary targets.

BUILDING THE LATIN AMERICAN DRUG NETWORK

The Czechoslovak component of the Soviet drug offensive began in 1960 on two fronts, Asia (Indonesia, India and Burma) and Latin America (Cuba). Because of the special relevance of Cuba to the growth in illegal drugs and narcotics in the United States, the Soviet-Czechoslovak-Cuban operation deserves close scrutiny.

In the late summer of 1960, just a year and a half after Fidel Castro seized power, his brother Raúl Castro visited Czechoslovakia in search of military aid and assistance. At that time, Fidel and the Soviets distrusted each other, which is why the Cubans first approached Czechoslovakia rather than the Soviet Union. Sejna was responsible for receiving the Cuban delegation and serving as their host during their visit. One of his first actions was to arrange for Raúl to visit the Soviet Union and meet Khrushchev[1]. Following that visit, the Soviets directed Czechoslovakia to work with the Cubans and pave the way for an eventual Soviet takeover of Cuba. The Soviets wanted Czechoslovakia to take the lead, hiding the rôle of the Soviet Union. They did not want Fidel Castro to be aware of the Soviet operation to infiltrate and take over Cuba and they did not want the United States to be alerted to what would be happening.

Cuba and Czechoslovakia signed an agreement whereby the Czechoslovaks would help the Cubans obtain military equipment, train the Cubans in military planning and operations, and help organise Cuban intelligence and counter-intelligence[2]. In return, Cuba agreed to become a revolutionary centre[3] in the West and to allow Czechoslovakia to establish an intelligence station in Cuba. Sixteen Czechoslovak advisors went to Cuba to provide training and help establish their intelligence and counter-intelligence operations. Roughly fifty percent of the Czechoslovak advisors and intelligence agents who went to Cuba were actually Soviets operating under Czechoslovak cover. Within three years, all Czechoslovaks in key positions would be replaced by Soviets. Thus, from the beginning, Cuban intelligence and military structures were heavily influenced by the Soviets. In less than ten years, the Soviets were in complete control.

After the first Cubans had been trained as intelligence agents, they received their first directions from Moscow via Czechoslovakia: to infiltrate the United States and all Latin American countries[4] and to produce and distribute drugs and narcotics into the United

States. The instructions from the Soviet Defence Council went to the Czechoslovak Defence Council and thence to Cuba. Czechoslovak advisers helped the Cubans initiate the production of drugs and narcotics as a matter of the highest priority and also assisted them in setting up transportation routes through Canada and Mexico, where the Czechoslovaks had good agent networks, into the United States. Rudolph Barak, the Czechoslovak Minister of Interior and as such the head of civilian intelligence, personally helped establish the Cuban operation. From the beginning, Barak was constantly pushing the Soviets to go faster and farther. He wanted to speed production and make more effective use of the Czechoslovak agent networks in Latin America, Asia, Austria and West Germany[5].

No sooner had the basic Cuban drug production and trafficking operation started up than instructions were received from the Soviet Defence Council to expand the offensive. In 1961, Czechoslovakia received directions from the Soviet Defence Council for Cuban intelligence to infiltrate existing drug operations in Latin America and the United States and to prepare the base for 'recruiting' these independent operations. The order was presented to the Czechoslovak Defence Council by the Ministers of Defence and Interior. As Secretary of the Czechoslovak Defence Council, Sejna was responsible for coordinating and scheduling such directions and subsequent assignments. The Czechoslovak plan to implement the order had been coordinated and approved by the Soviet Administrative Organs Department of the Central Committee of the CPSU.

The *main objective* of the infiltration was to obtain information on individuals who had been corrupted by drug and narcotics trafficking. Key target groups that were identified were the military, police, government, politics, religions and business. Additional targets were scientific institutions, military industry, and universities. *A secondary objective* was to obtain intelligence on all drug and narcotics production and distribution activity, to enable the Soviets to exert strategic control and help prevent the various independent operations from interfering with one another. Intelligence derived from organised crime penetrations also contributed to this objective. The first meeting to coordinate the infiltration and collection of data on drug and narcotics corruption that Sejna was aware of occurred in 1962 during the Second Havana Conference, at a secret meeting of Soviet and Soviet-trained strategic intelligence agents from all the Latin American organisations. The secret meeting was managed by Cuban and Czechoslovak intelligence. Czechoslovak officials from military intelligence, Zs, organised the meeting. Other Czechoslovak officials attending the conference were from the Ministry of Interior, Second Administration (the KGB intelligence counterpart in Czechoslovakia) and military counter-intelligence.

In collecting data on individuals corrupted by drug-trafficking, both those using drugs or profiting from the trafficking, the Soviets identified large numbers of people who could be bribed, who were susceptible to influence, and, most important, as Sejna elaborated, who were '*not concerned about the consequences of their actions*'. The resulting information in the dossiers provided an excellent base for recruiting 'agents of influence' or spies. This information was also used to expose and damage the reputations of individuals and organisations considered hostile to Soviet interests.

The use of corruption data for blackmail and for recruiting agents of influence is a long-standing Marxist-Leninist tactic which is used on a global scale. Czechoslovak intelligence divided its dossiers on corruption into two categories: people already in positions of power, and people at lower levels who were likely to advance into positions of power. By 1967, Czechoslovak intelligence had about 2,500 dossiers on people in the first category.

Their files did not duplicate the dossiers maintained by others who were active in Latin America – the Cubans, East Germans, Hungarians, Bulgarians and Soviets – because of cooperation among the intelligence services. Thus, by the late 1960s, the Soviets already possessed corruption data on upwards of 10,000 influential people throughout Latin America.

As an indication that these numbers are not unreasonable, in 1971 a Frenchman by the name of Batkoun was caught bringing heroin into Canada. He was deported to France and convicted there of exporting heroin. During the trial, Batkoun was identified as a member of the French Communist Party and an agent of the subsection '*Groupement Cinq*' of the Soviet KGB. During his trial, *Valeurs Actuelles* reported that when arrested he had in his possession a list of 2,000 heroin addicts in Canada, many of whom were prominent civil servants, artists, radio and television entertainers, and university professors[6].

Corruption, of course, is not confined to Latin America, but includes North America and European countries such as France, Sweden, Austria, Switzerland, Italy, Great Britain and Germany, of which the last two were identified by the head of the CPSU's International Department, Boris Ponomarëv, as the most corrupt. Recognising that the financial institutions that help launder illicit money are part of this network of corruption, the potential for Soviet blackmail and influence operations becomes mind-numbing. Indeed, as will be discussed later, part of the Soviet strategy was to involve people in drugs who were in positions of influence, especially people in banks, financial institutions, politics, the military, and middle-level management in industry, *precisely* because of the subsequent potential for blackmail and influence operations[7].

Knowledge of how various 'independent' drug operations work, what their trafficking networks are, and who their contacts are, is also used in pursuit of the second objective mentioned on page 26, to exercise strategic control over the operations. In general, the Soviets do not want or need tactical, day-to-day control. So long as drugs and narcotics are flowing in the right direction, into bourgeois societies, Soviet objectives are being accomplished. What is important to the Soviets is to prevent such activities from interfering with other Soviet Bloc operations and certainly to prevent such operations from causing the spotlight of publicity to be shone in the 'wrong' direction.

The information collected via this process was impressive. In 1963, General Sejna, the Minister of Defence, and the chief of military intelligence visited the Zs drug-trafficking training centre at Bratislava. Their host and escort was Colonel Karel Borsky, the military intelligence political officer who was in charge of the training centres. At the time, Sejna was amazed at the scope of the detail on drug-trafficking around the world, but especially throughout Latin America, that had been assembled at the Bratislava training location. For example, extensive data had been acquired on numerous companies in Mexico the main business of which was drug smuggling – including pictures of the trucks and the names of the drivers used to transport the drugs into the United States.

Armed with knowledge of how drug operations work, the Soviets watch an operation and exert control only when necessary. The potential for strategic control is evident from testimony given in 1983 by Juan Crump, a Colombian lawyer and narcotics trafficker. In response to questions by Senator Dennis DeConcini (D-AZ) on the importance of contacts with Colombian officials, Crump responded that contact (bribery) was essential in order to exist and survive[8]. Through Soviet knowledge of these officials, and intelligence on their illegal activities, the Soviets obtain the leverage to exert control over the 'independent' drug operations when necessary.

Another mechanism employed to deal with organisations or individuals who do not cooperate is to set them up for arrest by drug enforcement authorities. That has been rumoured to be what enabled the US authorities to bring to trial the Colombian drug lord, Carlos Lehder Rivas. Possible reasons for his betrayal are easy to imagine. For example, either the Soviets or the other members of the Medellín Cartel could have concluded that Lehder had become too vocal, too political[9]. Lehder was giving radio interviews and calling cocaine the 'Latin American atomic bomb'[10]. Cocaine was a revolutionary weapon to be used against the imperialists, he explained. The problem with what he was saying was that it focused unnecessary attention on the drug operations, specifically on the Medellín Cartel of which he was a member, and was close enough to the truth about the Soviet operation, that either party could have concluded that Lehder had to be silenced[11]. The beauty of simply turning him over to American law enforcement authorities was that it improved the public image of these authorities, even though all they were really doing was acting as disciplinary agents for the drug-trafficking organisation.

Another example of this practice was provided by Ramon Milian Rodriguez, a Miami-based CPA who managed a significant proportion of the drug money earned by Colombia's Medellín Cartel [see page 97]. While in the process of taking $5.3 million in cash out of the United States in May 1983, he was arrested and subsequently convicted of racketeering[12]. Rodriguez was employed by the cartel to set up safe houses for collecting, counting and packaging the cash. He then arranged shipment of the money, a complex laundering process, to various banks. All the banks in Panama were used by Rodriguez in the process. Eventually, he explained, most of the money returned to him, which he then invested in real estate, stocks, bonds and Certificates of Deposit for the cartel.

When Rodriguez first set up the operation, Manuel Antonio Noriega was an army colonel in charge of Panama's intelligence service. Rodriguez testified before a US Senate Subcommittee in 1988 that he believed General Noriega had 'very adroitly used the American law enforcement agencies to surgically extract me from the operation, while leaving the operation intact for him and his cronies to continue working'[13]. The tip-off for Rodriguez's arrest was an anonymous wire, presumably sent by Noriega, from Panama to the South Florida Task Force on drug interdiction, alerting them to Rodriguez's plans[14].

But there are other possibilities worth considering. Rodriguez states throughout his testimony that he was strongly anti-Communist. In 1980 or 1981, Cuban intelligence, the DGI, had tried to recruit him to their operation, but he had turned them down. At about the same time, a war started between the Medellín Cartel and the Cuban-sponsored M-19 revolutionaries. Rodriguez states that he advised the Cartel on how to fight the war using terrorist tactics, and then advised against cooperating with the M-19 after the dispute was resolved. Rodriguez further explains how he cautioned the Cartel about the measures he saw being taken by Cuban intelligence to penetrate and obtain control of the Cartel. Finally, Rodriguez explained how he was especially careful in his dealings with Noriega to ensure that 'Noriega was powerful enough to serve us but never let him get powerful enough to control us'. While the telex to Miami that triggered Rodriguez's arrest may have come from Noriega, under the circumstances it would also be logical to suspect that a Cuban or Soviet intelligence agent might have been behind it.

Through the use of information gained by infiltrating the various drug organisations, the Soviets have no need for direct (tactical) control of all Latin American operations. Indeed, it is better that they maintain their distance and that even insiders should remain unaware of the leverage (control) the Soviets can exert when necessary. This operating principle can be seen reflected in a secret resolution adopted at the Tri-Continental Conference held in Cuba in 1966, which stated as the sixth operating principle:

'To back up resolutely the campaign of the drug addicts, defending it in the name of respect for individual rights. *To maintain completely apart the cadres of the Communist Party from the channels for narcotics and their traffic, so that this source of income could not be linked with the revolutionary action of the Communist Party* although we must combine fostering the fear of atomic war with pacifism and with the demoralisation of youth by means of hallucinating agents'[15] [emphasis added].

Following the decision to have Cuban intelligence agents infiltrate all Latin American operations, the Soviet Defence Council gave further instructions, again through the Czechoslovak Defence Council, this time for Cuba to establish its own production and trafficking operations in various Latin American countries. This provided a first-level backup to the indigenous operations. Cuba now moved rapidly to establish narcotics activities in Mexico and Colombia. The resulting Cuban drug network set up in Colombia was manned by Colombians but directed by Cuba. Czechoslovak intelligence helped establish the operation and the Soviets were involved in both planning and approval. As soon as the new arrangements were underway in Mexico and Colombia, the Cubans, with the assistance of the Czechoslovaks, expanded into Panama and Argentina, and, with the assistance of East Germany, into Uruguay and Jamaica.

Cuba and Czechoslovakia also developed joint operations in Chile. Danislav Lhotsky, a Czechoslovak intelligence agent, was in Chile officially under an economic cover. His instructions were to develop in concert with the Cubans production and distribution networks in Chile first, and then to expand the network into Argentina and Brazil. When Lhotsky returned to Czechoslovakia in 1967, he was awarded the Order of Red Star for his successful work in building the drug network in Chile.

One of Cuba's early contributions to the drug operation in Chile – identified in a US Drug Enforcement Administration (DEA) intelligence report – was the recruitment of the Marxist Senator Salvador Allende, who would later become President. Allende was also present at the Tri-Continental Conference. He proposed creation of OLAS – the Latin American Solidarity Organisation – as a 'united front advocating armed revolution' and was elected its first leader. During Allende s presidency drug-trafficking flourished. In 1973, US authorities seized $309 million worth of cocaine produced in Chilean laboratories[16].

In Argentina, the Czechoslovak drug operation was established by one of Czechoslovakia's most successful agents, Oldrick Limbursky, who was functioning in Argentina as a representative of a Czechoslovak export company. He built the drug network in Argentina and then expanded it into Brazil.

In short, the Cubans were highly effective in establishing operations throughout Latin America. Both Fidel and Raúl Castro were enthusiastic and pushed hard to have drug activities expanded faster than the Soviets deemed prudent. Fidel Castro's first visit to Czechoslovakia was particularly noteworthy in this respect. His visit coincided with an extended visit to Moscow following the Cuban Missile Crisis. He was annoyed, to say the least, and spent roughly ten days complaining to top Soviet leaders about their general lack of consultation with him. Then he went on to Czechoslovakia.

The conversations with Fidel were most difficult, Sejna explains. Fidel thought he could destroy capitalism overnight. He wanted to exploit crime for revolution and use the knowledge of people already corrupted by drugs, which was flowing in from the Cuban infiltration operation, to help speed the sale of drugs. The drugs will help us, Sejna recalls Castro emphasising, in our defence, in obtaining money, and in liquidating capitalism.

Fidel was absolutely adamant. This episode, in fact, was one reason why the Soviets regarded him as an anarchist more than as a Communist. The Czechoslovak officials argued long and hard to convince Fidel that they needed to prepare for the next twenty years, not just for tomorrow. It was not possible, they stressed, to change the old generation. We can corrupt them and exploit them through crime to obtain information and to influence decisions. But the focus for significant change had to be the younger generation. These were the people that we needed to work on to change the military, to retard scientific development, and to influence government leadership. This is why American youth had been selected as the primary target for the drug offensive.

To communicate Soviet drugs strategy more decisively and clearly to Fidel, Czechoslovak officials organised a detailed briefing on Khrushchev's strategy of 'peaceful coexistence', which was designed, as Khrushchev had explained to high-level Czechoslovak officials in 1954, not to befriend the Americans, **but to lead them to the grave more quickly**. The whole operation was laid out so that Fidel would understand how the use of drugs was integrated into the overall strategy and, therefore, why it was not possible simply to isolate drugs and treat drug-trafficking as an independent operation. drug-trafficking had been designed as an integral part of a coordinated strategy, and it was essential that Fidel understood the importance of this strategy for the long-range, systematic destruction of capitalism.

In addition to production and trafficking, Cuba was also involved in research and development of new drugs. In the fall of 1963, Raúl Castro's deputy went to Czechoslovakia for assistance in obtaining special equipment for producing drugs in Colombia and for manufacturing synthetic drugs as part of an experimental program in Cuba. The actual equipment was picked up by Raúl Castro in April 1964, when he stopped over in Prague after a visit to Moscow. Subsequently, the Czechoslovak chief of the Health Administration of the Rear Services, Colonel-General Miroslav Hemalla, accompanied by two subordinates and two technicians, flew to Cuba to sign an agreement on medical cooperation (a cover for drug research), to teach the Cubans how to operate the equipment, and to instruct Castro to begin local production of drugs in the Dominican Republic. This was part of the Soviet decision to produce drugs locally whenever possible, rather than ship them in from the Soviet Union or Eastern Europe. Cubans were to be used as the operators, so as to keep the Soviets 'clean'.

Following these various measures to penetrate existing drug organisations and then to set up Cuban operations throughout Latin America, the Soviets ordered the formation of still another set of backup production and distribution networks all over the region – this one organised directly by selected East European intelligence services. Czechoslovakia's first target was Colombia. To kick-start the new operation, the Soviets recommended that the Czechoslovaks should recruit one of the key individuals from Cuba's drug network in Colombia, a retired Colombian military officer who went by the name of Kovaks. The Top Secret code name for the Czechoslovak operation in Colombia, **'Pyramid'**, was selected to mislead people into associating the new initiative with the Middle East. The Czechoslovak officer in charge of this operation was the first deputy at the Ministry of

Interior. Shortly afterwards, he became the Minister of Interior. Amazing through it may seem, some in the West do not even appreciate that in the overt Communist system, the Minister of Interior is not the person in charge of natural resources or parks, which is what Westerners usually associate with the title. Rather, the Minister of Interior is in charge of 'interior security'; that is, civilian intelligence and the secret police.

Kovaks travelled to Czechoslovakia in April 1964 with a plan for the new operation to be approved by Czechoslovak intelligence. To cover his trip, he first went to Mexico, where he was provided with a forged passport at the Czechoslovak Embassy. From Mexico he flew to Vienna, where he was provided with a Czechoslovak passport to use on the third leg of his journey.

The final plan that he brought with him for the new activities in Colombia was first taken to the Soviet Union for approval. Then the plan, modified to incorporate last-minute Soviet suggestions, was presented to the Czechoslovak Defence Council. The plan set forth guidelines and planning estimates, the most important of which were:

1. With help in obtaining the necessary equipment, production of cocaine would begin within six months.
2. The distribution network would be in operation in less than six months.
3. Initial distribution would be into the United States and Canada. Later, the distribution would be extended to Europe.
4. Distribution would be kept out of the local market.

At the presentation of the joint Ministry of Defence and Ministry of Interior plan, the Minister of Defence explained that twelve people had already been recruited for the operation and that eight of them had already been cleared in two ways: first, by the Communist Party of Colombia, and secondly, by a long-time Czechoslovak intelligence agent who was then a high official within Colombia's internal security ministry. The plan was unanimously approved by the Czechoslovak Defence Council.

Because the most effective Cuban drug operation was developing in Mexico, the Soviets now directed the Czechoslovaks to infiltrate and gain control of this operation. The Czechoslovak Top Secret code name for this operation, **'Rhine'**, was selected to mislead people into associating it with Europe. The Czechoslovak agent who was responsible for this initiative, Major Jidrich Strnad, had been operating in Mexico under cover of an export company. His Zs control officer was Colonel Borsky.

The Cubans had been especially effective in recruiting Mexicans to establish production and distribution networks and in using the associated corruption information for blackmailing Mexican officials. The Soviets were especially impressed, and one of the main reasons for directing Czechoslovak intelligence to infiltrate the Cuban operation was to learn the secrets of their success in Mexico.

Recognising the strategic location of Mexico, the Soviets further directed the establishment of a *second* Czechoslovak operation in Mexico which was designed to complement the **'Rhine'** initiative. The code name of this second operation was **'Full Moon'**.

This drug campaign had two purposes. The *first* was to develop an extensive network for smuggling drugs into the United States. The *second* was to train intelligence agents who would then be inserted into the United States and Canada, with instructions to penetrate drug distribution networks. Through their contacts into supply networks in Mexico, they were to access the supply network and gradually take control of the drug businesses in the United States and Canada. This was a 'push-pull' drug operation. The name **'Full Moon'** referred to the time when Soviet Bloc agents would be in control of most major groups in the United States and Canada. Mexico, it should be noted, has also been an important country in the Chinese drug offensive.

With both the Soviets (initially through the Cubans) and Chinese having targeted Mexico, it comes as no surprise that Mexico is one of the primary drug-trafficking routes into the United States for heroin, cocaine and marijuana. For identical reasons, Canada is another primary drug-trafficking route into the United States.

Czechoslovak intelligence was also involved in the Cuban operation in Panama, under the code name **'Pablo'**. A Cuban operation was set up, too, in El Salvador. At a meeting on the financing of the Communist Party of El Salvador, Sejna remembers that the Soviets directed the Cubans to provide the financing for that Party out of their profits from the El Salvador drug operation[17].

A separate Soviet operation intended for the 'benefit' of those who regularly seek the warm sands and seas of the Caribbean islands was directly targeted to take advantage of the booming Caribbean tourist trade. The Second Secretary of the French Communist Party (a long-time KGB agent), together with the First Secretary of the Communist Party of Guadeloupe, conceived the idea of distributing drugs to Caribbean tourists. Their objectives were to raise money out of the tourist trade and to obtain blackmail information on vacationing Americans and other members of the bourgeoisie.

They helped establish the operation and provided recommendations on whom to recruit to run it. The operation was then turned over to two Czechoslovak intelligence officers, one from military intelligence and one from the Ministry of Interior. Both officials had been born in France and spoke fluent French. Guadeloupe was the centre of the operation, which serviced Martinique and other islands. The monies earned in the late 1960s from this initiative proved adequate to finance all Communist intelligence operations in Guadeloupe, Martinique, Suriname, Haiti and most of France.

In the early 1960s, the Soviets were rapidly building organisations throughout North, Central and South America and the Caribbean. Other Soviet satellites directly involved as Soviet surrogates, in addition to Czechoslovakia and Cuba, were Hungary, East Germany, Bulgaria and Poland. Understandably, most of Sejna's knowledge was of the Czechoslovak dimension of the drug strategy. The other East European satellites identified above are not dealt with in detail in this analysis, but they were all deeply involved in the Soviet drug offensive. Romania and Albania were not part of the formal Soviet-directed offensive because the Soviets did not trust their security. Albania had asked to participate, emphasising its strong intelligence network in the Balkans and the Middle East. But rather than bring Albania into the operation, the Soviets decided to provide Albania with the money to purchase the necessary equipment, so that Albania could proceed as an 'independent' drug promoter.

Countries where Sejna had direct knowledge of organisations which had been established by the mid-1960s included Canada, Mexico, Panama, Argentina, Chile, Brazil, Colombia, Costa Rica, Uruguay, Paraguay, Brazil, Peru, Guadeloupe, El Salvador, the Dominican Republic, Jamaica and quite naturally, the United States. To this list should be added countries where organised crime operations that were critical to the drug-trafficking network, were being developed. One example of such a country is Venezuela, which the Soviets had decided in 1960-61 to use as a centre for mafia organisation, operations and money-laundering in the Western hemisphere.

The drugs initially chosen for distribution were opium, heroin, morphine, marijuana and synthetics such as LSD. While cocaine was not prominent at that time, by 1961 the Soviets, in analysing the drug scene, had concluded that cocaine was, to borrow one of their favourite phrases, the 'wave of the future'[18]. This revelation to Sejna came during a meeting in Moscow in 1964 which had been convened to discuss and coordinate deception planning. In attendance from Czechoslovakia were the head of the Military Section of the Administrative Organs Department, the deputy chief of the Main Political Administration, the deputy chief of Zs (military intelligence) and head of strategic intelligence, and Jan Sejna. The Soviets present were the deputy chief of the Main Political Administration, the deputy chief of GRU [Soviet Military Intelligence] and head of strategic intelligence, and General Boris Shevchenko, the head of the Department of Special Propaganda, who ran the meeting.

It was at this meeting that Shevchenko introduced the term **'Pink Epidemic'**. In discussing the future, he stressed the potential of cocaine. It was highly preferable to heroin, he explained, because it was so much easier to produce and because they believed that many more people could be reached with cocaine than with heroin. The Soviets were so impressed with cocaine's potential, in fact, that they spoke in terms of its becoming an epidemic, a 'white epidemic'. To 'serve and extend' the epidemic, Shevchenko explained that a *separate* production and distribution base was to be built, commencing immediately.

This new cocaine operation was to be referred to by the aforementioned cover name, **'Pink Epidemic'**. In the beginning, the lead countries in establishing the cocaine production and distribution base were the Soviet Union, Czechoslovakia and Cuba. Czechoslovakia immediately began a special technology program to develop the necessary production techniques. This operation was run by military intelligence and the Health Administration, under the control of military counter-intelligence.

Necessary production experimentation was conducted at a top-secret scientific research centre at Milovice. The operation was facilitated by the Cubans, who learned the crude techniques that were used in South America and then passed the information to Czechoslovak intelligence. The Czechoslovak scientists took the procedures and developed more professional mass-production techniques.

Thus, between 1960 and 1965, the Soviet Bloc intelligence services, directed from Moscow, established drug production, distribution and money-laundering operations throughout South, Central and North America. Only local personnel who passed stringent security background investigations were used to run the operations, which were discreetly managed by Soviet Bloc or Cuban intelligence agents who, as a general rule, were specially trained in the Soviet Union. Future drug-traffickers from all over the world were taught the narcotics trade in East European and Soviet training centres. Additional training centres were later established in North Korea, North Vietnam and in Cuba. These graduate criminals became controlled Soviet narcotics trafficking agents. The initial trafficking was in heroin, marijuana, and synthetics. However, with effect from 1964, a special network was constructed specifically to serve and extend the coming cocaine epidemic. ∎

References to Chapter 3:

1. For a more detailed account, see *We Will Bury You, op. cit.*, pages 45-50.

2. Biographies of Fidel Castro describe the problems he had obtaining military equipment in 1959 from the Soviet Union, Yugoslavia, and the United States. Some arms and ammunition were obtained from Belgium in mid-1960. The first Czechoslovak weapons arrived in late 1960. Tad Szulc, *Fidel: A Critical Portrait* (New York: William Morrow and Company, Inc., 1986), page 498. Peter G. Bourne, *Fidel: A Biography of Fidel Castro* (New York: Dodd, Mead & Company, 1986), pages 188-189.

3. **'Revolutionary centre'** is the formal designation of a region selected and then prepared to promote the revolutionary situation throughout the zone in which the centre is located and to support Soviet military operations in the event of war. The basic criteria applied in establishing revolutionary centres are the need for such centres to have political influence throughout the zone, to supply revolutionary forces for deployment in other countries in the zone, to supply sabotage material for use throughout the zone, to be a centre for the education of cadres, and to be directly useful for Soviet military operations in the case of global war and for surrogate forces or neighbouring forces in revolutionary wars.

4. In the summer of 1963, a Czechoslovak intelligence report stated that Cuban intelligence agents had successfully penetrated 69 percent of the Latin American countries. In most cases, the penetration had been through Mexico. Additionally, with the help of Spanish communities, they had placed seven agents in the United States.

5. In 1984, Clyde D. Taylor, Acting Assistant Secretary, Bureau of International Narcotics Matters, Department of State, told Congress that reports on the involvement of the Cuban Government in narcotics trafficking had first reached the US Government in 1963. US Congress, Senate, *Drugs and Terrorism, 1984*, Hearing Before the Subcommittee on Alcoholism and Drug Abuse of the Committee on Labour and Human Resources, August 2, 1984 (Washington D.C.: US Government Printing Office, 1984), page 41. Rachel Ehrenfeld has written that a secret Drug Enforcement Agency [DEA] report leaked to the *Miami Herald*, November 20, 1983, identified 1961 as the beginning of Cuba's involvement in drug-trafficking: 'Narco-Terrorism and the Cuban Connection', *Strategic Review*, Summer 1988, page 57. Arthur M. Schlesinger, Jr. in *Robert Kennedy and His Times* (Boston: Houghton Mifflin Company, 1978), page 504, reports that a Federal Narcotics Bureau document of July 1961 reported rumours in the Florida Cuban exile community that Santos Trafficante, Jr., one of the organised crime bosses with ties into Cuba who was involved in the CIA assassination operation, was Castro's outlet for drugs in the United States. Another news report stated that DEA agent Avelino Fernandez broke open the Cuban drug connection to Noriega in 1978 and that Fidel Castro was specifically identified as having been involved with drug-trafficking since 1964. Michael Hedges, 'Picture Shows Castro, Noriega, del Cid at Secret Meeting', *Washington Post*, January 18, 1990, page A5.

6. Candlin, *Psycho-Chemical Warfare: The Chinese Communist Drug Offensive Against the West*, *op. cit.*, pages 182-183.

7. Infiltrating banks and financial institutions, while important when Khrushchev was in power, was made even more important when Brezhnev became General Secretary in 1964.

8. *The Cuban Government's Involvement in Facilitating International drug-traffic*, Joint Hearing Before the Subcommittee on Security and Terrorism of the Committee on the Judiciary and the Subcommittee on Western Hemisphere Affairs of the Foreign Relations Committee and the Senate Drug Enforcement Caucus, United States Senate, Miami, Florida, April 30, 1983 (Washington, D.C.: US Government Printing Office, 1983), pages 10, 26-27.

9. See Rensselaer W. Lee III, 'Why the US Cannot Stop South American Cocaine', *Orbis*, Fall 1988, page 11.

10. 'Interview with Carlos Lehder Rivas, Reputed Colombian drug-trafficker', in Uri Ra'anan et al., *Hydra of Carnage* (Lexington, Massachusetts: Lexington Books, 1986), pages 433-435.

11. As an example of this type of concern, the former Consul General of Panama, José I. Blandón Castillo, testified that 'we had information to the effect that the Medellín Cartel was... very concerned with Noriega because Noriega was being too visible. He was preventing them from what they call business, and they were trying to find a way to eliminate him'. US Congress, Senate, *Drugs, Law Enforcement and Foreign Policy: Panama*, Hearings Before the Subcommittee on Terrorism, Narcotics and International Operations of the Committee on Foreign Relations, February 10, 1988, Stenographic Transcript, pages 52-53.

12. US Congress, Senate, *Drugs, Law Enforcement and Foreign Policy: Panama*, Hearings Before the Subcommittee on Terrorism, Narcotics and International Operations of the Committee on Foreign Relations, February 11, 1988, Stenographic Transcript 1.

13. *Ibid.*, page 86.

14. It does not make logical sense for Noriega to turn in Rodriguez to gain control, because turning in Rodriguez would not accomplish that objective. If Noriega did turn in Rodriguez, therefore, it would seem logical to search for another reason. One possibility is that Noriega was simply assisting US drug control operations in Operation Pisces, which was investigating money-laundering in Panama, or appearing to be assisting while actually performing a favour for someone else. As in many situations, a combination of various considerations may well have been involved.

15. Candlin, *Psycho-Chemical Warfare: The Chinese Communist Drug Offensive Against the West*, *op. cit.*, pages 48-49, citing translations provided by Professor Herminio Portell-Vila, former history instructor of Fidel Castro at the University of Havana.

16. Data on Chile in the early 1960s is contained in the study by Robert Workman on narcotics trafficking for the National Defence University. He writes that a DEA intelligence report dated March 31, 1982, describes a 1961 meeting of high-ranking Cuban officials, 'including revolutionary leader and President of the National Bank of Cuba, Che Guevara, Captain Moises Crespo of the Cuban secret police, and Dr Salvador Allende, a senator and future Marxist President from Chile, to discuss establishing a cocaine trafficking network'. The report was described in a *Miami Herald* newspaper story, and Workman writes that intelligence agents stated that the article was accurate. Robert B. Workman, *International Drug-trafficking: A Threat to National Security* (Washington, D.C.: National Defence University, Research Publication Directorate, June 1984), unpublished.

Also, as James R. Whelan reported: 'At the Tri-Continental Conference in Havana, then-Senator Salvador Allende proposed the creation of OLAS – the Latin American Solidarity Organisation – as a 'united front… advocating armed revolution'. Allende was then elected to head OLAS. Once in the Chilean Presidency, he presided over a dramatic expansion of illicit drug activity in that country. According to one source, during the final year of Allende's presidency (1973), US authorities seized $309 million worth of cocaine from Chilean laboratories. The drug trade was said to yield $30,000 per month in pay-offs to the Popular Unity political parties in Allende's coalition. One of the first acts of the new military government headed by Gen. Augusto Pinochet was to crack down on the drug trade, working closely with US agencies to do so'. James R. Whelan, *Out of the Ashes: Life, Death and Transfiguration of Democracy in Chile, 1833-1988* (Washington, D.C.: Regnery-Gateway, 1989), pages 227-228, 592.

17. Robert Workman cited an interview with a US citizen who was kidnapped and held for ransom for about three months by the Revolutionary Armed Forces of Colombia (FARC), a Marxist guerrilla group. The victim reported as follows: 'The FARC, M-I9, and Ejercito Popular de Liberación (EPL) are all really consolidated, they are really one family controlled by Cuba…. I was in their camp when a Cuban was at a blackboard instructing some guerrillas. One of the guerrillas asked him: 'What happens to all of this money? You control the drug-traffic, you're taking in millions of dollars, and I don't see any money in our camp. They just give us bare necessities. You get food, clothes, and shells for your rifle and you do not get anything else'. The Cuban adviser's answer was that one half of the money was being sent to El Salvador. 'That we are liberating El Salvador. When El Salvador is liberated, then they will turn around and – using the economies of El Salvador, Nicaragua and Cuba – funnel funds into Colombia and help us, so we can overthrow the government here'. Robert B. Workman, *International Drug-trafficking A Threat to National Security* (Washington, D.C.: National Defence University, Research Publication Directorate, June 1984, unpublished, *op. cit.*), pages 13-14.

18. Many people are surprised that the Soviets recognised the potential of cocaine as early as 1961, especially since the problems posed by cocaine did not become well known in the United States until the late 1970s or early 1980s. This can be illustrated by recalling the attitude of President Carter's drug adviser, Peter Bourne, who viewed cocaine as pleasurable and benign and could not understand why DEA was making such a fuss over the increase in cocaine trafficking. The Yale University psychiatrist and drug historian David Musto has reminded us, however, how easily we forget. Early in this century, he explains, cocaine was legal and its use began to grow. Prices fell, and 'sniffing, swallowing and injecting of cocaine became widespread'. By 1910, cocaine had been transformed from 'a miracle drug to the most dangerous drug in America'. In his annual message to Congress that year, President William Howard Taft said: 'Cocaine is more appalling in its effects than any other habit-forming drug used in the United States'. Constance Holden, 'Past and Present Cocaine Epidemics', *Science*, December 15, 1989, page 1377, citing David F. Musto, *The American Disease: Origins of Narcotic Control* (New York: Oxford University Press, 1987).

KHRUSHCHEV INSTRUCTS THE SATELLITES

In 1962, Khrushchev formally extended the Soviet narcotics operation to the East European satellites. The strategic leaders (First Secretaries, Premier Ministers, Ministers of Defence, Chiefs of General Staff, and special assistants) of the satellites were summoned to attend a secret meeting in Moscow to discuss negative developments in the socialist economies. Romania, Albania and Yugoslavia were not present. Sejna was one of the officials in attendance. High-level Soviet officials attending the meeting included Nikita Khrushchev, Leonid Brezhnev, Mikhail Suslov and Andrei Kirilenko. It was at this meeting that Khrushchev formally laid out the Soviet strategy. Mao Tse-tung and the Chinese were smart, he began, referring to the drug business. They were also more imaginative and operative. Why should we let the Chinese have a free hand in this world market, he asked, and then he answered his own question. The Chinese were good, but the Soviet Bloc intelligence services had a much superior organisation and should move as fast as possible to use drugs and narcotics both to cripple capitalist society and to finance more revolutionary activities.

Khrushchev then discussed the many benefits to be derived from this business. It would provide a nice income and be a source of much-needed foreign exchange to finance intelligence operations. It would undermine the health and morale of American servicemen. Because people on drugs would be undependable in crises or emergencies, the drug business would 'weaken the human factor in the defence situation'.

Khrushchev dealt with the impact on education at length. American schools were high-priority targets, because this was where the future leaders of the bourgeoisie were to be found. Another high priority target Khrushchev identified was the American work ethic, pride and loyalty, all of which would be undermined through drugs. Finally, drugs and narcotics would lead to a decrease in the influence of religions and, he added, under certain conditions, could be used to create chaos.

'When we discussed this strategy', Khrushchev concluded, 'there were some who were concerned that this operation might be immoral. But we must state categorically', he stressed, 'that anything that speeds the destruction of capitalism is moral' [= Lenin – *Ed.*].

Only a few questions were raised by those attending the meeting. Janos Kadar, the

First Secretary from Hungary, expressed concern that the drug operation should not interfere with the progress that had been achieved under peaceful coexistence. He was referring to the economic and technical assistance that had begun flowing in from the West.
Accordingly, he suggested that Third World countries that were not regarded with suspi-
cion by the United States should be used to run the operations.

This, indeed, has been one of the techniques employed to maintain a safe distance
between the Soviet Bloc countries and the actual running of narcotics operations.
Throughout Latin America, for example, while Soviet Bloc intelligence agents exercise
overall control and direction, indigenous personnel are heavily relied upon to run the
actual operations. This technique can also be seen in respect of operations within the
Soviet Bloc that have been designed to service Western Europe. For example, the US Drug
Enforcement Agency prepared a summary report on the rôle of Bulgaria in international
narcotics trafficking in 1984 for Congressional hearings[1]. A variety of sources, all consistent, were referenced in the report, which covered the 1970-84 time period.

One organisation highlighted in the DEA report was KINTEX, a Bulgarian export-
import firm established in 1968. KINTEX was managed by the Bulgarian secret police and
acted 'on secret orders from Moscow'[2]. KINTEX was established, according to DEA
sources, mainly to provide a mechanism *for using foreign nationals* inside Bulgaria to manufacture and ship narcotics to Western Europe and munitions to the Near East. The foreign operatives were Turkish, Syrian and Jordanian nationals. Coordination meetings
included traffickers from Greece, Italy, Iraq and Iran. While Bulgaria was identified in the
early 1970s in a classified CIA study as being a 'new centre for directing narcotics and
arms trafficking'[3], all the data in the DEA report on people actually handling drugs refers
to foreigners operating inside Bulgaria. The Bulgarian Government's response to US complaints was to deny any involvement: the presence of foreign nationals on their soil constituted no crime and no Bulgarian nationals either inside or outside Bulgarian territory
have been implicated[4].

Another leader to speak at the Moscow meeting was Walter Ulbricht, the First Secretary from the German Democratic Republic. He used the occasion to press for greater German participation. At that time, the Germans did not have a charter to conduct strategic
intelligence and therefore, Ulbricht stressed, Germany would require assistance to exploit
its resources in Africa, the Middle East, and Latin America. Strategic intelligence, which
includes sabotage, terrorism, deception and espionage, was where the narcotics offensive
originated and had its home. By 1964, East Germany had been granted permission to
begin strategic intelligence operations.

Later in the day over drinks, Khrushchev nudged Sejna playfully with his elbow
and, with a gleam in his eye, he revealed the secret name of the Soviet drug-trafficking
operation, 'Druzhba Narodov' – which, roughly translated, means 'Friendship of Nations'.
The clever cover name with its deceptive play on words was pure Khrushchev.

This meeting in Moscow was a unique event. The Soviet narcotics strategy was considered exceedingly sensitive and was assigned the highest security classification. People
without an absolute need-to-know would not be told about the operation. Following the
meeting, which was the official beginning of the operation, with very few exceptions all
coordination and cooperation were handled on a bilateral basis.

The satellite leaders returned to their respective countries and proceeded to develop
their individual plans amid the tightest secrecy. Sejna has described the manner in which
the Czechoslovak plans were developed, briefed to the Defence Council, approved, and

then implemented. This description provides especially an interesting insight into the manner in which very sensitive operational plans were developed, controlled and kept secret.

The task of developing the plan was assigned to five people, one each from the Administrative Organs Department, civilian intelligence, military intelligence, the Foreign Department and the Military Health Administration. Sejna was in charge as Secretary of the Defence Council. The five people, plus a cook from Sejna's secretariat, were sequestered in a villa at Rusveltova No. 1, which incidentally was where Castro stayed when he came to visit Prague. Their work was monitored by the Soviet adviser to the chief of Zs and by Jiri Rudolf and Vaclav Havranek, who were the Administrative Organs Department officials in charge of military intelligence and military counter-intelligence. Only five other Czechoslovak officials had access to the villa, the Minister of Interior, the Minister of Defence, the Chief of the General Staff, the Chief of the Second Administration (civilian intelligence), and Sejna. After this group had assembled the overall plan, the only people who had access to it were the seven members of the Defence Council.

When the narcotics plan was finished, it was considered more sensitive even than even the annual intelligence plans. Nine copies were made and placed in sealed envelopes and taken to the Defence Council, where they were opened for the members to examine prior to their vote to approve the plan. The Minister of Defence and Minister of Interior jointly presented the plan to the Defence Council. The plan addressed research, development, influence of drugs on humans, testing, production, distribution, money handling, how the profits would be used, and the individuals who would have specific personal responsibilities. During the presentation, the Minister of Interior, Rudolph Barak, explained that 'Not only would this action serve to destroy Western society, but in addition the West will pay high money for it'. Antonin Novotny, First Secretary and Chairman of the Defence Council, asked how much, and Barak responded: 'Enough to finance the entire Czechoslovak intelligence service'.

As soon as the discussion was completed, not even waiting until the end of the meeting as was normally the case, Sejna collected all the copies and resealed them in their envelopes. All but three copies were destroyed. These three copies went to military intelligence (Zs), the Second Administration of the Minister of Interior, and the files of the Defence Council, which were in Sejna's secretariat. No written instructions to implement the plan were issued. The head of each department or agency that had a specific task came to one of the three offices where copies of the plan were held to read that portion on a 'need-to-know' basis. For example, for scientific development and production, the chiefs of the Rear Services and Medical Administration independently came to Sejna's office to read the pertinent portion of the plan. Sejna's job was to make certain each official understood his responsibility. The official was then required to sign a statement saying that he understood the directive, after which the official departed.

This process applied even to the Minister of Defence. All orders were verbal. Reports on progress were due back to Sejna in six months. Sejna himself then assembled and presented these reports to the Defence Council.

A year later, in 1963, Khrushchev, displeased with the speed with which the operation was progressing, directed General Major Nikolai Savinkin, the deputy head of the Administrative Organs Department of the Central Committee of the CPSU (he would become head in 1964 following General Mironov's death in a plane crash), to visit each satellite and Cuba personally and prepare a detailed plan to accelerate and coordinate the narcotics operation. The Administrative Organs Department is one of the two or three most important departments of the Central Committee[5]. It controls the Ministry of Defence, the Ministry of Interior (KGB), and the Ministry of Justice. This is the department that directed operation *'Druzhba Narodov'*[6]. Other organisations that participated are described in the next chapter.

Savinkin's plan was approved by the Soviet Defence Council and directives were sent to the various satellites. These directives, which came through Sejna as Secretary of the Czechoslovak Defence Council and Chief of Cabinet at the Ministry of Defence, covered a wide variety of actions: research, production, organisation of transportation, organisation of cooperation among satellites in different regions of the world, the need for cooperation in assisting Cuba to infiltrate all Latin American operations and what form that cooperation would take, names of specific people in different countries who would assist in the distribution, and associated propaganda and disinformation. Instructions were also received as to which specific financial institutions were to be used in laundering and transferring money. In the case of Czechoslovakia, at least fifteen different banks in nine countries (including Singapore, Vienna, Argentina and Holland) were identified. The Soviet bank in London became increasingly involved in the transfer of drug profits† [7].

The propaganda and disinformation instructions were especially interesting. Propaganda, disinformation and deception are exceptionally important dimensions of all Soviet operations. Each decision that is made is thoroughly prepared, including the monitoring or oversight, secrecy provisions (that is, who is to be told what), and the 'political plan' to facilitate the implementation.

The political plan is a euphemism for the deception that is to be employed. Disinformation and propaganda are developed to support the basic deception plan. In the narcotics and drug operation, the basic thrust of propaganda and disinformation was to cause the blame to be placed on 'society'. Additionally, and in support of this basic thrust, corruption data would be released to discredit individuals and organisations considered hostile to Soviet interests[8]. There were two different propaganda campaigns – one waged against youth and one against the population at large. This involved the Department of Special Propaganda, the Propaganda Department and the International (Foreign) Department, with a special coordination centre set up in the Administrative Organs Department.

The basic strategy for propaganda and deception had first been set forth in 1961 or 1962 by Soviet General Kalashnik, deputy to the Chief of the Main Political Administration, the ideological watchdog of the Soviet military establishment. Kalashnik was the chief ideologist at the Main Political Administration. Sejna recalls his simple instructions: 'Our propaganda must be directed to our enemy, not to our friends'. The word 'friends' meant drugs and narcotics. Propaganda and deception were to be used to divert attention away from drugs and narcotics, especially insofar as the middle and upper classes were concerned, and to cause these same people to focus their attention on problems of nuclear war, the Vietnam war and anti-Americanism.

† *Editor's Note:* In the late 1960s, UK employees of the Russian bank in London, Moscow Narodny Bank, observed that Russian officers of the institution were conspicuously liberal with entertainment and expense accounts, often inviting lowly members of staff to join them for extended 'liquid lunches'. For very many years, Viktor Geraschenko was either a senior officer or the head of the bank. Under Gorbachëv, Geraschenko was transferred to head the central banking institution and was accordingly seen at successive Annual Meetings of the International Monetary Fund and the World Bank after Russia had acceded to the Bretton Woods institutions. He was 'restored' to the position of head of the Russian Central Bank under President Yeltsin amid the turmoil which overwhelmed the Russian financial markets in August 1998.

These propaganda instructions were extended in 1964 in a letter signed by Leonid Brezhnev which was discussed at a meeting of the Czechoslovak Defence Council. The letter directed that data on the Chinese drug and narcotics trafficking operation should be made public, to advertise China's rôle as the source of illicit trafficking and thus to draw attention away from the Soviet operation. (One of the first articles written for this purpose appeared in *Pravda* on September 13, 1964. It was written by V. Ovchinnikov and was entitled *'The Drug Dealers': see also page 146, and Note 43, page 152*).

In September 1963 the top leadership (First Secretaries, Premier Ministers, Ministers of Defence and Interior and selected staff, a total of up to 15 from each country except for Romania, Albania and Yugoslavia, which were not present) met in Moscow for the annual conference on the plan and tactics to be followed in the coming year. The diplomatic, intelligence and party initiatives – the integrated process – for the coming year, were reviewed by the Soviet leadership.

The principal speaker was Mikhail Suslov, chief ideologist of the Communist Party and one of the key officials in the development of strategic plans. In discussing drugs, Suslov began by pointing out that the decision that had been taken earlier on drug and narcotics trafficking was the right course of action. As the Soviets had assessed Latin America in the 1950s, they had recognised that the Latin American countries were dependent on the bourgeoisie, especially the United States. The Soviets had decided that this had to change: the Latin American countries had to be made dependent on the Soviet Union. The primary instruments to be used were drugs and other forms of corruption, which the Soviets had concluded were widespread throughout the Americas.

The Soviets referred to the revolutionary movement in Latin America as the Second Liberation. The First Liberation had been the liberation from Spain and Portugal. The Second would be the intended liberation from the United States and the bourgeoisie [9]. The Third Liberation would be the transition into Communism.

Suslov explained that it was necessary to disarm anti-Communist and US friends before the Second Liberation could take place. The Soviets believed that the corrupted bourgeoisie had already accepted the idea of revolution, which was in fact a deliberate Soviet-induced deception. The approach taken to encourage acceptance of the notion of revolution was to argue that Latin American countries were destined to proceed through revolutionary stages, in which the changes that would be accomplished turn out to be beneficial. In these early stages, there was, by Soviet direction, to be no mention of socialism or even use of socialistic phrases – to avoid scaring people away from the concept of revolution.

The Soviets asserted that five factors would prove most instrumental in speeding the revolutionary process throughout Latin America:

1. *The US-USSR military balance.* The Soviet Union needed to be strong enough to stop the United States from interfering before the revolution could be started.

2. *Bankruptcy of colonialism.* Through propagandising the exploitation and impropriety of colonial policies and, naturally, the protectionism that went along with colonialism, the United States' ties to Latin America would be weakened and ultimately severed.

3. *Organisation of ideology and material supply of the liberation forces.* Better organisation and a united ideological offensive were required among the liberation forces. The movement had become disjointed under Stalin. Ideological unity was necessary and the supply of material assistance – money, arms, training, organisation – needed to be improved throughout Latin America.

4. *The defeat of the United States in Vietnam.* This was important to split the United States at home and to make it difficult for the United States ever to become involved in foreign wars again. Also, it was important for nationalistic forces to recognise that the United States could not be counted upon to assist its allies against the revolutionary process.

5. *The demoralisation of the United States and its neighbours on both sides, north and south.* Drugs were a principal instrument to be used in bringing about this demoralisation – with demoralisation by drugs to be referred to, as noted, as the **'Pink Epidemic'**[10] [*see page 33*]. The Soviets believed that when the **'Pink Epidemic'** covered the North and South American continents, the situation would be highly satisfactory for the revolution.

Suslov reviewed the situation in Latin America, using data gathered by Soviet intelligence, local Communist parties, and from Cuban and Warsaw Pact intelligence agents who had penetrated the Latin American drug operations. Making special reference to Paraguay, Jamaica, El Salvador, Guatemala, Honduras and Mexico, Suslov asserted that seventy percent of Latin American bureaucrats were tied into (that is corrupted by) drug operations. In Mexico, he said, eighty percent of the bureaucrats were tied into drugs or involved with other forms of corruption. In Latin America, sixty-five percent of Catholic priests used drugs, he said. Catholic priests have been a primary target of Soviet strategy in Latin America[11].

Four years later, at a meeting in 1967, Boris Ponomarëv explained to Czechoslovak officials that according to Soviet estimates, eighty percent of Latin American priests were anti-American, and slightly over sixty percent were inclined to the left[12]. This particular statistic was heavily weighted by young priests, whom the Soviets believed would exert important influence in Latin America over the ensuing twenty years. Boris Ponomarëv advanced three reasons for working with these younger priests: to help the revolution move forward, to use the church to help distribute drugs, and to use priests to gain additional information on drug-trafficking networks.

But, reverting to 1963: after reviewing intelligence statistics on the drug business, Suslov discussed two special groups against whom drugs were to be used. The *first* was the bourgeois leadership. *Second* was a group referred to as the 'lumpen proletariat' – the unemployed who often turned to crime or prostitution for survival; a somewhat equivalent term to describe this group might be the 'downtrodden proletariat'[13]. As Mikhail Suslov explained, this group was particularly vulnerable to the lure of drugs. That was all to the good, because it was to the advantage of the revolutionary war movement to destroy this group, as it was useless and a burden. Its members did not want to work. They were the main consumers of drugs and were to be destroyed. The key revolutionary tactic was to prepare a revolutionary élite and these downtrodden proletariat were not part of that élite.

To further the drug business, Mikhail Suslov also emphasised four points:

1. Use Cuba to help establish drug operations.

2. Be certain to obtain security clearances on all personnel first, before involving them in drug-trafficking and handling operations.

3. In the Communist Parties, brief only the First Secretaries on drug activities. The individual Communist Parties were to be kept at arms' length from drug operations, for two main reasons. First, the Communist Parties were believed to have been infiltrated by foreign agents. Accordingly, knowledge of drug operations was to be kept away from the Parties and all personnel were to be carefully cleared prior to their involvement in drug activities. Secondly, drug operations yielded money and this in turn meant possible fiscal independence. Drug operations were therefore to be kept out of the hands of the Communist Parties as a means of ensuring their continuing dependence on Moscow. Drug money used to finance foreign Communist Parties would first be channelled to Moscow and then to the various Parties according to their needs.

4. It was important to induce indigenous Latin American intelligence, counter-intelligence and military forces to become more involved in drug operations. These organisations represented important sources of pro-US feelings, and drug-assisted corruption was to be used to undermine such pro-American attitudes.

Khrushchev's style was to sit and interrupt the speaker to make additional points as he saw fit. He first interrupted Suslov to stress the need for caution. 'Comrade Suslov', he interjected, 'is particularly careful. I tried to force him to speed up the drug process – to make the bourgeoisie pay for the revolution – but I agree with him. We cannot take higher risk than we are taking now'. At another point Khrushchev interrupted and explained: 'Some people equate drugs and alcohol, but alcohol is not like drugs. We give vodka to Soviet soldiers and we proceed from success to success'.

Suslov also pointed out that it was necessary to begin creating reserves for the Latin American revolutionary forces, so that their needs would be satisfied when they were ready to step out from the underground. Accordingly, all Warsaw Pact countries were to begin contributing to a Latin America reserves account.

Suslov's speech left nothing to the imagination. Operation *'Druzhba Narodov'* was to be global in scope. The bourgeoisie in all countries were targets. Drugs and narcotics were to be primary weapons for use in the world revolutionary offensive.

As the Soviet *'Druzhba Narodov'* strategy took shape in 1962-64, probably the best, most succinct description of the targeting philosophy was provided to the Czechoslovak leadership in 1964 during a visit to Bulgaria. Todor Zhivkov, First Secretary of the Communist Party of Bulgaria, explained to the visiting Czechoslovak delegation that the United States was the primary target of the Soviet Bloc's drug offensive because it was the worst enemy ('the Main Enemy'), because it was simple to move drugs into the United States, and because there was an unlimited supply of hard money there. ∎

References to Chapter 4:

1. US Drug Enforcement Agency, 'The Involvement of the People's Republic of Bulgaria in International Narcotics Trafficking', in US Congress, Senate, *Drugs and Terrorism*, 1984, Hearing Before the Subcommittee on Alcoholism and Drug Abuse of the Committee on Labour and Human Resources, August 2, 1984 (US Government Printing Office: Washington, D.C., 1984).

2. *Ibid.*, page 66.

3. *Ibid.*, page 58.

4. *Ibid.*, page 61.

5. The importance of this department is also emphasised in John J. Dziak, *Chekisty: A History of the KGB* (Lexington, Massachusetts: Lexington Books, 1988), pages 148, 151-152.

6. The head of the Administrative Organs Department, incidentally, was also the Soviet official in charge of the Soviet arms control operation during the 1960s.

7. Dr Zdzislaw M. Rurarz was a member of Polish military intelligence (ZII) for 25 years, economic adviser to the Ministries of Foreign Trade and Foreign Affairs and to the First Secretary, and Ambassador to Japan before defecting to the United States in 1981. He explained to the author that before he left, he believed the number of Soviet banks, financial institutions, and joint ventures around the world that were available to assist in the money handling process was about 300. Subsequently, he learned from a French source that the number had risen to 400.

8. While there is no known connection, one example of an event which could have been triggered by the Soviets was the drug scandal involving the old Bureau of Narcotics in which US Federal agents were found to be selling heroin or protecting drug dealers. This scandal was disclosed by Attorney General Ramsey Clark in 1968. It resulted in almost every agent in the New York bureau being fired, forced to resign, or transferred. Edward Jay Epstein, *Agency of Fear: Opiates and Political Power in America* (New York: G. P. Putnam's Sons, 1977), page 105. See also US Congress, Senate, *International Traffic in Narcotics*, Hearing Before the Committee on Foreign Relations, July 1, 1971 (Washington, D.C.: US Government Printing Office, 1971), page 29.

9. Sejna first heard this view on the liberation phases in about 1962 from Andrei Kirilenko, Khrushchev's deputy, at a meeting of the Warsaw Pact leadership. Kirilenko explained that the Soviet strategy was to keep the United States out of the world revolutionary process by building a fire under the American window.

10. 'Pink Epidemic' was the codename for the operation to 'serve and extend' the cocaine epidemic which the Soviets believed would be the wave of the future. *See Chapter 3.*

11. Miguel Bolanos Hunter was a former counter-intelligence officer in the counterespionage section of the Nicaraguan state security apparatus. In an interview for the Oral History Project, International Security Studies Program, Fletcher School of Law and Diplomacy, Bolanos reviewed the origins, structure, and missions of the state security apparatus. With respect to the church, he said: 'To the Sandinistas, the [traditional Catholic] Church is Enemy Number One. There is no doubt about it'. [Testimony of Miguel Bolanos Hunter, in Uri Ra'anan *et al.*, *Hydra of Carnage* (Lexington, Massachusetts: Lexington Books, 1986), page 309].

As Jan Sejna explained religions are viewed as an especially dangerous force within socialist countries and in all countries being prepared for revolution, given the conflict between Marxist and religious morality. [The attack on religion is at the core of the revolution: Gorbachëv proclaimed on 15th December 1987, after all, that 'there must be no let-up in the war against religion because as long as religion exists, Communism cannot prevail. We must intensify the obliteration of all religions wherever they are being practiced or taught' – *Ed.*]. Within socialist countries, the long-term – 50-year – objective was to eliminate the importance and influence of religions. Outside the socialist countries, propaganda, deception, diplomacy and intelligence services were to be used to destroy, influence or use the various religions. Within the Third World countries, religions were viewed as 'temporary friends' because they supported the revolutionary spirit.

Overall, the principal directions of Soviet activity directed against religions were as follows:
● To encourage leading religious centres to support the Soviet policy of peaceful coexistence.
● To compel leading religious groups to deny their support for capitalism and to promote the idea that the rich countries must help the poor countries.
● To support desired political, social and economic changes which will bring the Communists to power in the various targeted countries.
● Through propaganda and deception, to show that socialism is allied with religious groups in the 'fight' for a better life generally.
● To use religious groups to exploit and further disarmament – that is, to exploit the idea that it is against the will of God to kill people. [For the revolutionaries are content invoke God, of course, when it suits their purposes to do so – *Ed.*].
● To build a mass psychological perception of nuclear warfare as signifying the end of the world.
● To infiltrate the religious centres with the following order of priority:
    (1). The Vatican;
    (2). Moslems;
    (3). Jews;
    (4). Buddhists;
    (5). Reactionary sects.

With reference to 'reactionary sects', Czechoslovak intelligence had three clerical agents within the Vatican in the late 1960s. They were located, Sejna asserted, within the sections responsible for foreign policy, finance and ideology. The Moslems were particularly important because of their rôle within the Middle East and Africa. One consequence of the Arab-Israeli War was that it enabled Soviet Bloc intelligence services to infiltrate all of the leading Moslem centres.

The Jewish community was regarded as an especially important target to assist the Soviet Union to gain economic influence over the West, and as an especially important source for intelligence information, and as a liberal counterweight against right-wing forces. The most difficult religion for the Soviets to manipulate was Buddhism because divergent physical characteristics made the religious order difficult to infiltrate. Reactionary (conservative) sects, which were also anti-Communist, were regarded as having considerable political influence. These sects also desired to achieve control and power, which the Communist plan exploited. In 1967, the Communists had obtained inside information on, or influence over, by their estimate, in excess of 40 percent of the various sects and other religions.

According to the *Communist Manual of Instruction of Psychological Warfare*: 'As it seems in foreign nations that the church is the most ennobling influence, each and every branch and activity of each and every church must, one way or another, be discredited. Religion must become unfashionable by demonstrating broadly, through psychopolitical indoctrination, that the soul is nonexistent, and that Man is an animal'. Reprinted in *Brain-Washing: A Synthesis of the Communist Textbook on Psychopolitics* (Melbourne, Victoria, Australia: New Times Ltd., 1956), page 35. [See also Introduction to the Second Edition of the present work, pages IX to XI – *Ed.*].

12. These figures are supported by Western surveys. For example, by the early 1970s, 78 percent of all Catholic priests in Chile identified themselves as being on the left politically. James R. Whelan, *Out of the Ashes, op. cit.*, page 712.

13. Sejna had first heard the term 'lumpen proletariat' in the early 1950s. At that time, it was the label attached to that portion of the proletariat who were not rising up to oppose the bourgeoisie; that is to say, those who were not easily recruited to the Communist movement.

In 1963, the term took on new meaning. It was now used to describe the unemployed and people who did not want to work or contribute. The Soviets believed that such people often turned to crime to support themselves and, indeed, in their view, being unemployed was almost synonymous with being a criminal. Communist studies also concluded that this group of people, in addition to crime, often turned to drugs – both the sale of drugs and their use. As a result of this linkage to crime, drugs, and other immoral activities, Soviet and East European analysts concluded that the lumpen proletariat could be profitably used to accelerate the destabilisation of the United States.

This conclusion was further strengthened because the big cities were considered to be the principal revolutionary centres within the United States, and life in these cities was becoming more and more dominated by the lumpen proletariat. Additionally, military service draftees were believed to be extensively recruited from the so-called lumpen proletariat, which was thus a high priority target for corruption because of their potentially adverse effect on the military. This was not a recruitment exercise. Members of the lumpen proletariat were still not considered suitable for the revolutionary movement. But they were a key target because of the damage they could do to capitalist society through destabilisation and demoralisation, and therefore were an asset to be used to help in the revolutionary process – before being destroyed following the revolution.

Within the lumpen proletariat, the minorities were identified as especially important because they constituted over 70 percent of it, according to the relevant Soviet studies. Accordingly, race became an integral dimension of the targeted class, with Black people and Hispanics being the two most important minorities. The Soviets believed that there were growing divisions between the Whites and the non-White minorities, and that the US Government could not solve the problem. As Moscow analysed the situation, capitalism was dying, and as the economic and social situation deteriorated, more and more members of the lumpen proletariat would be generated. The effect of this conclusion was to highlight the importance of the lumpen proletariat even further.

By 1967, the concept of lumpen proletariat was dominated by the image of the inner-city poor, especially the minorities. Most of the Third World was also regarded as lumpen proletariat. Even so, whereas, in 1963, this group was viewed as the main consumer of drugs, still, the main target to whom the drugs were to be marketed was not this group, but rather the élite. By 1967, this had also changed, with respect to discussions of Soviet narcotics strategy directed against the United States, and the lumpen proletariat, which by this time and in this context meant the inner-city poor and mainly Black people and Hispanics, became a key target for drug-trafficking and the main group to be recruited to do the marketing. Also, by 1967, Soviet strategy included the promotion of race warfare within the West, and this strategy was reflected in Soviet propaganda, disinformation and even industrial contracting policies.

ORGANISING FOR 'DRUZHBA NARODOV'

In the West, when people speak of intelligence operations, what they normally have in mind are covert operations run out of a nation's intelligence service, such as the CIA, KGB or GRU. This concept does a great disservice to Communist intelligence operations, which involve many agencies, not just the KGB or GRU, and which are generally not directed by the intelligence services, but rather by the Defence Council, Administrative Organs Department, or another appropriate Party organisation. **That is, intelligence operations are Communist Party operations designed to serve State interests, which only the Party can establish**[1]. The intelligence service is strictly an instrument of *Party* strategy, again in contrast to the United States which has no counterpart strategy. The operation known as *'Druzhba Narodov'* – Khrushchev's clever 'Friendship of Nations' plan – is especially interesting because of the insight it provides into the nature of Soviet intelligence operations.

Even in the beginning, in the mid-to late-1950s, the drug and narcotics operation involved more than intelligence officers. Medical science personnel were heavily involved in analysis, research and testing. The principal motivating force was Nikita Khrushchev, the First (later, General) Secretary of the Communist Party of the Soviet Union (CPSU). Initial planning was conducted by the special joint civilian/military Czechoslovak/Soviet team mentioned previously. The incorporation of drug-trafficking strategy into national security planning was handled by a special committee under the direction of Leonid Brezhnev. This committee, which met between the fall of 1956 and the spring of 1957, was responsible for a comprehensive upgrading of Soviet strategy to bring it into the nuclear age. Brezhnev's deputy was Mikhail Suslov, the head Soviet ideologist. Subcommittee leaders were Marshal V. D. Sokolovskiy (military), Dimitry Ustinov (military industry), Boris Ponomarëv (foreign affairs) and General Nikolai Mironov (intelligence).

Two revisions of Soviet strategy with respect to drugs and narcotics emerged during the course of this review. The *first* involved an official recognition that drugs could be important weapons for use in weakening opposing military forces[2]. *Secondly*, it was realised that drugs could be used to influence bourgeois leaderships in the Third World and among Social Democratic parties in particular, although none were to be excluded.

Responsibility for market analysis and targeting was assigned to the International Department of the CPSU. The International Department was also involved in the collection of corruption information on foreign leaders and its use in either blackmail, intimidation or exposure operations. This department was also heavily involved in propaganda planning and would probably have made the critical decision to release information on Chinese drug-trafficking to the propaganda operation.

The Main Political Administration of the Army and Navy, the department that keeps ideological watch over the military, was also involved in the drug-trafficking operation from the beginning. As early as 1956, the Czechoslovak leadership was advised by Soviet General Kalashnik, the ideologist at the Main Political Administration, about a new view on drugs and other chemicals capable of affecting the mind and behaviour of millions of people. This was one of five new weapons which could 'destroy the enemy before he can destroy us'. The other weapons included the ideological offensive, which meant propaganda and deception, good foreign policy designed to split the West, isolation of the United States, and economic and social chaos. It was essential, General Kalashnik explained, that the military should hasten to understand that there were weapons of great effectiveness, other than conventional and nuclear weapons.

A similar explanation was provided by Khrushchev in the early summer of 1963 in Moscow. During an informal discussion, Khrushchev had just criticised Marshal Rodion Ya. Malinovsky for being in far too much of a rush to push his tanks into the West. Then Khrushchev explained that *the Soviets were operating at two strategic levels simultaneously*, to engage the West in war. **The first echelon was deception, disinformation and propaganda. The second echelon was the destruction of capitalism by their own money through drugs.** Once these two echelons have been successful, Khrushchev emphasised, then you can use the third strategic echelon, Comrade Malinovsky – our tanks.

As the Soviet Bloc drug offensive grew and matured, the organisation became more complex – but with control and secrecy remaining extremely tight. This is another characteristic of Soviet operations: just because an operation expands , it does not follow that control over information becomes loose. The Defence Council itself is a case in point. The Defence Council remains small precisely in order to maintain tight control and good security. In the drug business, while many people were involved, few really knew the true purpose of the operation, or even of the massive Soviet involvement.

The principal Czechoslovak organisations that participated in the drug business are identified in *Figure 1* on page 49. The organisational structure applied in Czechoslovakia paralleled the organisational structure in the Soviet Union. Certain organisational names are different: for example, the Czechoslovak counterpart of the Soviet International Department was the Foreign Department; the First Secretary was the General Secretary in the Soviet Union; and the Czechoslovak Second Administration under the Ministry of Interior was the counterpart to the Soviet KGB. There are different research centres in the Soviet Union, and Soviet organisations are larger and more varied; but the essence of the two organisational structures is the same.

The principal differences are that the Soviet organisations make *strategic* decisions of *global* scope, and are larger, and that there are organisations in the Soviet Union which are responsible for foreign Communist Parties and which have no counterpart in Czechoslovakia. This particular distinction could be regarded as especially important.

For example, important inputs to the development of drug-trafficking strategy in Latin America were provided by the local Communist Parties, which would meet each year in Moscow and present their assessments of the progress of their drug operations, making recommendations for new techniques, markets and tactics.

As in all important Soviet operations, the General Secretary was not only informed,

**First Secretary
Czechoslovak Defence Council
Joint Committee**

GOVERNMENT	PARTY [Central Committee]
Ministry of Interior	Administrative Organs Department

Second Administration
  Strategic Intelligence
  Agent networks
Counter-intelligence
	Main Political
	Administration

Finance Administration	Foreign Department
Ministry of Defence	Health Department

Intelligence Administration [Zs]
  Strategic Intelligence
  Agent Networks
  Special Propaganda
  Finance
	Propaganda and
	Agitation Department
	
	Finance Department

Rear Services Health Administration	
Department of Technical Support for Foreign Countries	Science Department
Main Finance Administration	Highest Party School
Ministry of Finance *Military Section*	
Academy of Sciences	
Ministry of Foreign Trade *Main Technical Administration*	
Foreign Ministry	
State Plan Commission *Military Administration*	

Figure 1: Czechoslovak organisations involved in international offensive drug operations during overt Communism.

but played the lead rôle. In respect of planning and direction, the real power in the Soviet system resided in the Central Committee departments. One of the two or three most important departments was the Administrative Organs Department, which was the centre for planning and control of drug operations in both the Soviet Union and in Czechoslovakia. This was probably the case in the other satellites as well.

The Administrative Organs Department exercised control and oversight over the intelligence services, the military and (socialist) justice. Thus, it was only natural that the Administrative Organs Department would be the lead Central Committee department in respect of drug operations. It was no mere coincidence that when Khrushchev wanted the drugs offensive to be intensified in 1963, he called upon General Major Nikolai Savinkin, the Deputy Head of the Administrative Organs Department, to visit all participating countries and issue comprehensive instructions. Western analysts might well be advised to pay increased attention to the rôle of the Party and of the powerful Central Committee Departments, especially the Administrative Organs Department. In this regard, it is important to recognise that Savinkin became head of the Administrative Organs Department in 1964, running it until his retirement in 1987, twenty-three years later. (It was not until 1988 that the Soviet press announced that he had stepped down as head of the department).

Within the Administrative Organs Department there were officials whose responsibilities were, in effect, to watch over the military and intelligence organisations. Also, political officers were located within the military and intelligence organisations who, in addition, were members of the appropriate sections of the Administrative Organs Department and who kept their respective section chiefs informed on what was happening in their areas of responsibility within the military or intelligence services. For example, Sejna was the highest ranking political officer at the Czechoslovak Ministry of Defence and, as such, he was also a member of the military section of the Administrative Organs Department. Additionally, in the case of specially coordinated operations (such as drug-trafficking), important departments often had special coordination and control functions not only with respect to their normal responsibilities – for example, over the military and intelligence organisations in the case of the Administrative Organs Department – but over other participating organisations as well.

Another organisation of importance in maintaining control and internal security was counter-intelligence. In the headquarters of (Czechoslovak) military intelligence (Zs), there was a section of military counter-intelligence, which was really a section of the Ministry of Interior (KGB in the Soviet Union) and which also had a responsible controlling official in the Administrative Organs Department.

Also, within both civilian and military counter-intelligence, there were special departments that watched over the counter-intelligence operations and reported on them to the head of the Administrative Organs Department. **The Soviets trust nobody, and their organisational structure has always reflected this principle.** Everyone is controlled three ways. This is one reason why, when several officials from Cuba, Nicaragua, Bulgaria, or from some other Communist state, were found to be involved in drug-trafficking, it was always highly unlikely that these were 'just a few corrupt officials'. The Party was almost certainly well aware of what they were doing, and in fact not only approved of the operation but probably directed it to be carried out.

Indicative of the Party's oversight and discipline in drug operations was the fact that in 1959 the Chief of the Czechoslovak Zs, General Racek, was fired following an inspection by the Administrative Organs Department official who was in charge of Zs and military counter-intelligence. In his report, he criticised General Racek for not putting the best people into the drug business. Racek had failed to recognise how important the drug business would be for intelligence operations.

Both civilian and military intelligence had narcotics responsibilities. However, because production was controlled by and within the military and because the military was responsible for destroying the ability of an enemy population to support a war effort, primary responsibility for drug-trafficking resided within the military establishment. Civilian intelligence (the Second Administration in Czechoslovakia, the intelligence component[3] within the KGB in the Soviet Union) assisted whenever their resources were better suited to the task and where military intelligence, Zs in Czechoslovakia, did not have opportunities for trafficking in drugs.

Most of the narcotics agent operations were handled within the strategic intelligence sections of the civilian and military intelligence organisations. Agent recruitment, training, and administration were handled by the agent networks branch, but the narcotics operation was run by the strategic intelligence branch. This branch was responsible for establishing production quotas in respect of drugs produced in Czechoslovakia and for coordinating and directing overseas (local) drug production; for coordinating transportation; for managing agent operations; and for overall foreign operations planning.

Counter-intelligence and military counter-intelligence, the business of which is security, were also involved. Their mission was particularly complicated in overseas operations and required the assistance of foreign Communist Parties and strategic intelligence agents operating within the country of interest. Financial records, budgeting, and bookkeeping were handled by special finance sections within each intelligence service.

In the case of Cuba, both the Zs and the Second Administration (and Soviet GRU and KGB intelligence) helped to set up the relevant drugs operation. It was a joint venture from the outset. As explained earlier, when Raúl Castro was in Czechoslovakia in the summer of 1960, he signed assistance agreements with both the Minister of Interior and the Minister of Defence. When plans for expanding the drug operations or reporting on past progress were presented to the Czechoslovak Defence Council, the presentations were made jointly by the Ministries of Defence and Interior.

Between the Ministries of Defence and Interior there was a joint committee which coordinated intelligence operations. This committee decided who would run recruited agents, who would run a particular operation (civilian or military), who could work best in different regions, and so forth. In Czechoslovakia, the co-chairmen of the committee were the First Deputy Minister of Interior and the Chief of the General Staff. Other members were the Chief of Zs and the Chief of the Second Administration in the Ministry of Interior (chief of intelligence in the KGB in the Soviet Union), and their deputies in charge of strategic intelligence. In planning an operation, this committee in the Soviet Union first decided which satellites could do the job most effectively and, within each satellite, which intelligence service, civilian or military, had the best opportunity to do so.

In the late 1950s , a number of particularly important organisations were formed which were given critical responsibilities: the Departments of Special Propaganda in the Intelligence Administrations of the General Staffs. These departments reported jointly to the Intelligence Administration and to the Main Political Administration. They played especially important rôles in collecting data on individuals in foreign countries and in controlling such individuals in time of war. Narcotics strategy, especially that element associated with the gathering of information on associated corruption, was closely coupled with the mission of the Departments of Special Propaganda. These departments also had important rôles in deception and deception planning, and were often the principal agencies issuing such instructions.

Propaganda was run by the Central Committee's Department for Propaganda and the Departments of Special Propaganda. A special person (a special section in the Soviet Union) at the Administrative Organs Department provided intelligence data derived from the intelligence services and from the Department of Special Propaganda, and issued directions (orders) for the propaganda offensive. In the case of deception operations, again many organisations were involved – the most important of which were the Main Political Administration, the Department of Special Propaganda, the Foreign (International) Department, the strategic intelligence sections of both military and civilian intelligence, and the Elected Secretariat[4], which was responsible for the oversight of most deception operations.

Both East European and Soviet scientists participated heavily in military and intelligence R&D, including the development, production, and analysis of the consequences of drug and narcotics usage. In Czechoslovakia, the main research activities in support of narcotics trafficking were handled by the Academy of Sciences and by the military research centres. In the Academy, the primary activities were conducted at the Charles Medical University and at the Medical College at Bratislava. In the military, the primary focus or direction was provided by the Military Health Administration, with the work performed in the Central Military Hospital – the Military Medical Education Centre where doctors were trained – and the Air Force Medical Centre.

The Academy of Sciences' activities were governed by one-year, five-year and long-term (fifteen years and beyond) plans consisted of two parts, a regular part and a Top Secret element. The participants involved in putting together the Top Secret part outside the Academy of Sciences were the Administrative Organs Department of the Central Committee, the Health Department of the Central Committee, the Military Administration at the State Plan Commission, the Science Administration at the Ministry of Defence, the strategic intelligence section at the Ministry of Interior, the General Staff (Zs), and the military section of the Finance Department of the Central Committee.

Plans and objectives for research and development of improved drugs and narcotics (that is to say, drugs which would be more rapidly addictive, easier to manufacture, and which would offer 'improved' long-term debilitating mental effects)[5] were contained in the top secret segment of the plans, along with development plans for biological and chemical warfare agents, special chemicals for assassinations, and mind-control (behaviour modification) drugs. As indicated earlier, drugs and narcotics were regarded as chemical weapons.

Analysis of the effects of drug and narcotics trafficking – that is, market analysis – was an especially important Soviet Bloc activity. The most important analysis centres were the Military Political Academy of the Main Political Administration, the Highest Party School and the Academy of Sciences. At the Military Political Academy, the focus was on the military perspective, of course. The Highest Party School granted PhDs in a wide variety of subjects, including both physical and social sciences. Normally sixty percent of the schooling consisted of Marxism-Leninism and forty percent focused on the student's field of specialisation; for example, biology. These institutes were convenient locations for analytical programs because they were separately funded, had ready access to libraries and also had access to research facilities. The principal research was conducted by the faculty.

There were also joint research teams, the members of which came from all the Soviet

Bloc countries. These were usually directed by the Soviet participant, and in many cases the entire team was located at one of the universities or hospitals in Moscow. Over the years, the tendency was towards integration of Soviet Bloc research with increased emphasis on research teams housed in Moscow, probably reflecting the then-KGB chief Yuriy Andropov's interests in maintaining tight control over special activities. As will subsequently be described, research activity on drugs during the 1960s was effective in producing drugs which were intended to limit intellectual development. All Warsaw Pact countries were involved in this research. Cuba was also involved and indirectly attached to the Warsaw Pact research through Czechoslovakia with effect from 1967 onwards.

The Soviet Bloc's intelligence services also had special agents scattered around the world, but concentrated in Europe and the Western Hemisphere, who were not involved in drug-trafficking *per se*, but who observed its effects. General Sejna recalls a special training session for such individuals which was held at the Zs drug-trafficking training centre at Bratislava. The focus of the session's activities was to analyse market opportunities, to recommend measures which would mislead local and national authorities about the distribution of drugs, and to identify vulnerabilities in police organisations and, in particular, opportunities to corrupt or compromise police. Individuals who attended this special training session worked for either military or for civilian intelligence. They were not all Communists. But they were, as General Sejna observed, all very intelligent. One individual was a Canadian university professor.

These special studies were an especially important dimension of Soviet operations. The study activities were not one-shot, *ad hoc* studies, although such activities may be conducted from time to time. The main emphasis was placed on continuing activity involving the scientists, medical doctors, propagandists and intelligence specialists of several Soviet Bloc countries. They continuously examined developing tendencies around the world, as they would say, and identified new marketing opportunities and techniques. As part of Soviet directions to the satellites, specific points-of-contact were established to ensure that satellite intelligence and propaganda operations were kept informed of the conclusions arising from market analysis. This was necessary to ensure that the best possible ideas on global vulnerabilities and drug-trafficking techniques were being employed in *'Druzhba Narodov'*.

Under the Soviet Bloc's COMECON economic coordination organisation, there was a Health Section and under that, a *military* health subsection. The members of that subsection were all the military chiefs of Health Administrations in the Warsaw Pact countries and, for the Soviets, the chief of the Main Health Administration. **This group helped coordinate research and production of drugs and narcotics throughout the Warsaw Pact.** COMECON, like other Soviet organisations, was not a simple economic cooperation organisation. It also served as a cover for a total military command structure designed to take command of Warsaw Pact forces should the Warsaw Pact be 'dissolved'. This arrangement was designed to enable the Soviets to recommend that both NATO and the Warsaw Pact be dissolved in the interests of peace, without such action having an appreciable impact on Soviet Bloc military capabilities.

The centre for planning production and distribution of drugs and narcotics was the Main Health Administration of the Rear Services in the Soviet Union. In Czechoslovakia, the centre was located within the Health Administration under the Rear Services.

Distribution and transportation were managed by the Main Technical Administration at the Ministry of Foreign Trade. This administration was one of the most important organisations in both narcotics and terrorist operations. It was responsible for transporting and storing weapons, explosives and narcotics. The administration was heavily staffed by Zs officers. The organisations it controlled included trade bodies involved in transportation – for example, COBOL, CHEMEPOL and AEROFLOT. Logically, KINTEX, or its evident successor in Bulgaria, GLOBUS, almost certainly came under this administration.

The Main Technical Administration was given authority by the Defence Council to contract with foreign organisations for assistance where agreements were required, such as in the training of terrorists and others involved in sabotage and revolutionary war activities. This administration was, in effect, a cut-out organisation for strategic intelligence operations. It made the contracts and collected the monies. The administration was staffed mainly by Zs officers. The counterpart organisation in the General Staff was the Department of Technical Support for Foreign Countries, which coordinated the provision of weapons, explosives, terrorist supplies, etc. for shipment with the Main Technical Administration.

Within the satellites there were also Soviet intelligence stations, often located on the borders: in Czechoslovakia, for example, at Karlovy Vary, Liberec, Doupov, Cerchov and Bratislava. These stations acted beyond host country control or knowledge. When called upon to assist, the host would cooperate. The stations would engage in strategic intelligence operations, such as drug trafficking, without the host country's knowledge.

Illegal movement of goods across borders was maintained in peacetime so that sabotage agents could be moved in a similar manner during a crisis situation, without attracting undue attention. In this connection, it is useful to recall that all these operations – narcotics trafficking, military aid to terrorists, and sabotage – were handled by the strategic intelligence organisation within both military and civilian intelligence.

The Soviet Bloc negotiated a TIR (*Transports Internationals Routiers*) system with the West Europeans, to simplify customs and facilitate trade. Under this régime, in the country of departure, the customs officer seals the freight and signs the customs documents. Then the truck can be driven across all European frontiers. Customs inspectors are not allowed to examine the contents unless there are concrete indications that the seals or freight documents have been tampered with. This system began functioning in the late 1940s and expanded dramatically after 1949, with the greatest increase being the Soviet and East European share. By the 1970s, the Soviet Bloc's share of TIR transportation had risen to thirty percent. By the mid-1980s, it had increased to over fifty percent. This system is used to transport narcotics and terrorist supplies.

The TIR system also prevents Western officials from observing the shipments as they are transferred to other transportation means – such as ships, the preferred alternative. Czechoslovakia and other satellites rented part of Hamburg harbour. This segment of the harbour was treated as though it were Czechoslovak territory (or the territories of the other states concerned). The operations and facilities there were controlled by the Main Technical Administration of the Ministry of Foreign Trade. The Czechoslovaks paid rent to the Germans and the Czechoslovak ships used the docking and transportation links for shipping, including the shipment of materials for strategic intelligence operations, such as drugs and weapons for terrorism and sabotage, without any German interference or control, or customs. Large trucks were loaded in Czechoslovakia and sealed. They were then driven across Germany to the harbour. In the course of their journey, the trucks dropped off messages and packages, and passed by military installations. Despite the fact they were usually followed by German intelligence, the German authorities could do nothing because these arrangements were provided for in a German-Czechoslovak agreement. The satellites made full use of the Hamburg port, rather than of other available facilities such as those in Poland, because the West watched Polish, not German, ports.

In 1984, evidence of this system in operation surfaced in a report by the US House Select Committee on Narcotics Abuse and Control, which stated: 'Methaqualone... has mostly been smuggled from Colombia where it is formulated into tablets from methaqualone powder originating in The People's Republic of China and Hungary and *surreptitiously shipped to Colombia from the Free Port of Hamburg*' [6] (Emphasis added).

The use of the TIR system for transporting weapons and drugs was also illuminated by the defector and former chief of Romanian intelligence, Lt. General Ion Mihai Pacepa. He explained that most drivers of Romanian TIR trucks were agents of the Romanian foreign intelligence service, the *Departamentul de Informatii Externe*, or DIE, and that their operation was based upon the model set up by Bulgaria, which also used TIR cover for the transportation of drugs and weapons to the West. The DIE, which was run by Pacepa, made full use of TIR trucks:

'... for secretly bringing high-technology materials and military equipment into Romania, as well as for smuggling unmarked arms and drugs to the West. Most of these movements are carried out under the protection of international TIR agreements and for-eign customs seals. Over the years every kind of seal and form sheet used by Western customs authorities has been duplicated by the DIE and kept on hand to use to replace any original customs seals destroyed along the way for operational reasons [7].

A description of the process was also provided by Lt. General G. C. Berkhof, of the Royal Netherlands Army. He was Chief of Staff of NATO's Allied Forces Central Europe (AFCENT) until October 1986. Lt. Gen. Berkhof stated that there was much evidence of Bulgarian and East German involvement in drug-trafficking, and some evidence of Czechoslovak involvement. He confirmed that the TIR system was heavily exploited by the KGB and East Bloc intelligence services and that Dutch experts believed that over five percent of the TIR traffic was related to intelligence activities. He also said that similar findings emerged in Italy and other West European countries.

Thus, it would seem that the West European governments probably knew what was happening and yet 'officially' sanctioned the transportation of illicit drugs, narcotics and ter-rorist supplies across their territories. This TIR system and its use for the transportation of illicit goods, and a general awareness of what was happening, were further explained to the US Congress by General Lewis Walt in 1972, during hearings on global drug-trafficking[8]. In 1984, the US Drug Enforcement Administration [DEA], acknowledged in Congressional hearings that they had known about the use of Iranian, Turkish and Bulgarian TIR trucks for smuggling drugs and other contraband since 1972. They pointed out that 50,000 trucks per year transited Bulgaria and Yugoslavia, either to or from the Middle East and Europe. Of these vehicles, the DEA added, approximately half were TIR trucks. The DEA report also stated that Bulgarian customs officials had been implicated in assisting drug-traffickers[9].

Drugs and narcotics trafficking were, as is the case with all intelligence operations, incorporated into the entire planning process. A long-term plan established priorities and cooperation for the development of scientific projects in parallel with the production of narcotics and drugs. The targeted countries and their order of priority were identified. The long-term plan described how the distribution networks in different countries would be developed and when and how to exploit their vulnerabilities. The short-term plan was more specific and tactical. It specified which groups to cooperate with; who the agents were; and what the production and shipping schedules would be.

The monies were controlled via six highly classified organisations. The Interior Ministry and Intelligence Administration of the General Staff had their own Finance Administrations. Additionally, there was a special Main Finance Administration at the Ministry of Defence. Within this administration there was a special branch that handled the secret element of the budget, which included the budgeting of narcotics and other strategic intelligence operations. This part of the budget was kept secret from everyone else within the Main Finance Administration and from even the Politburo and Central Committee.

Only the Defence Council and special military sections of the State Plan Commission and Finance Department had access to the secret part of the budget. At the Ministry of Finance and the State Plan Commission there were special military sections, within which were intelligence subsections that handled the intelligence components of the budget, which were then coordinated directly and only with the Defence Council. To complete the circle, within the Finance Administration of military and civilian intelligence were special sections that handled the secret part of the budget. These special organisations were the only places where complete figures on the intelligence budget could be found.

In reviewing the way the Soviet drug operation was organised, several important conclusions stand out. **Clearly, the narcotics offensive is an intelligence operation of the highest importance.** It is evident that the operation is directed by the State, specifically by the Administrative Organs Department, and that many agencies are involved – in the case of Czechoslovakia, no less than twenty agencies or organisations, as shown in *Figure 1* on page 49. It is especially noteworthy that notwithstanding the distributed nature of the operation, security was very well maintained and access to information was tightly controlled. Again, in the case of Czechoslovakia, less than thirty people **really** understood the full nature of the operation. To illustrate the effectiveness of Communist security measures, while the Soviet Bloc drug dimension was launched in 1955, and by 1965 at least five satellites and numerous surrogate organisations were participating, there was apparently was no knowledge of the operation or even a suggestion of its existence within US or other Western intelligence services until 1986. ■

References to Chapter 5:

1. One example is a definition of strategic disinformation (deception) taken from a KGB training manual: 'Strategic disinformation assists in the execution of State tasks, and is directed at misleading the enemy concerning the basic questions of the State policy...' quoted in US Congress, House, *Soviet Covert Action (The Forgery Offensive)*, Hearings Before the Subcommittee on Oversight on the Permanent Select Committee on Intelligence (Washington, D.C.: US Government Printing Office, 1980), page 63.

2. The principal initial objective of the Soviet narcotics strategy was to weaken the military forces of the capitalists by attacking the population from which the military recruits its forces. An interesting elaboration of this objective was provided by Major Juan Rodriguez Menier, Chief of Security at the Cuban Embassy in Budapest, Hungary, who defected in January 1987. In an interview published in Miami's *El Nuevo Herald*, June 5-6, 1988, which was translated into English and reprinted by the Cuban American National Foundation, Rodriguez explained Cuba's drug-trafficking objectives as follows: '**Drugs are the best way to destroy the United States. The [Cuban] Government is convinced that by undermining the will of American youth to resist, they can destroy the enemy without firing one bullet. The foundation of any army is the youth and he who is able to morally destroy the youth, destroys the army**'. This doctrine is **identical** to Soviet Leninist teaching in general, and to the programme for military and societal demoralisation described in satanic detail by **Lavrentiy Beria**, as cited in the *Communist Manual of Instructions of Psychological Warfare*: see *Brain-Washing: A Synthesis of the Communist Textbook on Psychopolitics*, published by Goff, 1956: see Introduction to the Second Edition of the present work, pages IX-XI; Note 10, page 23; and Note 11, page 44.

3. 'Intelligence component' or 'KGB intelligence' is used to refer to that element of the KGB that handles intelligence, in contrast to counter-intelligence and other non-intelligence functions.

4. For an insider's description of Communist organisations, see Jan Sejna and Joseph D. Douglass, Jr., *Decision-Making in Communist Countries. An Inside View* (Cambridge, Massachusetts: Pergamon-Brassey's, 1985).

5. Crack is a form of cocaine which suddenly appeared in the United States and spread rapidly across the country. It is cheap, easy to use, very rapidly addictive, and has serious medical side-effects. It is an example of the new drugs that the Soviet Bloc's research programs were designed to develop. 'Ice', a crystalline methamphetamine, is an even nastier example – as it is still cheaper, much easier to manufacture, has longer-lasting highs, and even more serious side-effects.

6. US Congress, House, Select Committee on Narcotics Abuse and Control, *International Study Missions Summary Report 1984* (Washington, D.C.: US Government Printing Office, 1984), page 2.

7. Ion Mihai Pacepa, *Red Horizons* (Washington, D.C.: Regnery Gateway, 1987), pages 87-88.

8. US Congress, Senate, *World drug-traffic and Its impact on US Security*, Hearings Before the Subcommittee to Investigate the Administration of the Internal Security Act and other Internal Security Laws of the Committee on the Judiciary (Washington, D.C.: Government Printing Office, 1972), Part 4, page 134.

9. *Drugs and Terrorism*, 1984, *op. cit.*, pages 62-63, 69-70.

POLITICAL WARFARE & DRUGS IN VIETNAM

China and the Soviet Union competed for the drug business of US servicemen during the Vietnam War[1]. The Chinese dimension of this trafficking represented an extension of what they had learned in the early 1950s, not only in the Korean War, but in the French Indochina War as well.

During the Indochina War, which culminated with the defeat of the French at Dien Bien Phu, the Chinese worked with the Vietnamese Communists to promote drug use by French troops. The tactic was even more successful in Indochina than it had been in Korea. In January 1954, the French Lt. General Cogny explained to an American Army operations officer, Molloy Vaughan, that drugs from China were having a serious effect on the morale of French combat units and that the growing use of drugs among French soldiers was also eroding support for the war back home in France. One of the chief distribution centres was the Chinese gambling city of Cholon, a suburb of Saigon, where the troops went for rest and recreation. Prostitutes there were especially effective in pushing drugs on the French servicemen.

This was the first time that the French had run into this use of drugs, Lt. Colonel Cogny explained to Vaughan, and the effects of trafficking were proving to be extremely serious. Not only had drugs upset morale and fighting efficiency, but additionally, many soldiers were too ashamed to return to France and, instead, had elected to be discharged in Indochina – where they remained, which had a further debilitating effect on morale[2].

According to Soviet intelligence, in 1957, at the third meeting of the Central Committee of the Chinese Communist Party, the Chinese decided to expand their narcotics offensive. This expansion was designed as part of the 'Great Leap Forward'. The principal subject discussed at the meeting was the economy. The decision to expand drug production was adopted as one solution to China's economic problems[3]. In the decision document, one paragraph reviewed Chinese experience in Indochina and explained that drug-trafficking was beneficial because it had undermined the morale of French troops, had introduced combat weaknesses, and had provided the Chinese with a significant profit.

The decision was now made to expand opium poppy farms by 100 percent and, similarly, to double research and production activities. To further ease economic problems, instructions were sent out to have emigrants invest in business in China and support China's policy and interests – including the marketing of drugs and narcotics. Primary targets were to be Mexico, the United States and Canada.

In addition to stated economic objectives, there was another motivation of particular importance from a US perspective: preparation for the growing US military presence in Vietnam. As Chou En-lai explained in 1958 during a pep talk he delivered at a meeting in Wuhan to discuss increasing opium production:

'The Centre has decided to promote poppy cultivation on a large scale.... Every one of you must awake to the fact that the war in Vietnam is likely to escalate and US imperialism has determined to fight against our revolutionary camp by increasing its military force in Vietnam....From the revolutionary point of view, the poppy is a great force to assist the course of our revolution and should be used; from the class point of view, the poppy can also become a powerful weapon to win the proletarian revolution.... By exporting large quantities of morphine and heroin, we are able to weaken the US combat force and to defeat it without even fighting at all...'[4].

Chou's observations on what was likely to happen in Vietnam were not without justification. Following the Korean Armistice, US shipments of military equipment headed to Korea were re-routed to Vietnam to support the French operation. Simultaneously, the US military presence in South Vietnam began to expand. By 1957, the steady increase in US military personnel in South Vietnam was clear to the people at the headquarters of the US Pacific Command who were responsible for war plans. Indeed, 1957 was the year when the first war plans for US forces in Vietnam were developed. Given the highly successful use of drugs against the French troops in Vietnam, and the success of the Chinese in promoting drug usage by US forces in Korea, Chou's remarks should come as no surprise[5].

Chou's observations at the 1958 meeting were remarkably consistent with reports on his discussions with President Gamal Abdel Nasser during a visit to Egypt seven years later, in 1965. At a banquet given in his honour, Chou is reported to have said:

'We think that US involvement in the Vietnam War provides a good chance for us to fight against US imperialism. Thus, the more troops it sends to Vietnam, the more satisfied we are.... At present US servicemen are experimenting with opium eating and we are helping them in this respect. We have already grown the best quality opium for them.... We will use opium to shatter the morale of the US troops in Vietnam and the effects on the United States will indeed be beyond prediction'[6].

The Soviets and Czechs were rather well-informed about Chinese trafficking, both through Soviet intelligence agents in China and North Korea, and through intelligence collection operations in Vietnam, Laos, Burma and Afghanistan, where Czechoslovak agents were assisted by the North Vietnamese, Laotians, Burmese, Cambodians and Afghans. The development of Soviet intelligence capabilities in China specifically oriented to the drug trade was the product of a long-term recruitment operation. Even before Mao Tse-tung came to power in 1949, the Soviets had become concerned about Mao's loyalties and had initiated measures to recruit spies among the Chinese Communists. During the Korean War, these efforts were expanded, specifically to collect data on Chinese drug-trafficking operations.

As discussed earlier, the Soviets became extremely interested in the Chinese drug strategy and its effectiveness during the Korean War. With effect from 1951 and continuing until 1962, a significant focus of Soviet espionage activity was to recruit spies to report on the Chinese drug business – research, production, manufacturing techniques, distribution and finance. Sejna first learned of this Soviet espionage operation during a Defence Council meeting, while planning for a forthcoming visit by a delegation of the Communist Party of Japan.

In preparation for discussions with the visiting delegation, a joint Ministry of Defence and Interior report on political relations among the Communist Parties of Japan, China and the Soviet Union was prepared for the Czechoslovak Defence Council. The drug business was one of the items covered in this report.

The report described Soviet measures (in which Czechoslovak intelligence participated) to recruit Chinese spies. The targets of this recruitment operation were Chinese scientists, students, engineers and technicians whom the Soviets believed might go into some aspect of the drug business. Recruitment took place in China and in the Soviet Union and Eastern Europe, where numerous Chinese were temporarily stationed. The cadre of intelligence agents so recruited provided the Soviets with extensive data on China's drug operations, notwithstanding Chinese security practices associated with the drug business.

While China tried to hide its activities from the Soviets, by the late 1950s Soviet intelligence had identified almost 100 Chinese factories manufacturing heroin and drugs for use against the bourgeoisie. They also knew about new laboratories in Shanghai, Katong and Tibet where synthetic drugs were prepared and tested. The Chinese also controlled factories in different countries which participated in the Chinese drug strategy. The Soviet recruitment program had produced a particularly valuable source in one such company located in Saigon. Through this source, information was obtained on Chinese drug-trafficking in Vietnam. The company also provided narcotics to various Middle East and African countries. This was in fact the source of much of the original Soviet intelligence on drug-related corruption in Africa and the Middle East.

Through their agents, the Soviets were also alerted to the Chinese decision in 1957 to expand their drug offensive. By 1958, the Soviets had grown concerned about the expansion of Chinese trafficking because of its possible adverse effects on Soviet plans. Accordingly, in late 1958 or early 1959, the Chinese Minister of Defence, Marshal P'eng Te-huai, who was also a member of the Politburo, was invited to tour the Soviet Union and Eastern Europe. During his visit, deficiencies in Chinese industry and collective farms were pointed out to him to make him appreciate the potential value of Soviet assistance, and, of course, of Soviet 'good faith' and interest.

Then, midway through his visit, the subject of drugs and narcotics was raised. The Soviets suggested that the two countries and Parties should coordinate their foreign policies. In particular, the Soviets suggested dividing up the drug market, with the Chinese getting Asia and Africa, and the Soviets taking the Americas and Europe. When the Defence Minister returned to China, he sent a personal letter to Mao, criticising some of Mao's policies and recommending certain improvements, based on his visit to the Soviet Union and Eastern Europe. The letter was classified Top Secret because it discussed cooperation in foreign policy, military policy and drugs. Not only did the suggestion fall on deaf ears, but Mao Tse-tung liquidated the Defence Minister, not for criticising him, but rather, for even acknowledging to the Soviets that China was in the drug business[7].

While the Chinese were first to recognise the potential for the use of drugs in Vietnam, the Soviets were not far behind. In 1963, the Soviets had arranged for Czechoslovak intelligence to assist the North Vietnamese in setting up a training centre for drug-traffickers. Then, in 1964 when the school was in operation, the Soviets prevailed upon the the Czechoslovaks to negotiate an agreement with North Vietnam to produce narcotics and drugs in that country and to ship the material via the Viet Cong and through Thailand to US forces throughout Southeast Asia. The North Vietnamese were pleased with the arrangements finalised in 1965 because, among other considerations, Sejna recalls, it put them in competition with the Chinese. The agreement within which the narcotics agreement was concealed dealt with the production of natural rubber. It was signed by Premier Pham Van Dong and Prime Minister Josef Lenart. The details were worked out by the chiefs of North Vietnamese and Czechoslovak military intelligence.

Through its intelligence sources in China, who were reporting back through a Czechoslovak Zs agent stationed at their embassy in Peking, the Czechoslovaks learned that the Chinese had also expanded their narcotics trafficking operation in 1964. Specifically, an agreement had been signed between the Communist Party of Japan and China in which the Japanese would assist China in supplying drugs to US soldiers in Japan and Okinawa. Under the terms of the agreement, China's counter-intelligence would perform background security checks on all Japanese who were scheduled to be recruited for this operation. In return for their assistance, the Communist Party of Japan was to receive twenty five percent of the profits.

In 1965, the Soviets expanded their Vietnam narcotics trafficking operations to ensure that drugs were available in nearby locations which US servicemen and officers would visit during vacations to 'rest and recuperate'. One leg of this trafficking operation in which the Czechoslovak intelligence service assisted was located in Australia. The Czechoslovaks were called upon to assist because they were able to operate in Australia more flexibly than the Soviets and were not watched as closely as the Soviets.

The Czechoslovaks had also established better relations with the Australians, particularly with the Labour Party, and had several commercial operations in Australia which helped to provide cover. Finally, the Czechoslovaks had additional resources, namely Australian soldiers whom the Czechoslovak intelligence services had recruited. The supply of drugs for this operation came from North Vietnam – which was another reason for Czechoslovak assistance, insofar as they were already involved in the North Vietnam drug production operation.

1965 was also the year when the Czechoslovak Chief of the General Staff and Chief of the Main Political Administration learned that the Czechoslovak operation had been criticised in a Soviet Defence Council report. The Soviet complaint was directed against the Czechoslovak intelligence service, and accused it of placing more attention on profits than on the real objective of the drug business, which was the liquidation of capitalism. The two Czechoslovak officials were in Moscow attending a meeting when they were informed about this concern by the Soviet Defence Council and were told to change their priorities. The first priority was to promote drug usage, not to make money. The specific subject addressed was the use of drugs against the US military in Southeast Asia.

The primary targets within the US military in Vietnam, the Soviet officials emphasised, were US military command staff officers, personnel associated with communications, personnel responsible for producing situation analyses, and intelligence officers. General Vaclav Prchlik subsequently reported to Sejna that Soviet General Yepishev, who headed the Main Political Administration, had told him that if the US military were inclined to take drugs, they should if necessary be given them free of charge. The money was far less important than influencing the military with drugs.

Western intelligence officers as well as political analysts have identified 1966 as the year when the trafficking of narcotics into Vietnam underwent a marked increase [8]. This would also be the year when the Soviet-Czechoslovak-North Vietnamese operation became fully operational. By 1967, narcotics had become a serious problem among the US military in Vietnam. One Soviet KGB intelligence study reported that 90 percent of US servicemen were using some form of drug, most commonly marijuana. However, the US military authorities refused to acknowledge the seriousness of the problem until it became so open and blatant that it could no longer be denied.

The drug challenge was brought out of the closet in 1970, immediately following the 'secret' bombing of Viet Cong sanctuaries in Cambodia in April-May that year. China responded with a stern warning which Henry Kissinger analysed in person. He then advised the President as follows: 'The Chinese have issued a statement, in effect saying that they wouldn't do anything' [9].

But, with effect from June 1970, heroin of almost pure quality suddenly appeared for sale at below wholesale prices outside the gates of every US installation in Southeast Asia. As General Lewis Walt has explained:

'In June of 1970, immediately after our Cambodian incursion, South Vietnam was flooded with heroin of remarkable purity – 94 to 97 percent – which sold at the ridiculously low price of first $1 and then $2 a vial. If profit-motivated criminals were in charge of the operation, the price made no sense at all – because no GI who wanted to get high on heroin would have batted an eyelash at paying $5, or even $10. The same amount of heroin in New York would have cost $250'.

'The only explanation that makes sense is that the epidemic was political rather than economic in inspiration – that whoever was behind the epidemic wanted to hook as many GI's as possible, as fast as possible, and as hard as possible' [10].

General Walt also made it clear that the trafficking operation appeared to be highly coordinated and centralised and that some group must have established virtually simultaneous contact with scores of ethnic Chinese entrepreneurs and other criminal elements throughout South Vietnam. He also examined reports of interrogations of Viet Cong defectors who claimed to have knowledge of large-scale opium production in North Vietnam and, in one case, of Viet Cong involvement in the heroin epidemic. Another defector described the North Vietnamese distribution of drugs as a direct means of undermining the morale and efficiency of US forces. The Vietnamese officers with whom Walt discussed the problem were all convinced that the heroin epidemic was political rather than criminal in origin [11].

The result was a mammoth rise in US military drug abuse. While previously there had been two deaths per month due to a drug overdose, suddenly the statistic rose to sixty per month. In 1970-1971, the US Air Force lost more people to drugs than to combat. The impact on morale, readiness, and support for the war at home was devastating [12]. During investigations of the new epidemic, Chinese trafficking, North Vietnamese production and Viet Cong trafficking were all identified by US intelligence.

And, based on simple free market economics, one is led to two conclusions: *First*, that the increase was the result of combined, albeit not necessarily coordinated, operations; *secondly*, that the trafficking was unquestionably a sign of political warfare and not greed- or profit-motivated.

The increase in US military consumption was driven by **supply**, not demand.

But, notwithstanding the overwhelming evidence concerning the rôle of China, the White House, as will be explained in Chapter 9, issued instructions in 1972 to US Government officials telling them that the rumours about Chinese drug-trafficking were without substance and should be disregarded. ■

References to Chapter 6:

1. Chinese trafficking during the Vietnam War is reported in Hamburger, *The Peking Bomb, op. cit.*, pages 117-148 and Candlin, *Psycho-Chemical Warfare: The Chinese Communist Drug Offensive Against the West*, *op. cit.*, pages 240-266. The rôle of China was also confirmed by US intelligence and fact-finding missions. Sejna corroborated these reports. His knowledge was based on detailed Soviet and Czechoslovak intelligence reports.

2. Interview with Molloy Vaughan, May 1989. General Sejna further reports that the successful use of narcotics by the Chinese and Vietnamese Communists in the Indochina War was also studied by the French Communist Party, based on reports from Communists in the French Army in Vietnam. This French study was reviewed in Czechoslovakia during a Czechoslovak study undertaken to intensify drug-trafficking in the mid-1960s. The French study also blamed the use of drugs on 'bourgeois officers', some of whom were involved in the trafficking.

3. Reported by Mikhail Suslov at the February 1964, Moscow meeting of high-level East European leaderships which Sejna attended. The effects of the decision were also reflected in Candlin, *Psycho-Chemical Warfare: The Chinese Communist Drug Offensive Against the West*, *op. cit.*, page 114.

4. T'ang Ming-chieh, Specialist, Bureau of Investigation, Ministry of Justice, Republic of China, 'The Maoist Production of Narcotics and Their Intrigue to Poison the World', *Issues and Studies*, June 1973, page 35.

5. Also, in 1959 a delegation of the armed forces of North Vietnam, led by the Chief of the General Staff, visited the Soviet Union and other Warsaw Pact countries. Sejna was the host for the visiting delegation in Czechoslovakia. The main purpose of the visit was to obtain military equipment for the North Vietnamese army. At that time, the North Vietnamese expected the United States to increase its commitment to South Vietnam and wanted to prepare for the coming war. As part of their preparation, they were planning to reorganise their whole country for general war.

6. 'The Maoist Production of Narcotics and Their Intrigue to Poison the World', *op. cit.*, page 36, citing an article in the French magazine *Histoire Pour Tous*, January 1973. The episode is also described in the more widely read reference book by Mohammed Hassanein Heikal, *Nasser: The Cairo Documents* (New York: Doubleday, 1971), pages 278-279. See also Hamburger, *The Peking Bomb, op. cit.*, pages 143-148 and Candlin, *Psycho-Chemical Warfare: The Chinese Communist Drug Offensive Against the West*, *op. cit.*, pages 21-24.

7. Sejna was responsible for the Chinese Minister's schedule in Czechoslovakia and for assisting in the Soviet attempt to recruit the Minister. In preparation for his visit, Novotny was instructed by officials from the Soviet International Department. Other Czechoslovak officials were instructed by their Soviet adviser. In February 1964, Suslov presented a major speech on China at a meeting of the Soviet Central Committee. This was the formal time at which the Soviets stated that they had concluded that China was 'not about to march in step' and that the rift between China and the Soviets was irreversible. Suslov discussed many aspects of Chinese foreign policy, including China's drug operation. It was during this discussion that Suslov explained the reasons behind the Chinese Defence Minister's liquidation. The information had been obtained by Soviet intelligence. The secret element of this speech contained details on Soviet operations against China. In 1965, China was added to the Soviet 'main enemies' list.

Editor's Note: Anatoliy Golitsyn's analysis reveals that, notwithstanding these facts, the Sino-Soviet split was indeed a dialectical ploy, based upon classical Leninist strategic deception theory.

8. See, for example, Stefan T. Possony, 'Maoist China and Heroin', *Issues and Studies*, November 1971. The increase is undoubtedly the product of the combined competing trafficking of the Chinese and North Vietnamese-Czech Soviet operations.

9. Henry Kissinger, *White House Years* (Boston: Little Brown and Company, 1979), page 509.

10 .US Congress, Senate, *World drug-traffic and its impact on US. Security*, Hearings Before the Subcommittee to Investigate the Administration of the Internal Security Act and other Internal Security Laws of the Committee on the Judiciary, August 14, 1972, Part 1, Southeast Asia, and September 14, 1972, Part 4, The Global Context; Report of General Walt (Washington, D.C.: Government Printing Office, 1972), Part 4, pages 157-158.

11. *Ibid.*, pages 54-58.

12. In 1971, Representative Robert Steel (R-CT) reported that the high rate of heroin addiction had prompted the Nixon Administration to step up its rate of troop withdrawals. 'Drugs Reported Tied to Vietnam Pullout', *New York Times*, June 7, 1971, page A6.

13. *World drug-traffic, op. cit.*, Part 1, pages 54-58, and Part 4, page 160.

MOSCOW INTENSIFIES DRUG WARFARE IN THE LATE 1960s

The Vietnam War provided an ideal opportunity for the extension of operation *'Druzhba Narodov'*. The alienation of youth which was proliferating in the United States and the preoccupation of the US Government and citizenry with the Vietnam War presented the distraction and cover which enabled the Soviet offensive to expand without attracting undue attention. The first leg of the expansion started in January 1967. This was when a new Soviet study on the impact of the new 'technical élite' in the industrialised countries was completed. One copy was given to the Czechoslovak Defence Council, along with instructions to apply the findings to the drug operation. The study pointed out the growing importance of the technical élite – the middle-level technical managers upon whom the growth of high-tech industries so critically depended. These managers had become one of the most important groups in 'bourgeois society'; in the Soviet view, they were on a par with finance and big business. Accordingly, the group had become a most important target to infiltrate and sabotage.

The Soviet study pointed out that this new élite worked under great pressure, and that as the pressure grew, new opportunities to use drugs and narcotics would arise. Drugs were regarded as especially important as a means of destroying or sabotaging this group, and, at the same time, as a blackmail or bribery mechanism to use against such people in connection with the Soviet Bloc's drive to obtain (steal) advanced technology.

The use of drugs and narcotics in connection with technology espionage and theft had been a long-standing practice, dating back to before Sejna's appointment to high office. The use of drugs in such operations was first significantly increased following a meeting in Moscow convened by Khrushchev in the fall of 1959. The top leadership from the East European satellites (with the exception of Romania) were present. The subject of the meeting was Pact technology; the key question, was how to use the developing East-West relationship to improve the Warsaw Pact's technology[1] as quickly as possible.

Sejna was present at the meeting. The first subject addressed was technology theft. Khrushchev stated that the cheapest and fastest way to improve Warsaw Pact technology was to take (that is, steal) as much technology from the 'imperialists' as possible. Its value was doubled if you just take it, he said, and added: why pay the capitalist a profit if we can just take it and use it? As part of this discussion, the use of drugs and narcotics as a mechanism for money and blackmail in technology theft was reviewed. This was the primary way drugs and narcotics had been used in the past. The targets were business executives, technical managers, and sales personnel.

Organised crime was also used to facilitate technology theft. In 1963 or 1964, the Czechoslovak Ministers of Defence and Interior presented a report to the Defence Council on the use of organised crime in technology transfer. The focus was on attempts to steal laser and computer technology. The report was forty pages long and included charts that listed target companies in different countries, different organised crime groups, and the potential for action in various regions. The Defence Council's task was to decide in each case whether civilian or military intelligence should take the lead and to identify situations where coordination with other intelligence services was appropriate.

By this time, all the Soviet Bloc intelligence services were active in organised crime in different regions of the world. The Czechoslovaks and East Germans were particularly effective in Switzerland, Mexico and India; the East Germans in South Africa; the Czechoslovaks in Austria and Egypt; the Bulgarians in the Middle East, Greece, Turkey, Italy and Cyprus; the Hungarians in Spain, Portugal, Belgium and the United States; the Soviet Union in Great Britain and France; the Soviets, Czechoslovaks and East Germans in West Germany. Czechoslovakia had roughly three organised crime groups in Switzerland, seven in Austria, two in Mexico, eleven or twelve in India, and one each in Argentina and Sweden. In the case of Austria, the head of one of the Czechoslovak groups was the chief of police in one of the sections of Vienna. Altogether, Czechoslovakia ran or had infiltrated about fifty organised crime groups around the world. Sejna believed this achievement was comparable to those of Bulgaria, Hungary and Poland, more than that of East Germany, but was less than the achievement of the Soviet Union. The Italian mafia had been penetrated by all the Soviet Bloc's intelligence services, although the Bulgarians and Soviets were by far the most successful.

The existence of a Soviet strategy to infiltrate organised crime, which was launched in 1955, is especially sobering when the extent to which US Presidents, intelligence officials, and other high-ranking political leaders are known to have requested favours from members of organised crime, is recalled. Consider, for example, the CIA's attempts to assassinate Fidel Castro in the early 1960s. In one exercise, individuals from no less than four organised criminal groups, centred in Las Vegas, Chicago, Miami and Havana, were involved. One of the principals had been freed from jail by Castro himself and then allowed to leave Cuba and settle in Miami. A Bureau of Narcotics report described this individual as a possible connection for Cuba's narcotics trafficking into the United States. Even if we disregard the covert Soviet Bloc intelligence penetration of organised crime groups, it does not require much imagination to recognise 'why', as historian Arthur M. Schlesinger, Jr. described the situation, 'Castro survived so comfortably the ministrations of the CIA'[2].

The tendency to turn to organised crime for special tasks is not an activity that is unique to the US strategic leadership. It is a rather common activity in many countries. It seems unlikely that any of the public officials concerned has been, or is, aware of the hidden risks in pursuing such activities which could arise because of the covert presence of Soviet Bloc intelligence agents. The huge potential value of this rather simple-appearing Soviet operation is a keen indication of Moscow's knowledge of other cultures, and of the Soviets' genius in developing effective strategic operations.

An intelligence study reviewed by Sejna described the manner in which organised crime was categorised in Soviet planning. There were three principal categories, the code names of which were blue, purple, and yellow butterfly. In the first category were relatively small groups involved in local crimes – for example, small narcotics distribution, banks and finance. In the second category were criminal groups related to drugs and to technology transfers. The third category contained the more traditional criminal operations, such as the mafia, which were penetrated for intelligence information of a military, political, or economic nature.

Each principal category was further broken down into three sub-groups referred to as alpha, beta and gamma. The first group consisted of organised crime networks which had been created and were fully controlled by Warsaw Pact intelligence services. Organisations in the second group were created by someone else but had been penetrated by Warsaw Pact intelligence agents and could be exploited. In the third group were known organisations that the Warsaw Pact intelligence services had been unable to penetrate.

At a Czechoslovak Defence Council meeting, Khrushchev's deputy, Andrei Kirilenko, spoke to top Czechoslovak officials about Khrushchev's concern over the program. He explained that Khrushchev had asked why the categories 'we cannot control completely' were the largest. 'Why do we not switch the statistics'? he asked. Kirilenko then inquired whether the Warsaw Pact intelligence services were scared of professional criminals. 'When you deal with the criminals', he stated firmly, 'you must be tougher than they are'.

The measures taken in 1967 to target the newly identified technical élite for sabotage, espionage and technology theft was the second important intensification of across-the-board technology theft operations using drugs and narcotics to which Sejna was a direct witness and participant.

Each year the Defence Council reviewed the technology stolen during the preceding year. It then met and approved a plan describing what was to be stolen during the subsequent year. In reviewing stolen technology at the end of 1967, Antonin Novotny, First Secretary of the Communist Party of Czechoslovakia, remarked to the Soviet General Secretary, Leonid Brezhnev, that drugs were of great help in stealing technology. General Oldrich Burda, the Zs chief, added that twenty to twenty-five percent of the technology stolen in 1967, the total value of which was estimated by the Zs at $300 million, had been acquired through the use of drugs.

In the spring of 1967, the Czechoslovak strategic leadership received additional guidance from the Soviet Union. In April, Sejna, Jiri Hendrich and Lt. General Vaclav Prchlik travelled to Moscow where they met Soviet General Aleksey A. Yepishev, Chief of the Main Political Administration, and General Shevchenko, Chief of the Department of Special Propaganda. At this meeting, **Shevchenko discussed the continued importance of infiltrating the banks and financial institutions.** Collecting data for military purposes was one objective. He also stressed the importance of using drugs to corrupt people in these institutions and indicated that such infiltration would also facilitate the use of the banks as handlers of money for foreign operations, including drug-money-laundering.

The financial institutions were so important, Shevchenko emphasised, that careful attention was to be exercised by the satellite propaganda apparatus to keep these institutions out of the limelight [3]. Individuals in these institutions assisting the Soviet Bloc operations represented a long-term investment which would serve Soviet interests for many years and, thus, corruption in these institutions was not to be publicised. The Soviets did not want any light to be thrown on the banks' operations.

Previously, in 1963, during a meeting of the Czechoslovak Defence Council when money-laundering was being discussed, the Chief of the General Staff had stated that the Soviets had decided that officials in the Soviet finance department should not be informed about the precise sources of the funds they were handling because there was too great a risk of compromise. **At risk, the Soviet adviser had explained, were people in seventy-five percent of the banks in Latin America and in forty-five percent of the banks in the United States and Canada.** When the amount of money involved was considered, around $300 billion per year in the United States in the late 1980s, $500 billion or more per year worldwide, these percentages certainly do not seem high.

Furthermore, in the spring of 1967, General Savinkin, head of the Soviet Administrative Organs Department, convened a meeting in Moscow of the top leadership of the Warsaw Pact drug-trafficking countries, plus Cuba. Savinkin chaired the meetings, which continued for several days. Numerous Soviet military and intelligence generals were present at different times. In addition to Sejna, Josef Kudrna, the Czech Minister of Interior, and General Bohimir Lomsky, the Minister of Defence, were present. Four Cubans attended the meeting: Raúl Castro, Cuba's Minister of Interior, the deputy military intelligence chief in charge of narcotics, and one other. The other countries represented were East Germany, Hungary, Bulgaria and Poland.

One of the most important topics addressed at this particular meeting was the importance of attacking NATO and US military forces more aggressively with drugs. Detailed studies of all NATO forces were presented, and their vulnerabilities discussed. In his remarks, General Savinkin identified three primary objectives: To corrupt officers, to recruit agents and to impair the functioning of troops.

The offensive against US troops based overseas, received special emphasis. Savinkin explained that areas where US troops were based – Germany, Turkey, Greece, Panama and so forth – were, to use a military term, to become *zones of strategic destruction*. This task was so important that Soviet Major General Vasil Fedorenko was placed in charge of coordinating the attack. Each country had a similar coordinator designated, who acted as the primary liaison with Fedorenko. And as will be described shortly, the need to corrupt US forces in NATO received additional emphasis in the fall of 1967. (By 1970, the standard of US command of forces in NATO had in fact already fallen to dangerously low levels and was soon to trigger far-reaching disciplinary measures).

In this operation, Panama received special emphasis because of the Panama Canal and because of the presence in Panama of several US military bases. Colonel Frantisek Penc, of Czechoslovak military intelligence, was in charge of the Czechoslovak operation in Panama. He was also the liaison to Fedorenko for drug-trafficking against US bases in other regions of the world.

At one of the special sessions focused on Latin America, General Shevchenko, head of the Department of Special Propaganda [*see page 65*], explained that the Soviets believed that over seventy percent of the top-level Panamanian military (Lt. Colonel and above) were anti-American. A list of these officers had been drawn up with the assistance of the Communist Party of Panama. They had all operated with the Communist Party and some had contributed money to the Party. The officers were not targets to be destroyed, General Shevchenko emphasised, but to be protected because some of them were our 'Gold Reserve'. Many, if not most, of them were involved with drugs. One of the Panamanian military officers on the list was Omar Torrijos Herrera, who was to seize control of Panama in 1969. Raúl Castro said that Cuba believed that anti-American sentiments were even stronger among lower level officers, and that the Cubans would like to focus more attention on recruiting lower level officers. The Soviets concurred with this proposal.

By 1972, Panama had developed such a severe drug problem that special measures were discussed at the US Bureau of Narcotics and Dangerous Drugs [BNDD, subsequently absorbed into the DEA]. In an attack on Noriega in 1986, the *New York Times* published a detailed account of these anxieties. John E. Ingersoll, who was then head of the Bureau of National Dangerous Drugs, confirmed that BNDD had hard intelligence that Noriega was trafficking in drugs – adding that the BNDD had been frustrated in its attempts to persuade General Torrijos to take action against Noriega. According to a 1978 Senate Intelligence Committee report, five measures had been discussed to deal with the *'Guardia Nacional* official', which was the Committee's description of Noriega: Link Noriega to a fictitious plot against Torrijos, leak information on Noriega's drug-trafficking to the press, link negotiations over the Panama Canal to Noriega's removal, secretly encourage powerful groups in Panama to raise the issue, and 'total and complete immobilisation', which was of course an euphemism for assassination[4].

Colombia was another country which the Moscow meeting held in the spring of 1967 discussed in detail. With respect to Colombia, Raúl recommended that Cuba should develop more than one group to control drug-trafficking. (At that time, there were two Soviet-controlled operations: the Cuban operation and the Czechoslovak operation). Savinkin pointed out that the number of groups should be kept to a minimum. The more groups there were, the more people there would be in the know, and the greater was the risk of exposure. He was referring to exposure of the *Soviet operation*†. Castro agreed, but said the risk was also high with just one group because of the internal politics involved. Savinkin approved Castro's recommendation and emphasised that it was the Cubans' responsibility and he would trust their judgment in this matter – but that Havana should be careful not to go too far.

Raúl also raised the question of how much the Communist Party of Colombia should be told and presented a long list of people corrupted by the drug trade in Colombia which had been assembled by Cuban intelligence agents who had infiltrated the indigenous Colombian drug-trafficking networks. The Soviets were concerned about some of the names on the list whom they believed to be among various 'double agents' whom the indigenous drug-trafficking organisations had corrupted and were using against the Soviet-Cuban drug operation. Savinkin said that these people were all criminals. They don't trust anybody except themselves, he explained. We are in the same position and cannot trust any of them, either.

In his review of Mexico, Savinkin said that there were no corrections to be made in respect to the corruption of Mexican political officials. For all practical purposes, they had all been corrupted. The next priority was to work on the Mexican business élite.

There were also discussions about the networks into Western Europe. The principal distribution outlets into the European market were Switzerland, Austria (Vienna) and

---

† *Editor's Note:* This revealing admission of the obvious – that *exposure must be avoided at all costs* – points the way for serious Western observers and for all who are determined, even at this late stage, to confront the drug offensive against civilisation. The *one hazard* that the perpetrators fear is, precisely, *exposure*. Hence the present work, intended by the Author to expose this long-term act of war against humanity. Note also that Savinkin was concerned about the *Soviet* drug programme being exposed, not so much the ultimately expendable ones of the satellites, which existed in part to provide Moscow with a veneer of deniability.

Sweden (Stockholm). All the Soviet Bloc intelligence services operated in these regions, which served as centres for drug distribution and for the covert transfer of stolen technology to the Soviet Bloc. (Panama was also to become a centre for these two activities). Intelligence linkages into other countries favoured certain national intelligence services; for example, the Germans were particularly active in marketing drugs through the Netherlands.

Another topic discussed was the increased use of drugs to corrupt the élite classes in Third World countries. Bulgarian officials said that Turkey and Iran had posed no problem. They had destroyed themselves. Savinkin criticised this remark and told the Bulgarians to listen more carefully – he was referring to the élite class. They must improve the quality of drugs and push their use into the upper classes.

In 1967, the head of the Health Administration briefed the Czechoslovak Defence Council on seven or eight new drugs which had been developed in the course of their drug research and development program. The research activity had been started five years earlier, in a facility constructed next to the Central Military Hospital in Prague specifically for the development of chemical and biological warfare agents, mind-control drugs, assassination weapons, and more effective narcotics.

The drugs reviewed in 1967 were a product of this program. They had been developed by scientists and medical doctors from the Central Military Hospital and the Air Force Scientific Centre and tested on prisoners. The new drugs were considered more effective because their immediate effects were longer lasting, and, as a bonus, they caused long-term damage in the capacity of humans to think logically. Sejna was particularly impressed with one of the more effective drugs that left the user optimistic and put him in a 'no worries, don't care' frame of mind. When tested on prisoners, the prisoners became unconcerned about penalties or having to spend their whole lives in jail. The longer-term effects, tested after two to three years, were residual mental attitudes of passivity and resignation. The test subjects did not even try to make intelligent decisions. Evidently, the drug attacked the centre of motivation.

At the briefing, the Czechoslovak doctors recommended three drugs that they believed would be the drugs of the future. The Soviet adviser, who also attended the meeting, said the drugs should not be marketed then because they might cause questions to be asked. **At that time, the Soviets believed that the blame for the drug epidemic, as desired, had been successfully placed on organised crime.** If we put new drugs on the market, the Soviets reasoned, people in the West might become suspicious. We need to be very careful to wait until the correct time; for example, when there are other potential co-producers who can be blamed as the source for the new drugs.

Another especially interesting new dimension arose in September 1967, in connection with a visit by Raúl Castro to Czechoslovakia. This event was the annual development and approval of the next one-year plan. Accompanying Castro were several high-level Cuban officials: the Chief of Military Intelligence, Chief of the Military Medical Administration, Deputy Head of the Administrative Organs Department, Deputy Chief of the General Staff for Armaments and Technology, and the Deputy Chief of the Main Political Administration. As in the past, Sejna was the Czechoslovak official who hosted the entourage. The principal subject of the meeting was the drug and narcotics operation. A sizeable expansion of Cuban and Soviet Bloc drug and narcotics trafficking activity was agreed. At this meeting, too, a protocol was signed which enabled Cuban scientists (seventeen or eighteen of them) to assist joint Soviet Bloc research teams working on drugs and narcotics. Henceforth the Cuban scientists would be working with Czechoslovak scientists, but not with the other Soviet Bloc teams. This was an indirect way of bringing the Cubans into the Soviet Bloc program.

One of the principal areas in which the Cuban scientists had been conducting research and one that they would be working on in cooperation with other Warsaw Pact scientists was an analysis of the influence of drugs on the 'intellectual stagnation' of society. The idea was that drugs would inhibit the development of the mind (intellect) and this would in turn help to bring about a stagnation of bourgeois society. The questions of interest involved what drugs or combinations of drugs were most effective in crippling the mind and how many drugs, over how many years, were required to cripple a society. That is, what drug-trafficking was required to achieve the desired effect?

This was part of a highly important Soviet operation; and all the Soviet Bloc countries had programs underway to develop the best drugs and accompanying analyses. Czechoslovakia, East Germany, Bulgaria, Hungary and the Soviet Union itself were heavily involved. The crippling of bourgeois society was the 'main order'.

The efficacy of this strategy could only be appreciated in the West after the event, since the long-term debilitating effects of nearly all drugs on the brain, even (indeed, especially) including those of marijuana, have since become better known and gained publicity and recognition. One factor of special relevance that is now recognised is the neurological effect on infants born to women on marijuana or cocaine, including long-term behavioural impairment and learning disabilities[5].

Castro was particularly forceful in presenting his position to Czechoslovak and Soviet officials. He argued that it was important to push this aspect of drug-trafficking operations even harder, and to advance the onset of stagnation by targeting younger students, specifically, high school students and children[6]. **The Soviets were thinking in terms of forty to fifty years to bring about the desired results.** Castro believed they could be accomplished in thirty-five years[7]. The Soviets were more conservative because of the social changes they believed would have to be achieved in parallel, and because they had coordinated these changes with other events in their long-range plan to destroy the West.

The Soviets were also concerned that pushing drugs on high school students and children might be too radical and cause an undesirable counter-reaction. In their plan, the Soviet-preferred bourgeois targets were the technical élite, intellectuals, soldiers and college students.

Following the meeting between Cuban and Czechoslovak officials in Prague described above, a Czechoslovak delegation went to Havana to work out details for the participation of Cuban scientists in the joint studies, to explore the possibility of including even more than seventeen scientists, and to determine if it would be possible through Castro to recruit more 'progressive' scientists throughout Latin America to assist (unwittingly) in analysing the impact of drugs on society. The delegation was headed by General Oldrich Burda, Chief of the Zs. Accompanying him were the deputy chief of the Health Administration, the chief of research at the main military hospital (his speciality being neurology), and the deputy head of the Department of Science.

Castro also believed that more emphasis in Latin America should be placed on corrupting and recruiting the military. This was necessary in order to push the revolutionary movement forward, he argued; the politicians were already thoroughly corrupted. By 1988, resources throughout Latin America were reporting the heavy involvement of military officers and police officials in drug-trafficking. This was particularly true in Colombia, its neighbours, and in Panama, Honduras and Mexico [8].

Additionally, by 1967 the Cuban campaign to penetrate the 'independent' Latin American drug operations was nearing completion. Cuban intelligence now estimated that ninety percent of the targeted organisations had already been penetrated and Castro argued that the time had come to destroy the Latin American drug groups which still resisted penetration and were 'uncooperative'.

Sejna further reported that in the fall of 1967, the Soviets called a meeting of the Warsaw Pact intelligence chiefs in Moscow to discuss expanding the drug and narcotics offensive to take advantage of the Vietnam War and disaffection of American youth. This meeting was especially noteworthy, because it may have been the same meeting on which a Bulgarian intelligence officer reported following his defection to the West in 1970. There has been considerable data from Bulgaria, all of which, in essence, confirms Sejna's testimony. This particular source was Stefan Sverdlev, a colonel in the Bulgarian Committee for State Security (secret police), the *Komitet Darzhavna Sigurnost* (KDS). Sverdlev had been directly involved in Bulgarian drug-trafficking. He described the rôle of KINTEX, a 'private' concern formed as a covert subsidiary of Bulgarian intelligence to handle parts of the drug operation. He stated that in 1967, the heads of the Warsaw Pact security services met in Moscow to **'exploit and hasten the inherent 'corruption' of Western society'**.

A subsequent meeting of Bulgarian State Security officers in Sofia, Bulgaria, was held to devise a three-year plan for the implementation of the strategy. This plan led to a State Security directive issued in July 1970, the subject of which was 'the destabilisation of Western society through, among other tools, the narcotics trade'[9]. When he defected, Sverdlev brought with him KDS directive M-120/00-0050, which dealt with the movement of narcotics from the Middle East through Bulgaria to Western Europe and North America[10]. Further, in December 1969, West Germany captured 200 kilograms of morphine base in Frankfurt. Through chemical analysis, the West Germans were able to conclude that the base had been produced in Sofia, Bulgaria[11].

By the early 1970s, discipline had been eroded in the US Army in Europe to the extent that serious questions of command had arisen. Even the mail service, which was used to distribute drugs, was corrupted[12]. A major clampdown ensued. Many soldiers were dishonourably discharged or reassigned. During the crackdown, the trafficking trail which was uncovered led back from American servicemen to Eastern Europe, with East Berlin, the German Democratic Republic, Hungary and Bulgaria prominently identified[13].

Robin Bruce Lockhart, the son of the well-known (in intelligence circles) British diplomatic agent, R. H. Bruce Lockhart, has also reported on the movement of drugs across Europe to the US armed forces. 'The finest and most powerful heroin', he writes, 'comes from East Germany and is marketed in West Germany, where the West German police estimate that the US armed forces account for no less than sixty-five percent of its consumption and at a price one-thirtieth of that obtaining in the streets of New York'[14].

What was especially noteworthy, again, was the low price. The objective is **political warfare**, *not the simple lure of high profits*, and the targets, in this case, are members of the US armed forces. As a further example of the tactics employed, opium was secretly added to marijuana – which was widely touted as being non-addictive and rather harmless at the time – to generate addiction covertly, without the user's knowledge. Similar tactics were also employed against US servicemen in Southeast Asia during the Vietnam War. High quality (white) heroin was sold to US servicemen as cocaine, which, at the time, many people believed was a harmless, non-addictive drug.

It is particularly important that these kinds of tactics should be kept in mind when assessing what happened during the 1980s in the United States. Trafficking is not a simple case of demand stimulating supply. More often it is the reverse situation, with **the suppliers working hard to** *create demand.* This helps to explain the failures of the interdiction programs of the 1980s. Notwithstanding attempts to crack down on trafficking and the seizure each year of ever higher quantities of cocaine, the purity of cocaine on the market has steadily *increased* and the price has *decreased* – which is *exactly the opposite* of what US authorities had expected.

The casual explanation is increased supply and competition. The more informed observer might question this explanation and consider *other possibilities*; for example, political warfare and measures calculated to defeat the so-called war on drugs.

The last event in 1967 of significance that General Sejna recalled was the completion of an important study, the report on which was entitled *Minorities and Immigrants in the United States.* The study was prepared for the Czechoslovak Defence Council. The study had been triggered by a talk given by the Soviet Ambassador, Stepan Cervoneiko, to the Czechoslovak Defence Council. His message was simple. 'The minorities will help us change the white to the red'. **'White'** referred to cocaine and **'red'** referred to the Red Revolution. The report formalised the rôle of drugging the minorities in the revolutionary process. The two key minorities to be targeted were Black people and Hispanics.

The importance of minorities had long been recognised in Soviet strategy, but the previous focus had been on the East European minorities and on their use in espionage. After Brezhnev became General Secretary, policies under Khrushchev were reviewed and new priorities were established. During this review, Khrushchev was criticised for not placing more focus on the use of non-European minorities, particularly Black people.

The need to make greater use of Black people in drug-trafficking first surfaced as a major topic of discussion during a visit by Raúl Castro to the Soviet Union and Czechoslovakia in 1965. In preparation for that visit, the Soviets instructed Czechoslovak officials on the need to criticise Castro for his anti-Black bias and to convince him of the importance of bringing more Black people into the drug-distribution and sales business. While in Moscow, Castro met General Savinkin (head of the Administrative Organs Department: *see above*), who took the Soviet lead in the education of Raúl Castro.

Castro stopped off in Czechoslovakia after leaving Moscow, and the 'education' continued. Raúl persisted in complaining that the problem with Black people was that they were more Black than Communist. In response, the Soviet General who advised Czechoslovak military intelligence told Castro that business was business, and that not all spies were Communist. Indeed, he pointed out, most spies were not Communist.

During private conversations with General Sejna, Castro criticised Savinkin and the Soviets in general. Obviously, we cannot exist without the Soviets, Raúl told Sejna, but they are stupid and need to listen to us. The Soviets do not understand the psychology of the Caribbean. Raúl was referring to Savinkin's push to have Cuba use both Cuban and Caribbean Black people in the drug distribution process. This was bad strategy, Raúl argued. Cuban Black people should not be used for several reasons.

First, he would have to infiltrate them through Mexico, and he believed this would upset the Mexicans. *Secondly,* Cuban Black people would be readily identified as Cubans because of their accent. *Thirdly,* it was a good idea to use just Caribbean Black people in the drug business, because the United States did not watch the Jamaicans, Haitians, Dominicans and other Caribbean nationals the way they watched the Cubans. *Fourthly*, many Black people in the United States were from other parts of the Caribbean and Blacks from those other parts of the Caribbean would have an easier job fitting in and selling drugs.

And *in the fifth place*, Castro was concerned about the reliability of Cuban Blacks. Here, Raúl was implicitly recognising the anti-Black bias of many of Fidel Castro's policies, which he believed militated against their use in such a sensitive operation. Raúl was not adverse to setting up a training program, which would include the resettlement of Cuban Black people on other Caribbean Islands for several years, until they had mastered local dialects. But for the immediate future, he was strongly opposed to using Cuban Black people in the drug program.

In the end, Castro agreed to use Cuban Blacks in intelligence operations that were not as sensitive as the drug business, and to begin training and using Caribbean Black people in the drug business. 'If you want more Black people, you will have more Blacks', Sejna recalls Castro finally agreeing, 'there is an inexhaustible supply in the Caribbean. But Caribbean Black people, not Cuban Blacks'[15].

This strategy reached its maturity with the 1967 report on the use of minorities. The specific objectives in targeting the minorities set forth in the report, as recalled by General Sejna, were as follows:

● To speed up the revolutionary process,
● To create political instabilities,
● To force the United States to pay more attention to domestic issues
  and less to international problems, and:
● To create eco-racism.

The concept of eco-racism was a product of several years' research and study. The Soviet idea was that in the United States, it is money that is most important. This was especially true among the Black people whom the Soviets believed were more motivated by material (economic) factors than by political ideals.

That is, they thought in economic terms rather than in political terms. Moreover, their anger was directed more at economic issues than at perceived political inadequacies. As a Czechoslovak delegation reported after visiting the United States in September 1967, the minorities, mostly Black people, did not understand that freedom for them meant socialism (Communism).

When we spoke to them about Communism, we were met with hostility and anger, the delegation explained. But, when we discussed economics, the anger of representatives from the minorities immediately focused on the inequities of the capitalist system. Accordingly, the delegates recommended that propaganda work should indeed focus on economic inequities – rather than on Communism and its 'benefits'.

The 1967 report, which was completed in December, addressed the importance of using minorities to 'speed the revolutionary process'. With respect to Black people, numerous tactics were identified. Racism was to be promoted because it was a destabilising factor. Operatives were to be directed at youth, since older Black people were believed to be too intimidated by the White establishment. Narcotics and propaganda were to be employed to 'revolutionise' the Black people. Black unemployment was to be promoted. Emphasis was to be placed on the concept of 'taking' or making the Whites 'give', in opposition to the concept of Black people working for a living.

This report also emphasised the need to bring Hispanic and Black minorities together. Hispanics were believed to be already well into drugs and by bringing them into closer contact with the US Black people, the use of drugs in the Black communities would be accelerated. The principal target of drugs would be the 'lumpen proletariat' – that is, the unemployed who were concentrated in the inner city ghettos. By pushing drugs into this group, crime and the general erosion of Western moral values would be stimulated because the use of drugs destroyed judgment and led people into crime, homosexuality, and other activities conventionally considered immoral.

The drug distribution chain or sequence in the United States was analysed in the report. The problem with the chain was that the majority of top bosses were White, while most of those who made up the base of the sales pyramid were Black. Two changes were therefore required. *First*, it was necessary to promote more Black people from street level into the organisation and management level. *Secondly*, it was necessary to bring Hispanics into the organisation. This was deemed advisable to avoid upsetting the Hispanics and also to avoid the undesirable problem of Black people being the only minority in control.

The report recommended making these changes as operations expanded, by promoting and training Black people and by bringing in Hispanics as new markets were opened. The combination of Black people and Hispanics would then be more effective in pushing drugs into the lumpen proletariat, which the Soviets believed was dominated by Black people and Hispanics. Together, Black people and Hispanics would form a *'spojena obcanska ohrana fronta'* or united citizen's defence front.

The thesis of the report was that drugs pushed into the minorities would create 'incurable political destruction'. The estimate presented in the report was that by the year 2000, people with a lack of morals created mainly through drugs, people who were willing to take whatever measures were necessary to support the revolution, would have expanded to encompass an estimated forty-two percent of the population.

In its 1989 report on the crack epidemic, the US Drug Enforcement Agency [DEA] concluded that: 'Large-scale, interstate trafficking networks controlled by Jamaicans, Haitians and Black street gangs dominate the manufacture and distribution of crack'[16]. The distribution of crack, which grew so rapidly in 1986, appears to be much more of an organised operation than a simple 'natural' phenomenon[17].

Crack rapidly became recognised as the most dangerous drug to hit America. As William Bennett, director of the Office of National Drug Control Policy, explained on CBS's *'Face the Nation'* on August 13, 1989, drug crime is up, drug-trafficking is up, drug deaths are up, drug emergencies in US hospitals are up. The reason for all this is crack.

Two appendices to the DEA report on crack[18] contained data provided by field agents on individual cities. Throughout these brief city summaries, the groups dominating the manufacture and distribution were shown to be Haitians, Jamaicans, Dominicans and US Black people. Trafficking was most prominent within the lower income inner-city areas, particularly in Black and Hispanic neighbourhoods[19]. While little was said about the wholesalers, two groups were identified: Cubans and Colombians.

The entire discussion of the nature of distribution and sales suggested a well-organised and managed operation – an operation designed to use Black people against Black people. The reality in 1989 thus wholly matched Soviet strategy, operations, and the underlying rationale laid down more than twenty years previously.

Could this really have been *just mere coincidence?* ∎

References to Chapter 7:

1. The fall 1959 meeting was preceded by a May 1959 KGB meeting which resulted in a decision to increase the number of KGB agents targeted against Western technology by a factor of ten, according to the recollection of a former CIA counter-intelligence official.

2. Arthur M. Schlesinger, Jr., *Robert Kennedy and His Times, op. cit.*, page 504.

3. Under Brezhnev, the banks and financial institutions became the third highest priority targets for intelligence infiltration.

4. Seymour M. Hersch, 'US Aides in '72 Weighed Killing Officer Who Now Leads Panama', *New York Times*, June 13, 1986, page 1.

5. See, for example, Michael Abramowitz, 'Pregnant Cocaine Users Reduce Risk by Stopping', *Washington Post*, March 24, 1989, page A10.

6. 'There is something of a consensus that the present serious drug crisis in the high schools – primarily marijuana, LSD, mescaline, and a few others such as amphetamines and barbiturates – began about 1967'. *Psycho-Chemical Warfare: The Chinese Communist Drug Offensive Against the West* (New Rochelle, New York: Arlington House, 1973), *op. cit.*, page 63. It is also interesting to note that in 1967, the Scholastic Aptitude Test scores used as college entrance exams began a decline which reached a low of 890 in 1980, down from the previous normal range of 965-975. Given the intensity of Castro's argument and his tendency to act without awaiting Soviet approval, it is logical to assume that Cuba had already begun the process of pushing drugs into US high schools at the time of the meeting in Moscow.

7. In a speech on international terrorism at the Congress of the European Christian Democratic Union held in Madrid in June 1986, Llaminio Piccoli, President of the Italian National Council of Christian Democracy, dwelt at some length on collusion between terrorists and the international narcotics trade. He also quoted Raúl Castro as stating towards the end of the 1960s that drugs would be a decisive weapon to disrupt the fabric of Western democracies. He also mentioned the narcotics trade organised by Cuba and certain countries of Central America, under the dominant influence of Cuba and the USSR.

8. See also, Merrill Collett, 'Colombia's Drug Cartel Said to Aim at Military', *Washington Post*, April 11, 1988, page A17.

9. *Drugs and Terrorism*, 1984, *op. cit.*, page 58.

10. Nathan M. Adams, 'Drugs for Guns: The Bulgarian Connection', *Reader's Digest*, November 1983.

11. *Drugs and Terrorism*, 1984, *op. cit.*, page 59.

12. Times have not changed. In 1988, investigations of drug-trafficking by Panama-based US soldiers uncovered the use of the military mail system to ship cocaine. Michael Isikoff, 'Drugs Allegedly Shipped in Army Planes, Mail', *Washington Post*, June 2, 1988, page A3.

13. Additional details are available in Joseph D. Douglass, Jr. and Neil C. Livingstone, *America the Vulnerable: The Threat of Chemical/Biological Warfare* (Lexington, Massachusetts: Lexington Books, D.C. Heath and Company, 1987), pages 113-144.

14. Robin Bruce Lockhart, *Reilly: The First Man* (New York: Penguin Books, 1987), page 99.

15. In 1980, a Jamaican, Mr. Earlston Spencer, participated in a hearing held by the National Committee To Restore Internal Security. He explained how in 1974, the year after Michael Manley became Prime Minister of Jamaica, young people were openly recruited to go to Cuba for training, which included training in guerrilla warfare. The first Jamaican gangs or *posses* are believed by the US Justice Department to have appeared in the United States around 1974. These Jamaican *posses* subsequently became some of the main distributors of crack cocaine in the mid-1980s.

16. US Department of Justice, Drug Enforcement Agency, *Crack Cocaine Review 1989* (Washington D.C.: US Department of Justice, 1989), page 13.

17. Observations in the 1989 *National Drug Control Strategy* are quite interesting in this respect. 'Crack is an innovation in cocaine retailing that takes uncanny advantage of the nation's changing drug use patterns'. The White House, *National Drug Control Strategy* (Washington, D.C.: US Government Printing Office, September 1989), page 4.

18. *Crack Cocaine Overview* 1989, *op. cit.*

19. Consider, for example, the following extracts taken from the city and state summaries in Appendix A and B of *Crack Cocaine Overview 1989, op. cit.*:

✖ Amarillo: Crack houses are run by American Black people who sell the majority of their product to Black buyers.

✖ Atlanta: Crack cocaine has literally taken over the lower income drug market throughout the State of Georgia.

✖ Baltimore: Haitians and Black people are the main traffickers.

✖ Boston: Crack rapidly spread through the major cities in Connecticut, Massachusetts, Rhode Island and New Hampshire, confined to the Black inner-city areas. Subsequent intelligence disclosed that out-of-state Black gangs were vying for control. Availability of crack... is principally controlled by Dominican and Puerto Rican groups.

✖ Bridgeport: Black people are still the main sources for crack. High-level Hispanic cocaine traffickers import cocaine and convert it into crack.

✖ **Cape Cod:** In 1988, Black violators surfaced as key suppliers of cocaine to the Mid-Cape area.

✖ **Dallas:** Crack distribution is controlled by a 500-700 member Jamaican-controlled cartel. Crack cocaine trafficking is primarily centred around the lower income, urban Black and Hispanic population.

✖ **Denver:** Crack houses are run by Jamaicans with the assistance of locally recruited Black females.

✖ **Fort Myers:** The cooks and distributors of the crack are mostly Black and the buyers cross all ethnic boundaries.

✖ **Hartford:** Black and Hispanic traffickers controlled the crack distribution to the Hartford area when it first surfaced.

✖ **Houston:** The crack problem is essentially situated in predominantly Black neighbourhoods.

✖ **Kansas City:** Reports substantial involvement of Jamaican traffickers.

✖ **Los Angeles:** Crack cocaine manufacture and distribution are primarily controlled by Black street gangs (the Bloods or the Crips) who have distribution networks throughout the northwestern and southwestern United States.

✖ **Lubbock:** Crack houses are typically motel rooms or empty houses run by American Black people who are supplied by Cuban wholesalers.

✖ **Miami:** Haitian and Jamaican illegal aliens are, for the most part, responsible for this phase [import and manufacture] of the operation. Local Black violators are responsible for local distribution, with some White assistance.

✖ **New Orleans:** A Black street gang (Crips) from Los Angeles has emerged as the main source of crack.

✖ **New York:** Primary crack traffickers are Dominicans and Black people. Dominicans are most active in upper Manhattan and the Bronx. Black traffickers control large areas of crack trafficking in middle-class and inner-city sections of Brooklyn, Queens and parts of the Bronx. Jamaicans and Haitian crack groups are not as large as the Dominican and Black groups, but they are involved in significant activity.

✖ **Newark:** Black and Jamaican gangs are the principal groups involved in street sales and distribution. Caucasians and Hispanics (predominately Dominicans) are active, but to a lesser degree.

✖ **Orlando:** The problem is located in poor Black neighbourhoods and Haitians are directly involved in many of the areas.

✖ **Philadelphia:** Crack cocaine houses, under control of Jamaican trafficking organisation,are beginning to surface.

✖ **Phoenix:** Crack cocaine is available in the public housing areas and is dealt entirely by Black people. Crack is supplied by the Crips and Bloods gangs of Los Angeles.

✖ **Providence:** Dominicans and out-of-state Black people control the distribution of crack. Most defendants are Dominican or US Black people.

✖ **San Diego:** Crack remains a serious problem in minority enclaves.

✖ **San Francisco:** Crack is an overwhelming problem in urban, lower class Black neighbourhoods.

✖ **Seattle:** Widespread availability of crack cocaine among all ethnic groups.

✖ **Tallahassee:** The majority of the crack cocaine clientèle are from the Black community. Suppliers are primarily Black traffickers in the Miami area, many of whom are either Jamaican or closely connected to Jamaican traffickers.

✖ **Tulsa:** Crack cocaine is readily available within the Black community.

✖ **Tyler:** Crack houses are managed by American Black people. Trafficking is primarily concentrated in Black communities.

✖ **Washington D.C.:** Utilisation of juvenile couriers, primarily Black teenagers, is a noted trend. A growing number of Jamaican distributors has entered the cocaine trade.

✖ **Wilmington:** Haitian crack distribution has grown from a limited market confined to Black Americans to open street selling in at least ten small communities. Most of the distributors are connected to the Haitian community located in the Fort Pierce, Florida, area.

CUBA AND THE RISE OF NARCO-TERRORISM

On November 15, 1982, the American public was treated to a rare display of candour. That was the date on which four important Cuban officials, including two influential members of the Central Committee of the Communist Party of Cuba, were indicted by a Federal grand jury in Miami on charges of conspiring to bring drugs illegally into the United States.

The indictments of high-ranking Cubans opened the floodgates. A stream of additional indictments followed, the more important of which were those of Jorge Ochoa and Carlos Lehder Rivas, reputed Colombian drug kingpins; Norman B. Saunders, the Chief Minister of the Turks and Caicos Islands; Frederick Nigel Bowe, a high-ranking Bahamas Minister; Everette Bannister, Chairman of Bahamas World Airlines and a close associate of the Prime Minister, Lynden O. Pindling; Colonel Jean-Claude Paul, the strongman of Haiti; Frederico Vaughan, a high official in Nicaragua's intelligence service; Panama's military dictator, General Manuel Antonio Noriega; Manuel Ibarra Herrera, former head of the Mexican Federal Judicial Police; and Miguel Aldana-Ibarra, former head of the Mexican branch of Interpol.

As a result of the evidence presented in the indictments, a picture of many interconnected drug operations gradually emerged – a picture which, while admittedly incomplete, bears a striking resemblance to the overall description of what Soviet strategy, as described by Sejna, was intended to produce. The picture contained four primary features.

First, there are close linkages between drug-trafficking and terrorist-revolutionary activities; hence, the term narco-terrorism. These have led to the breakdown in law and order that, when coupled with drug-related corruption, is bringing about the destabilisation of a growing number of important countries, most notably Colombia, Venezuela, Peru and Mexico. In many cases the terrorists or guerrillas control or manage drug production and distribution. This basic phenomenon is not limited to Latin America. It is also present in varying degrees in the Middle East, Southeast Asia and Africa.

Secondly, while the vast number of people involved in drug-trafficking do not appear to hold any particular political philosophy, there is a disproportionate involvement of Communist party officials, government officials from Communist countries, agents from

Communist intelligence services, and Marxist revolutionary and terrorist organisations.

Thirdly, within the Americas, Cuba stands out. Cuba is clearly involved with numerous drug-trafficking operations and provides many functions, from recruitment to transshipment facilities, command posts, equipment supply, production and manufacture, transportation, sales and marketing, and finance[1].

And *finally*, while money is always present as an obvious motivation, insofar as the higher officials involved with trafficking are concerned, the political dimension, specifically political warfare against the United States, is even more important than the money.

As a Soviet revolutionary centre[2] in the Caribbean, Cuba is the operational centre for drug-trafficking and for the training of revolutionary terrorists. (Nicaragua was becoming a second revolutionary centre, and was also active in drug-trafficking and in harbouring and training revolutionaries). Cuba provides a safe haven for Latin American drug-traffickers *en route* to the United States. For this, the drug-traffickers pay a fee. On their return trip to South America to pick up more drugs, they transport ammunition and supplies from Cuba to the revolutionary terrorists; for example, to the M-19 forces in Colombia[3].

The manner in which narcotics trafficking and revolutionary or terrorist organisations operate together can be seen in the reports on Colombian[4] and Cuban operations. Terrorist or revolutionary groups provide protection for the drug-traffickers. The drug-traffickers help finance the terrorists and revolutionaries and furnish them with information (intelligence) and transportation assistance. In Colombia, the Marxist M-19 revolutionaries have close ties to Cuba and various drug-traffickers, of which the most highly publicised over the years has been the organisation known as the Medellín Cartel.

The Cartel has close ties to Cuba, Nicaragua and other countries. The principal linkage between the Medellín Cartel and the M-l9, as explained by José I. Blandón Castillo, former Consul General of Panama, is the Cuban Ambassador, Fernando Ravelo Renedo. Ravelo works for Manuel Pineiro Losada, the head the Americas Department of the Central Committee of the Communist Party of Cuba[5] and former head of the DGI. The Americas Department (*Departamento de America*) has special responsibility for subversion and sabotage operations in the Western Hemisphere, including disinformation, terrorism, and drugs[6]. [*Editor's Note:* This was the position prevailing, of course, in 1990].

In Colombia and other countries, such as Peru, terrorists provide the drug producers with protection from the local police and military forces. The drug producers are alerted to possible raids on their facilities. They pass data to terrorists, who then ambush and kill the forces conducting the raids. This is good for the terrorists and for the producers, who in return provide funds, territory, and the supplies the terrorists need. As another example, when government officials decide to clamp down on drug-traffickers, the terrorists assist the traffickers by terrorising and killing officials, as they did in the case of the mass murder of the Colombian Ministers of Justice who were taking steps to extradite certain Colombian drug lords[7].

The terrorists provide additional muscle when bribery is inadequate. Generally, bribery has worked quite well. Corruption through bribery is rampant in the Bahamas, Mexico, Colombia, Bolivia, Peru, Costa Rica, Haiti, Panama, the Caymans and Brazil. By using terrorists to perform violent acts, drug-traffickers are able to maintain their image as businessmen – businessmen with wide-ranging influence, but still just businessmen. The drug-traffickers are, therefore, from a government official's point of view, *good people to get along with*, people who can *pay for services*.

They bring money into the country and provide jobs. So what, if they also provide a product which damages 'capitalists'? It is the *terrorists* who are the bad guys. While this logic is blatantly fallacious, it is amazing how many people accept it and promote it, including many high-ranking officials in the United States.

The precise origins of narco-terrorism are uncertain. However, there are a variety of facts that point to its gradual emergence, perhaps more as a result of evolution and circumstance than direct planning. First, as reported by Sejna, the current Soviet strategy involving narcotics trafficking, terrorism and organised crime had its origins in about 1955, when Khrushchev set about modernising Soviet subversion and putting the world Communist movement back on course following Stalin's death.

The three activities – drug-trafficking, terrorism, and organised crime – provided complementary functions; and the Soviet Bloc activities in all three areas were managed by the strategic intelligence sections in the KGB and GRU intelligence services. These strategic intelligence sections perform only special tasks of strategic importance, the most important of which, as indicated earlier, are strategic espionage, drugs and narcotics, terrorism, deception and sabotage.

The combination of narcotics and terrorism was also identified in the 1950s and 1960s by Dr Ray Cline, the former Deputy Director of Intelligence, Central Intelligence Agency, who explained:

'I have observed with horror the growing links in many areas between the three groups: the revolutionary political groups, who are, for the most part, Marxist-Leninist, anxious to create a state subordinate to the Soviet Union or one of its surrogate states, like Cuba; the narcotics traffickers, who need the protection that such revolutionary groups can give them and are willing to pay for it, and, in fact, are willing to finance the political revolutions with the proceeds of drug-traffic; and then the gun runners, the people involved in the illegal passing of guns to revolutionary groups and to narcotics traffickers'[8].

In the case of Bulgaria, the connection between drug-trafficking and terrorism was clearly evident in the early 1970s. Indeed, KINTEX is described by various sources as having dual tasks, the movement of drugs into Western Europe and the movement of guns and ammunition into the Middle East[9]. These are not totally independent activities, insofar as drugs are often accepted as payment for the guns and ammunition.

This method of operation has been connected with many terrorist organisations. For example, Jacques Kiere, Director of the Drug Enforcement Administration's national intelligence centre at El Paso, Texas, gave unpublished testimony on November 19, 1975, to the House Armed Services Committee on such swaps. He stated that 'five out of the ten known Mexican Marxist groups are known to trade Mexican heroin and other drugs for US guns'[10]. Similar data exists on revolutionary groups in Venezuela, the Dominican Republic, Brazil, Colombia, Peru, Burma, Panama and Bolivia.

But notwithstanding its early origins, the United States did not begin to wake up to what was happening concerning narco-terrorism until November 15, 1982, when four senior Cuban officials were indicted, along with ten others, by a Federal grand jury in Miami, Florida on charges of 'conspiracy to import marijuana and methaqualone from Colombia to the United States by way of Cuba'. The Cubans charged were Rene

Rodriguez-Cruz, an intelligence official and member of the Central Committee of the Communist Party of Cuba; Aldo Santamaria-Cuadrado, a Vice-Admiral in the Cuban Navy and also a member of the Central Committee; Fernando Ravelo Renedo, the Cuban Ambassador to Colombia, subsequently Ambassador to Nicaragua; and Gonzalo Bassols-Suarez, a former Minister-Counsellor of the Cuban Embassy in Bogotà and member of the Communist Party of Cuba. The ensuing publicity brought narco-terrorism out into the open for the first time.

The witnesses who provided the principal evidence at the ensuing trial (February 1983) were Juan Crump, a Colombian lawyer and drug-trafficker who negotiated with ranking Cuban officials for Jaimé Guillot-Lara, a leading Colombian drug-trafficker; David Perez, a Cuban-American drug-trafficker who met the boats and delivered the goods into the United States; and Mario Estevez Gonzalez, a Cuban intelligence agent who was infiltrated into the United States during the Mariel boat lift, who received narcotics from Cuba, sold them in the United States, and then returned the proceeds to Cuban intelligence.

Colombian Juan (Johnny) Crump was asked to use his influence to obtain Cuba's assistance for the trafficker Jaimé Guillot-Lara. During the ensuing negotiations with Cuba's Ambassador Fernando Ravelo Renedo and his deputy, Gonzalo Bassols-Suarez, Guillot-Lara wanted confirmation that 'if a drug shipment were lost, he would not have to pay the fee to Cuba. Then they say, Ravelo and Bassols, they, don't worry [sic], that they can wait, and they don't care about the money – OK? – that – **because his goal was hurt the United States full with drugs**' [sic][11].

This trafficking philosophy was also reported by Mario Estevez, who said he was ordered 'to load up the United States with drugs'[12]. The philosophy is especially interesting when considered alongside the known Soviet strategy, the objective of which was to bring about the intellectual stagnation of the United States, by means of the mechanism of achieving a maximum flow of drugs into the country, as discussed in Chapter 7.

Estevez further testified that he was directed by his DGI superior to make contact with drug-traffickers in Bimini and in the United States. During his drug-trafficking career, he imported over 270 kilogrammes of cocaine from Cuba, he said. He sold this cocaine to individuals in Miami, Chicago, Ohio, New Jersey, New York and other cities. He took the money he was paid to Cuba, where he delivered it to the Cuban Government. It was during one such trip that Rene Rodriguez-Cruz, a senior official of the DGI and a ranking member of the Cuban Communist Party Central Committee, put his arm on Estevez's shoulder and said how nice it was now that Cuba 'had a drugstore in the United States'[13]. Incidentally, Rodriguez-Cruz was one of the Cuban officials who had helped organise the Mariel boatlift used to infiltrate Cuban intelligence agents into the United States.

According to testimony provided to the US Grand Jury in Miami, it is the Government of Cuba that is trafficking drugs and narcotics into the United States. Cuba is also providing support to terrorist operations throughout Latin America. Both Fidel and Raúl Castro are directly involved, with Raúl the more active participant. The operation is secret and is run by Cuban intelligence, with other agencies participating on an 'as needed' basis[14].

Further, as was explained in Congressional testimony on February 26, 1982, by Gerardo Peraza, a former official in Cuban intelligence, throughout the 1960s there was extensive cooperation between the Cuban DGI and the Soviet KGB. Subsequently, with effect from 1970, the Cuban intelligence service was placed directly under the direction of KGB Colonel Viktor Simenov. Mr Peraza stated that after 1970, the DGI had ceased to be a partner of the KGB; rather, it had become a subordinate entity of the Soviet KGB[15]. Sejna explained that Cuban intelligence planning was integrated into overall Soviet Bloc planning in the 1968 intelligence plan which he reviewed in the fall of 1967. According to a Defence Intelligence Agency (DIA) report on international terrorism, the DGI has been 'essentially under the control of the KGB since 1969'[16].

Major Florentino Aspillaga Lombard was a career officer in the Cuban DGI until his defection (ultimately to the United States) via Vienna on June 6, 1987, from Czechoslovakia, where he had been stationed. He confirmed that a powerful drug syndicate had been using Cuba since 1978 as a transshipment point for illegal narcotics into the United States[17]. Protection was provided by José Abrahantes, a Castro deputy who was Minister of Interior. None of the drug-related activities could have been carried out without the personal approval of Fidel Castro, he explained[18].

In 1988 the rôle of Cuba in drug-trafficking was further confirmed by Major Antonio Rodriguez Menier, a Cuban intelligence officer and Chief of Security at the Cuban Embassy in Budapest, who defected in January 1987 [see page 56, Note 2 to Chapter 5].

He elaborated that the Cuban Government participated both directly and indirectly in narco-trafficking and that the Special Troops[19] of the Interior Ministry were used to coordinate operations. Rodriguez quoted the Chief of the DGI, General German Barreiro, as saying that **'drugs are the best way to destroy the United States'**. Their primary target was American youth. By undermining the will of American youth to resist, the United States could be destroyed *'without firing one bullet. The foundation of any army is the youth and he who is able to morally destroy the youth, destroys the army'*[20].

In 1989, Rodriguez repeated his charges and confirmed what Aspillaga had said; namely, that drug operations could not have been carried out without Raúl and Fidel Castro's personal approval. He added that **'Fidel is not doing that only for money. His philosophy is to use anything to destroy the United States. For example, drugs are regarded as the best way to destroy American society without troops or guns, because the younger people who are the future leaders, if they are drug addicts, they are very weak'**[21]. What is especially noteworthy about such statements, of course, is that they precisely reflect Soviet drugs strategy.

In March 1989, two Colombian drug dealers pleaded guilty to smuggling cocaine into Florida through Cuba. Videotaped evidence included conversations of how the Cuban military and civilian officials aided the traffickers. Reinaldo Ruíz and his son Ruben are shown telling a DEA informant how Cuba guarantees the success of cocaine loads run through the island and how the money paid for the service goes to Fidel Castro. The US Attorney, Dexter Lehtinen, stated: 'We believe the evidence presented in court details complicity on behalf of high-ranking Cuban officials'[22].

Besides Colombia, Cuba has also been closely linked with Panama and Nicaragua in drug-trafficking and gun-running. In the case of Panama, General Noriega was indicted on February 4, 1988. The indictment named 15 others and directly tied Noriega to Colombia's Medellín Cartel. Following the indictment, the US Government tried to force Noriega out of office. Suddenly there emerged a flood of information on Noriega's questionable activities. Drug-trafficking was the first of these; and this had been the case extending as far back as 1970. Gun-running was the second; and not just to non-Communist dissident forces, but to terrorists and Communist revolutionaries. This data also extended back to the early 1970s.

But the activity of greatest concern appears to have been Noriega's growing links to

Cuba and Cuban operations in Panama. Noriega had allowed Cuban intelligence to set up several hundred bogus corporations in Panama to circumvent the US trade embargo against Cuba[23]. Panama became a conduit for theft by the Soviet Bloc of US high technology. Even more serious was the growing Cuban military presence, which involved the shipment of weapons by Cuba – automatic rifles, rocket-propelled grenades, hand grenades and ammunition – into Panama, and often through Panama to revolutionary forces in other Latin American countries; guerrilla and special forces training given to Noriega's military (referred to as 'Dignity Battalions'); Cuban commando units which were reported to be conducting limited attacks on US military installations in Panama (for example, Howard Air Force Base was the target of an assault on April 12, 1988); and Cuban military advisers and intelligence support officials, whose numbers US officials estimated to be between thirty and fifty, although one defector put the number at 3,000 [24].

When the United States finally intervened in Panama on December 20, 1989, it would seem that far more impetus was provided by the need to bring an end to the growing military presence of Cuba (and, hence, of the Soviet Union) than to the assistance Noriega was providing to drug-traffickers and money-launderers. The drug business provided the rationale to remove Noriega; but the growing potential of Cuban and Soviet control mechanisms in Panama was even more serious[25].

The importance of Panama is obvious. Panama occupies a geostrategic position of exceptional importance, which may well explain why Panama was one of the first targets for the Soviet-Czechoslovak-Cuban drug-trafficking expansion into Latin America.

Evidence also surfaced concerning drug and narcotics trafficking by the Government of Nicaragua, and of its close relationship with Cuba. This evidence was provided, among other sources, by Antonio Farach, Former Minister Counsellor to the Nicaraguan Embassies in Venezuela and Honduras; by James Herring, an American who assisted the Government of Nicaragua in establishing cocaine production and transportation; by Ubi Dekker, a European hashish trafficker who dealt with Nicaraguan officials in establishing trade routes for Nicaraguan drug-trafficking into Europe; and by Alvaro José Baldizón Aviles, an official in the Nicaraguan intelligence service.

Antonio Farach's first knowledge of Nicaraguan drug-trafficking materialised in 1981, when he learned that Raúl Castro had visited Nicaragua in September that year and had met Humberto Ortega. The visit signalled the beginning of a 'new and special business' relationship. Farach deduced from other information that Cuba had offered to guarantee in a reasonable and safe manner the entry of the Nicaraguan Government into drug-trafficking. When asked whether Castro offered or ordered the Nicaraguans' entry into the drug business, Farach could not state which. But he did say that the relationship between the two countries was never one of respect. 'The Cubans always spoke as if they were the bosses. They were always very arrogant and demanding. They do not suggest in Nicaragua. They order in Nicaragua'[26].

Baldizón, a former Nicaraguan counter-intelligence officer, confirmed the arrogant rôle of Cuban advisers in the Nicaraguan intelligence and military services. The presence of Cuban advisers and instructors was 'pervasive', he explained. Their mission was to provide substantive advice, to implement security systems and methods employed in Cuba, to support the Nicaraguan leadership in the planning and execution of combat operations, to oversee ideological development, to ensure close coordination between Nicaraguan and Cuban security services, and to prepare war plans. 'The Cuban influence on decision-making in the Ministry is virtually complete and Cuban advice and observations are treated as though they were orders'. Cubans operating out of the Cuban mission also performed a counter-intelligence rôle in Nicaragua. Other advisers and technicians identified by Baldizón were from East Germany, North Korea, Bulgaria, and the USSR [27].

Similar observations were provided in 1988 by Major Aspillaga [*see page 81*], who described the Marxist Sandinistas as being under Castro's 'complete control'. In particular, he described communications intercepts from 1980 in which Castro ordered the Nicaraguan Defence Minister, Humberto Ortega, to arrange for his brother, Daniel Ortega, to assume the post of Nicaragua's political leader, so that Humberto could maintain control of the armed forces. The key advisers in the Nicaraguan Government, including the intelligence chief, were Cuban intelligence officers, Aspillaga [*see page 81*] explained[28]. He also said that the Cubans were training Nicaraguan Sandinista agents and performing counter-intelligence work. Moreover, a key intelligence official in the Nicaraguan Interior Ministry is a Cuban who married a Nicaraguan woman, but who still works for Cuban intelligence[29]. Additionally, Colombian drug-traffickers met Raúl Castro regularly in Cuba, Aspillaga said. Raúl is Fidel's right-hand man for all clandestine operations and Fidel viewed drugs as **'a very important weapon against the United States, because drugs demoralise people and undermine society'**[30].

The nature of Cuban advisers in Nicaragua as described by Farach, Baldizón, and Aspillaga appeared to be remarkably similar to the nature of Czechoslovak advisers in Cuba in the early 1960s who launched the Soviet takeover, with the Cubans in Nicaragua performing the rôle that the Czechoslovaks had played in Cuba. In line with this, one should suspect that half of the 'Cuban' advisers and instructors in Nicaragua might well have been Soviets operating under Cuban cover and that the real Cubans present were probably recruited and trained by the Soviets and now operated as Soviet intelligence agents. This might help to explain the arrogance observed by Farach and Baldizón.

When Farach asked other Nicaraguan officials why their revolutionary government should become involved in drug-trafficking, he was told: 'In the first place, drugs did not remain in Nicaragua. The drugs were destined for the United States. **Our youth would not be harmed, but rather the youth of the United States, the youth of our enemies. There-fore, *drugs were used as a political weapon because in that way we were delivering a blow to our principal enemy*'**[31]. The second reason he was given was 'in addition to a political weapon against the United States, drug-trafficking produced a very good economic benefit which we needed for our revolution. Again, in a few words, we wanted to provide food for our people with the suffering and death of the youth of the United States'[32].

Nicaragua's participation in drug and narcotics trafficking into the United States sprang from Raúl Castro's meeting with Humberto Ortega. The narcotics operation itself was placed under the Nicaraguan intelligence service, with Tomas Borge, the Minister of Interior and head of the intelligence service, in charge of the operation, and his deputy, Frederico Vaughan, the chief of staff.

Frederico Vaughan was indicted in 1986 in the US District Court, Southern District of Florida, along with Carlos Lehder, the Ochoa family, Pablo Escobar Gaviría, and others, on twenty-four counts of producing and smuggling cocaine into the United States, conspiracy, obstructing justice, and related crimes. James Herring, an American who was recruited by Robert Vesco for various nefarious tasks, has described how he was introduced to Nicaraguan and Cuban Government officials, and his work in 'drugs and high-tech smuggling'. He made a total of four trips to Cuba and four trips to Nicaragua. He was always 'escorted and treated very well by dignitaries from both governments'. In Herring's opinion, the operation was government-initiated[33].

Ubi Dekker is a cover name for a European who was a prominent Interpol fugitive and international narcotics trafficker; his true identity is concealed for security reasons. When he was asked if the trafficking was not really just the work of a few corrupt officials, Dekker responded, 'Completely doubtful. It's impossible…. It is the total [Cuban] Government'. The Cuban Government provided security, facilities, manpower, in short, everything; and there was a direct linkage between Cuba and Nicaragua[34].

Baldizón's debriefing by US officials was particularly revealing. From 1982 until his defection on July 1, 1985, Baldizón was the chief investigator of internal abuses within the Nicaraguan Ministry of Interior. In 1984, Baldizón's office received reports linking Interior Minister Tomas Borge with cocaine trafficking. Baldizón was instructed to investigate this as a compromise of a state secret. He thought this was a mistake, because he could not believe his government was involved in narcotics trafficking. Thus, he went to the chief of his office, Captain Charlotte Baltodano Egner, and asked her if the matter should not be investigated as a slander against the Minister. Baltodano was taken aback and said that the office should not have received the report.

The fact that Borge had involved the government in narcotics trafficking was highly classified, she explained, and known in the Ministry only to Borge, his assistant [Frederico Vaughan], the chiefs of police and state security, and to her. Outside the Ministry it was known only to members of the FSLN's National Directorate. Baldizón also provided additional details concerning Borge and cocaine trafficking and the use of the money 'for mounting clandestine operations by the Intelligence and State Security Department outside Nicaragua'[35]. Baldizón died in 1988, in California[36].

In 1987, another high-ranking official from the Nicaraguan Government defected to the United States: Major Roger Miranda Bengoechea. Miranda also confirmed Nicaragua's involvement in drug-trafficking. He reported how, one day, the Defence Minister, Humberto Ortega, told him that trafficking was Borge's operation, and added: '*It's a way of waging war on the United States*. It also provides a profit'[37].

Reports on narcotics trafficking in other Latin American (and Caribbean) countries, including Mexico, Panama, Colombia, Peru, Bolivia, the Bahamas, Haiti, Jamaica, Honduras, Brazil, Venezuela and Argentina are similar, differing mainly in degree and in respect of how advanced the trafficking operation has become. The primary similarities are drug-related corruption, participation of high government officials, the growing involvement of the military or police, and linkages to Cuba or Nicaragua. Communist involvement tends to be present, but is not as directly evident as is the case in Cuba and Nicaragua.

The principal differences between reported conditions in the non-Communist countries listed above and in Cuba and Nicaragua are that, in the case of Cuba and Nicaragua, drug-related activities are directly performed as initiatives of the Communist Government – so that there are no problems between the government and the drug-traffickers, nor do serious instabilities arise because of drug-trafficking.

The destabilisation potential inherent in the corruption which accompanies drug production, trafficking, and money-laundering may be even more dangerous and damning than the social problems caused by drugs, because it provides the foundation for revolution and takeover. This is where narco-terrorism has its primary impact, with the narcotics operations sabotaging law, order, economics and societal cohesion. When the situation has sufficiently deteriorated, the revolutionary terrorists can proceed to overthrow the government.

This destabilisation process was described in 1985 by Jon Thomas, Assistant Secretary for International Narcotics Matters, US Department of State, as follows: 'The traffickers in fact may have killed their golden goose. They have polluted their own countries with their drugs. Now added to the incentives for controls... [are] the undermining of economies, the erosion of public institutions, the corruption of law and order, the violence and the threats of narco-terrorists, and insurgent groups who capitalise on the drug trade, and the destabilisation of governments'[38]. In one sense, Thomas is absolutely correct. However, there is another dimension – namely, that these 'incentives' which contribute to destabilisation are not unwanted results, but rather desired objectives. **They are not killing the golden goose; they are building a revolutionary base for their own golden goose.**

Nor is this where the story ends, because there is an even more important dimension. In his testimony, Thomas was addressing the situation in Latin America. But what is happening is not limited to Latin America. It is happening around the world, including the United States. The breakdown of law and order is especially evident in those US States most closely associated with drug-trafficking and money-laundering; for example, Florida, Arizona, New Mexico and California. A prime example of the erosion of police capabilities, for a time, was evident in Washington, D.C., where the police frankly admitted they were out-gunned. On March 24, 1989, D.C. Police Chief Maurice T. Turner, Jr. said that the police could do little about the escalating homicide rate, other than wait until local drug dealers finished carving up the city into markets[39]. This echoes the sentiments of police in more than a dozen major cities. In a special report published in 1989 on growing anarchy within urban America, *US. News & World Report* concluded that 'combat like conditions' exist in New York, Boston, Philadelphia, Baltimore, Washington, Miami, Cleveland, New Orleans, East St. Louis, Detroit, Chicago, Atlanta, Houston, Dallas, Oakland and Los Angeles[40].

The challenges and human frailties that give rise to these problems are not limited to Latin America. They exist everywhere, the United States being of course no exception, which is another reason why drug-trafficking is far more serious than public and official government perceptions of the problem allow. ■

References to Chapter 8:

1. Cuba's participation in all these activities has been explained by numerous defectors and former narcotics traffickers. A collection of news media reports following the November 1982, indictment has been published as *Castro and the Narcotics Connection* (Washington, D.C.: The Cuban American National Foundation, Inc., 1983) and *Castro's Narcotics Trade* (Washington, D.C.: The Cuban American National Foundation, Inc., 1983). See also Ra'anan, *Hydra of Carnage, op. cit.*, pages 431-476.

2. A **'revolutionary centre'** is a base for the training and export of revolutionary activity. See Footnote 3, Chapter 3, for further information about **'revolutionary centres'**.

3. See US Congress, Senate, *The Cuban Government's Involvement in Facilitating International drug-traffic*, Joint Hearing Before the Subcommittee on Security and Terrorism of the Committee on the Judiciary and the Subcommittee on Western Hemisphere Affairs of the Foreign Relations Committee and the Senate Drug Enforcement Caucus, Miami, Florida, April 30, 1983 (Washington, D.C.: US Government Printing Office, 1983). Detail on the Soviet connection by former Cuban intelligence agents can be found in US Congress, Senate, *The Rôle of Cuba in International Terrorism and Subversion*, Hearings Before the Subcommittee on Security and Terrorism of the Committee on the Judiciary, February 26, March 4, 11, and 12, 1982 (Washington, D.C.: US Government Printing Office, 1982).

4. For a presentation of the growth of the Colombian cocaine cartels and linkages to terrorists, see Gugliotta and Leen, *Kings of Cocaine, op. cit.*

5. US Senate, *Hearings Before the Subcommittee on Terrorism, Narcotics and International Operations of the Committee on Foreign Relations*, February 9, 1988, unpublished stenographic transcript, morning session, pages 68, 71, afternoon session, page 41.

6. See US Congress, Senate, *Terrorism: The Rôle of Moscow and Its Subcontractors*, Hearing

Before the Subcommittee on Security and Terrorism of the Committee on the Judiciary, June 26, 1981 (Washington, D.C.: US Government Printing Office, 1982), page 10. For an excellent review of the evolution of the Americas Department, see Rex A. Hudson, *Castro's Americas Department* (Washington, D.C.: The Cuban American National Foundation, Inc., 1988).

Interestingly, Pineiro was one of two men Castro despatched on a secret mission to Chile's embattled Marxist-Leninist President, Salvador Allende, only six weeks before Allende's overthrow in 1973. Pineiro and the Cuban Deputy Prime Minister, Carlos Rafael Rodriguez – who also headed Cuba's Communist Party – bore a hand written note from Castro urging Allende to fight to the death should revolution materialise. Pineiro succeeded as secret police chief Luís Fernandes Ona, sent by Castro to aid in shoring up the Allende regime in its early days, and who subsequently married one of Allende's daughters. Whelan, *Out of the Ashes, op. cit.*, page 407.

7. See, for example, Bradley Graham, 'Colombian Supreme Court Overturns Extradition Pact With US', *Washington Post*, June 27, 1987, page A 16.

8. US Senate, *International Terrorism, Insurgency, and drug-trafficking: Present Trends in Terrorist Activity*, Joint Hearings Before the Committee on Foreign Relations and the Committee on the Judiciary, May 13, 14 and 15, 1985 (Washington, D.C.: US Government Printing Office, 1986), page 31.

9. *Drugs and Terrorism*, 1984, *op. cit.*

10. Workman, *International Drug-trafficking op. cit.*, pages 2, 28.

11. US Congress, Senate, *The Cuban Government's Involvement in Facilitating International drug-traffic*, Joint Hearing Before the Subcommittee on Security and Terrorism of the Committee on the Judiciary and the Subcommittee on Western Hemisphere Affairs of the Foreign Relations Committee and the Senate Drug Enforcement Caucus, Miami, Florida, April 30, 1983 (Washington D.C.: US Government Printing Office, 1983), page 23.

12. *Ibid.*, page 45.

13. *Ibid.*

14. Testimony of the witnesses is contained in *The Cuban Government's Involvement in Facilitating International Drug Traffic, op. cit.*

15. US Congress, Senate, *The Rôle of Cuba in International Terrorism and Subversion*, Hearings Before the Subcommittee on Security and Terrorism of the Committee on the Judiciary, February 26, March 4, 11 and 12, 1982 (Washington, D.C.: US Government Printing Office, 1982), pages 6-26.

16. US Defence Intelligence Agency, *The International Terrorist Network*, Report 6 010 5026 83, May 6, 1983, cited in Workman, *International Drug-trafficking, op. cit.*, page C-1.

17. The expansion of the Cuban drug operation in about 1978, followed by the Mariel boatlift, a Cuban intelligence operation, in 1980, may have been facilitated by the massive destruction of US internal security that began in the early 1960s and had reached about 95 percent of its peak by 1978. There was no mistaking what was happening, and it included a massive curtailment of FBI internal security investigations. In 1974, the FBI had over 55,000 open cases on subversives and extremists. As a result of the Privacy Act, self-policing during the Church and Pike committee investigations, and the initial impact of the Levi guidelines, the number of domestic security cases had fallen to roughly 20,000 by the summer of 1976. One year later, the number had plummeted to 102. By 1982, the number of active FBI cases was only 14; four organisations and 10 individuals. By 1978, the United States was a ripe and vulnerable target for foreign intelligence operations, which the Mariel boatlift could well have been designed to exploit. See Joseph D. Douglass, Jr. and Neil C. Livingstone, 'Terrorists Find That US Offers Inviting Targets', *Detroit News*, April 29, 1984, page 23A. 1976 also appears to be the year when the first Jamaican gangs (*posses*) which figure so prominently in the distribution and sales of crack, entered the country. DEA, *Crack Cocaine Overview 1989* (Washington, D.C.: US Department of Justice, 1989), page 7.

18. Bill Gertz, 'Castro Runs a Resort for Narcotics Dealers', *Washington Times*, March 23, 1988, A1.

19. As explained by Sejna, special troops, or *spetsnaz* in the Soviet vernacular, are specially trained intelligence sabotage forces whose missions support strategic intelligence operations. Their work is performed for the strategic intelligence directorates in civilian and military intelligence, which is also responsible for narcotics trafficking. The duty of *spetsnaz* units is to undermine the political, economic, military and moral stability of the enemy.

20. Carlos Alberto Montaner, 'A Conversation with a Cuban Intelligence Agent', *El Nuevo Herald*, Miami, June 5-6, 1988, translation by Cuban American National Foundation.

21. Bill Gertz, 'Castro Wants to Destroy US with Drugs, Defector Charges', *Washington Times*, August 28, 1989, page A3. See also Don Podesta, 'Ex-Cuban Officer Says Castro Profited from drug-trafficking', *Washington Post*, August 26, 1989, page A17.

22. Michael Hedges, 'Drug Money Ends Up in 'Drawer of Fidel'', *Washington Times*, March 10, 1989, page A5.

23. See, for example, Joe Pichirallo, 'Cuba Used Noriega to Obtain High-Tech US Goods, Defector Says', *Washington Post*, April 27, 1988, page A24.

24. See, for example, Lou Marano, 'Marxist Brigade Infiltrates Panama to Defend Noriega', *Washington Times*, April 5, 1988, page A1; Peter Almond and Bill Gertz, 'Shadow of Cuba Grows in Panama', *Washington Times*, April 29, 1988, page A1; Peter Samuel, 'Cuba Tightens Grip on Panama', *Washington*

Inquirer, June 24, 1988, page 1; Georgie Anne Geyer, 'Castro's Insidious Hand in Panama', *Washington Times*, December 27, 1989, page F1; and Roger W. Fontaine, 'Who Is Manuel Antonio Noriega?', in Victor H. Krulak, editor, *Panama: An Assessment* (Washington, D.C.: United States Strategic Institute, 1990).

25. In an action such as this, there are usually a number of motivating factors. Certainly, Noriega's drug operations and his growing links to Cuba are two very persuasive and obvious ones. But, there are others, not so evident, that may be equally, if not more, important. For example, there was almost certainly a growing antagonism towards Noriega within the US policymaking establishment. This establishment is generally anti-military, and is strongly against military dictators. The strong bias against military leadership in Latin America which came out into the open in 1969, is reported by Richard A. Ware, then- Principal Deputy Secretary of Defence (International Security Affairs): 'In 1969 individuals in State were allied with some in ISA in an almost messianic mission of social reform in Latin American countries. Essentially, this meant removing the military from positions of authority, with the resultant ascendancy of left-wing forces. Contacts with the military were minimised, and Defence was substantially removed from any rôle in the formulation of US policy. It was as if there were no national security interests south of the border'. Richard A. Ware, *The Pentagon's Office of International Security Affairs 1969-1973* or *Two Citizens Go to Washington* (Washington, D.C.: American Enterprise Institute for Public Policy Research, 1986).

Juan B. Sosa was Ambassador of Panama to the United States from October 1987 until the closing of the Embassy following the May 1989 election. He writes that 'Noriega's difficulties mounted during 1986, even as he continued to tighten the reins of his control over the military and political sectors of Panamanian society. His image abroad was damaged by a series of articles in the *New York Times* linking him to the narcotics trafficking. 'The Political and Economic Crisis of Panama', *Panama: An Assessment* (Washington, D.C.: United States Strategic Institute, 1990), page 18.

The articles Sosa probably referred to were: Seymour M. Hersch, 'Panama Strongman Said to Trade in Drugs, Arms and Illicit Money', *New York Times*, June 12, 1986; Seymour M. Hersch, 'US Aides in '72 Weighed Killing Officer Who Now Leads Panama', *New York Times*, June 13, 1986; and Seymour M. Hersch, 'Panama General Said to Have Told Army to Rig Vote', *New York Times*, June 22,1986. The first article appeared in the week that Noriega was visiting the United States. The articles were not just focused on drug-trafficking and money-laundering. Equal weight was given to a wide variety of activities, including providing arms to South American guerrillas, notably the Colombian M-I9, assassinating a political opponent, providing intelligence information to Cuba, enabling and profiting from Cuban technology theft operations run out of Panama, buying secret National Security Agency [NSA] documents from a US Army sergeant and transferring them to Cuba, and overturning the results of the 1984 election. As an interesting aside, when the US forces took over Noriega's office and home following the invasion on December 20, 1989, they found a variety of witchcraft or voodoo paraphernalia. Among the collection was a *tamale* inside which were two pieces of paper with the names Seymour Hersch and John Poindexter written on them.

In the five years prior to the attack on Noriega in the *New York Times*, Noriega ousted several civilian challengers and tightened his grip on Panama. As part of this operation, he also appears to have been asserting his control (and profit sharing) of the money-laundering process that involved all the banks in Panama. This may have further antagonised the US policymaking establishment. Additionally, William R. Gianelli, former Chairman of the Panama Canal Commission wrote that the economic sanctions imposed in April 1988, extended for an additional year in April 1989, to drive Noriega out, were unsuccessful; and that, as a result, American businesses were having to curtail or close activities, so that the international banking community was also seriously affected. 'The Panama Canal and the Canal Zone: Status and Prospects', *Panama: An Assessment, op. cit.*, page 10. Adding insult to injury, in January 1989, Noriega opened his own bank, Banco Institucional J1. These events may also have contributed significantly to the decision to invade Panama implemented in December 1989.

26. US Senate, *Drugs and Terrorism, 1984*, Hearing Before the Subcommittee on Alcoholism and Drug Abuse of the Committee on Labour and Human Resources, August 2, 1984 (Washington, D.C.: US Government Printing Office, 1984), page 83.

27. *Information Supplied by Alvaro Baldizón Aviles*, unedited and unpublished draft produced during debriefings with US Government representatives, S/LPD 6326751, pages 16-17. Testimony by Miguel Bolanos, a counter-intelligence officer in the Sandinista State Security apparatus, also supports the important rôle of Soviet Bloc advisers in Nicaraguan intelligence. In Bolanos's counter-intelligence section there were two Soviet advisers and one Cuban adviser. Bolanos reported that in State Security there were 70 Soviet, 400 Cuban, 40-50 East German and 20-25 Bulgarian advisers. *Inside Communist Nicaragua: The Miguel Bolanos Transcripts* (Washington, D.C.: Heritage Foundation, September 30, 1983), pages 8-9).

28. Gertz, 'Castro Runs a Resort for Narcotics Dealers', *op. cit.*, page A6.

29. Joe Pichirallo, 'Cuba Used Noriega to Obtain High-Tech US Goods, Defector Says', *Washington Post*, April 27, 1988, page A24.

30. David Brock, 'The World of Narco-terrorism', *The American Spectator*, June 1989, page 27.

31. *Drugs and Terrorism, 1984, op. cit.*, page 79.

32. *Ibid.*, page 80.

33. US Congress, Senate, *Rôle of Nicaragua in drug-trafficking*, Hearing Before the Subcommittee on Children, Family, Drugs and Alcoholism of the Committee on Labour and Human Resources, April 19,1985 (Washington, D.C.: US Government Printing Office, 1985), pages 27, 32 and 34.

34. *Rôle of Nicaragua in drug-trafficking, op. cit.*, page 41.

35. *Information Supplied by Alvaro Baldizón Aviles, op. cit.*, page 11.

36. The coroner's report states that death was caused by an aneurysm in the brain (stroke). Unofficial reports say that this happened several hours after Baldizón had dinner at his favourite Nicaraguan restaurant. There is, of course, the possibility of assassination. A class of Soviet-preferred assassination weapons are poisons that result in deaths by apparently natural causes hours to days after the poisons are administered. The types of 'causes' employed include heart attacks, strokes, and fast-acting cancers and hard-to-treat diseases.

37. Trevor Armbrister, 'Nicaragua's Secret Plan', *Reader's Digest*, April 1988, page 76.

38. US Congress, Senate, *International Narcotics Control Report*, Hearing Before the Subcommittee on Children, Family, Drugs and Alcoholism of the Committee on Labour and Human Resources, March 13, 1985 (Washington, D.C.: US Government Printing Office, 1985), page 8.

39. Eric Pianin, 'Turner Says Police Can't Halt Killings', *Washington Post*, March 25, 1989, page A1. See also Sari Horwitz, 'Berry Says Slayings Are Unstoppable', *Washington Post*, October 20, 1989, D1.

40. Thomas Moore et al., 'Dead Zones', *US News & World Report*, April 10, 1989, page 22.

HEAR NO EVIL, SEE NO EVIL, SPEAK NO EVIL

Throughout the 1950s, Harry Anslinger, the US Commissioner of Narcotics, worked hard to make people recognise that Communist China was the primary force responsible for narcotics trafficking[1]. 'The mafia ', he explained in response to misleading press reports, 'was not the biggest drug dealer. This was a false impression. By far the biggest drug dealer was Peking'. Anslinger provided extensive data to the United Nations and to the US Congress. He identified the Chinese government agencies that were involved, as well as numerous trafficking routes out of China through North Korea and Southeast Asia into Japan, the Philippines, Hawaii, Alaska, Mexico and the United States. He led operations to attack known distribution nets. But while he was unable to stop the flow, at least he did identify the source of the offensive: **Communist China**.

Then, in the early 1960s, something happened. In a study of Chinese narcotics trafficking, Stefan T. Possony observed: 'Beginning in the early 1960s, the subject [Communist China's drug offensive against the United States], which originally had attracted great attention, became an 'unsubject', to paraphrase Orwell'[2].

In a detailed analysis of the problem, A. H. Stanton Candlin observed the same phenomenon, which he explained in the following terms:

'The matter was handled differently until about 1962, before which year the United States showed signs of official comprehension of the problem. Since then, the threat has apparently been concealed from the public by persons who have evidently had the desire to cultivate better relations with the Red Chinese. The Chinese are the principal miscreants in this criminal conspiracy and they have been able, of late, to obtain protection and support in unexpected quarters'[3].

It is, perhaps, no mere coincidence that 1962 is the year in which Harry Anslinger retired and that in 1961 the pro-China interests moved into the State Department[4]. This coincidence is interesting, especially when coupled with the Soviet intelligence on the 1957 meeting of China's Central Committee, when it was decided to encourage overseas investment in China.

In 1969, President Nixon declared war on drugs. One of the first measures taken was to identify the sources of the problem. In one instance, analysts at the Central Intelligence Agency began looking at drug-trafficking emanating from Southeast Asia. Drawing on a massive amount of detail from a wide spectrum of sources, the first map was drawn of the 'Golden Triangle' – then regarded as the main source of drugs and narcotics[5].

The triangle included parts of Thailand, Burma, Laos, and, especially, Yunnan Province, China, as shown by the solid line triangle in *Figure 2* below. The northeast tip of the triangle was located well up in Yunnan Province, near Kunming. Yunnan Province was, indeed, the dominant source, both in its own right and through its control of and assistance to operations in northern Burma and Thailand. As the CIA Far East specialist who constructed the map described the position, the triangle was really a 'Golden V' the apex of which was in the region where Thailand, Burma and Laos came together. Most of the area, the funnel of the V, was in Yunnan Province.

This assessment was identical to the information provided by Sejna, based on Czechoslovak and Soviet intelligence studies. He also reported that in 1960 China signed a 'Treaty of Friendship and Cooperation' with Burma, which provided China with the opportunity to operate openly in Burma. According to KGB estimates, fifty

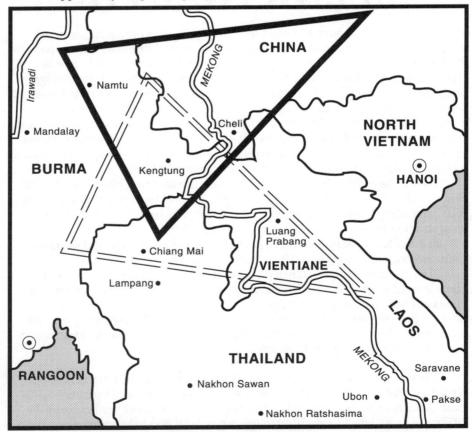

Figure 2: The Golden Triangle. *Bold Triangle:* Original CIA Analysis. *Dashed Triangle:* Modified 'politically correct' White House version, virtually bypassing Communist China.

percent of the Chinese representatives in Burma were involved (officially) in the drug business in the early 1960s.

In 1970, the CIA map of the Golden Triangle was passed to the Bureau of Narcotics and Dangerous Drugs [BNDD], a forerunner of the Drug Enforcement Administration [DEA: *see page 67*]. **Months later, a new version of the map emerged from the White House.** The tip of the triangle had been moved from 25 degrees north latitude in China down to 20 degrees north latitude, in Laos. The new designation is shown by the dashed-line triangle in *Figure 2*. With a few strokes of a pen, Communist China had been effectively excluded from the Golden Triangle.

At that time, the top national-level US organisation concerned with illegal narcotics trafficking was the Ad Hoc Committee on Narcotics, chaired by Henry Kissinger. As Edward Jay Epstein observed, Kissinger evidenced little interest in the heroin problem and rarely attended committee meetings. General Alexander Haig usually chaired the meetings in Kissinger's absence. Kissinger, [Under Secretary of State Elliot] Richardson and Haig spent most of their energies dampening the enthusiasm of White House zealots to launch a new heroin crusade which might again threaten diplomatic relations with important allies[6]. Certainly, the initiative towards China was one of the high-priority diplomatic initiatives at that time. Epstein also noted that after the Department of Defence began using reconnaissance planes to help identify poppy fields in Burma and Laos, Kissinger stopped the overflights of Burma specifically to avoid threatening *détente* with China[7].

In September 1971, the Cabinet Committee on International Narcotics Control was formed, headed by Secretary of State William P. Rogers. The committee seldom met and was quietly phased out in 1972. While in existence, it was run by Nelson Gross, a Republican from Saddle River, New Jersey, who had been defeated in his quest for a Senate seat in 1970 and who President Nixon had then appointed as senior adviser and coordinator for international narcotics matters at the State Department. In August 1972, shortly before the committee's demise, Secretary Rogers released a study which had been prepared under its auspices, *World Opium Survey – 1972*.

The primary producers of illicit opium identified in this report were India, Afghanistan, Turkey, Pakistan, Burma, Thailand, Laos, Mexico, Eastern Europe, North Africa and Latin America. The geographies of the Southeast Asian network as presented in the study are reproduced in *Figure 3* on page 92. As can be seen, both China and North Vietnam are effectively excluded in this representation of the opium network[8].

Moreover, the text, which specifically addresses the People's Republic of China, was quite revealing. The text explained that in February 1950, China introduced stringent controls over the production of opium poppy and the use of opiates, that the measures were strictly enforced, and that the problem of opium use had been effectively eliminated. Some small-scale illicit production might remain, the text allowed, and, along with it, 'perhaps, minor amounts of cross-border trade in the commodity'[9].

However, 'there is no reliable evidence that China has either engaged in or sanctioned the illicit export of opium and its derivatives nor are there any indications of government participation in the opium trade of Southeast Asia and adjacent markets'[10].

Similar statements were also made during the timeframe 1971-73 by the Strategic Intelligence Office of the Bureau of Narcotics and Dangerous Drugs (BNDD); for example: 'Not one investigation into heroin traffic in the area during the past two years indicates Chinese Communist involvement. In each case, the traffickers were people engaged in criminal activity for the usual profit motive'[11].

While statements such as these can be explained as the results of naiveté or incompetence[12], it seems quite clear that there was also present a continuing intent to cover up Chinese Communist drug-trafficking. One of the favourite words used to avoid the existence of intelligence information is 'evidence'. What really constitutes 'evidence'?

Does a report in draft form constitute an 'investigation'? A former CIA analyst who was detailed to the Strategic Intelligence Office of BNDD (which became the DEA in July 1973) was writing a report on Communist China's intelligence service, and specifically its involvement in narcotics trafficking, at the time the above denial was written.

The report picked up the Chinese narcotics trail back in the days of Anslinger and brought the story forward to the date of the report. It identified names, dates, places, organisations and so forth. The extensive and deliberate involvement of Communist China was obvious. The report was suppressed by DEA officials in 1973 while still in draft stage.

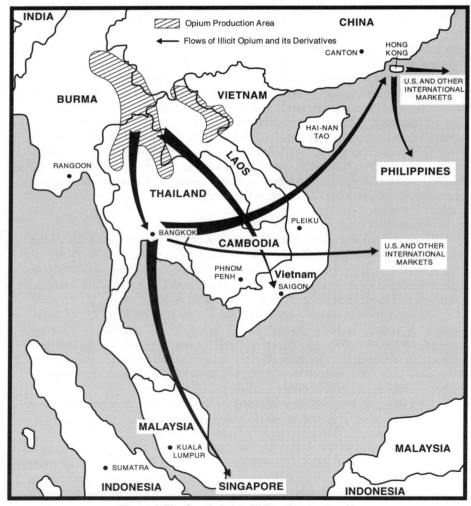

Figure 3: The South Asian illicit opium network[9].

The cover-up of Communist China's drug and narcotics trafficking appears to have started in the early 1960s. It took on greatly increased scope during the Nixon Administration, and it appears to be continuing today.

Never in reports from the State Department, Customs, or the DEA is China included in the Golden Triangle. About the only mention of Communist China in Congressional hearings on drug-trafficking over the decade to 1990 occurred in the testimony of Dr Ray Cline, the CIA's former Deputy Director for Intelligence. Discussing the combination of revolutionaries (mostly Marxist-Leninists), drug-traffickers, and gun runners, Cline explained:

'I became familiar with it [the combination] in Southeast Asia because, back in the 1950s and 1960s, we observed that most drugs, most opium, was coming from that triangle which is the southern part of Communist China, Burma, where the Communist Party of Burma controls most of the drug-growing area, and some parts of Laos and Thailand'[13].

Dr Cline's assertions parallel testimony in 1972 given by General Lewis Walt, who also recognised the important rôle of China in global drug operations:

'I have used the expression the 'Golden Triangle' because it has been used for many years, but I cannot help wondering, Mr. Chairman, whether it would not be more accurate to speak of the 'Golden Quadrangle', in view of the fact that the contiguous province of Yunnan in China is the site of a very substantial opium agriculture.... Yunnan might conceivably be responsible for a production in excess of the combined production of Burma, Thailand and Laos'[14].

While China has been, and probably remains, the most important producer and organiser in the Golden Triangle, China is rarely listed as a producing country in any of the reports issued by the State Department, the Drug Enforcement Administration, or US Customs[15]. Moreover, China is not the only country that is generally omitted from reports on drug- and narcotics-producing countries: most Communist countries are conveniently excluded, as well[16].

Another curiosity with respect to China involves the US Presidential commission directed to examine the trafficking into Vietnam which had emerged in the summer of 1970, and had caused narcotics addiction to grow like the plague among the US military. As indicated earlier, the primary source identified by the commission was China. But the commission's report was classified and suppressed[17]. As one member of the commission, General Lewis Walt, later confided to a close friend, keeping silent about the rôle of China was the most damnable order he had ever received.

Nor does this appear to have been the only such directive. On May 26, 1972, Jack Anderson reported on a White House document that had been making the rounds of the State, Defence and Treasury Departments and the US Information Agency. The confidential document referred to stories about Communist China's rôle in the world drug trade as 'arrant nonsense' and ordered US Government officials to cease making derogatory statements about the People's Republic of China. There was, the document stated, no evidence that Peking was bringing opium and heroin into Vietnam[18].

During the 1970s, the drug and narcotics problem continued to grow, notwithstanding the priority President Nixon had placed on addressing it. In retrospect, while the President may have been sincere in his statements about the need to wage war on illegal drug and narcotics trafficking, Epstein, in his analysis of US anti-narcotics trafficking activities during the Nixon Administration, was highly suspicious of the motivations of the bureaucracy and senior-level officials[19]. Following extensive research, he concluded that the drug issue was typically used to build empires, garner political headlines in the news media, and provide the rationale for the development of a national, White House-directed police force to be used for political tasks. No real interest in either understanding or combating the drug and narcotics problem during the Nixon Administration's war on drugs was discovered by Epstein. Moreover, he added, high-level officials involved with the war on drugs had a prior history of using the drug problem for personal political gain[20].

Meanwhile, the difficulties that the US Government encounters dealing with countries whose governments are involved with drug-trafficking seem to be almost independent of who is in office. Consider, for example, the strange case of Bulgaria. The Bulgarian intelligence (KDS) defector, Colonel Stefan Sverdlev, had been directly involved in drug-trafficking and, when he defected in 1970, brought with him official Bulgarian State Security documentation dealing with Sofia's narcotics trafficking activities.

Other US intelligence sources also identified the rôle of Bulgaria in drug-trafficking and explained how the company KINTEX was formed as a front for Bulgarian State Security to assist in narcotics trafficking and the flow of illicit arms and ammunition throughout Europe and the Middle East. Numerous sources also identified the Bulgarian plan to import large amounts of opium for conversion into heroin for trafficking. There was also a CIA study identifying Bulgaria as a new centre for directing narcotics and arms trafficking between Europe and the Near East[21]. Nonetheless, in June 1971 US Customs and the Bureau of Narcotics and Dangerous Drugs officials went to Sofia and proposed that the United States should train Bulgarian customs officials (who belong to State Security) on how to combat the drug-trafficking that was taking place across Bulgarian borders.

Even the Bulgarians must have been surprised[22], which may have accounted for their hosting a conference of customs directors from the Soviet Bloc nations in October 1971. A US-Bulgarian agreement was reached in November 1971, and in 1973 US Customs began holding training seminars in Varna, Bulgaria. They taught the Bulgarians US customs techniques and identified to Bulgarian officials[23] those individuals living in Bulgaria whom US officials believed were involved in drug-trafficking.

Not until 1981 did US officials decide they were not obtaining full cooperation from the Government of Bulgaria in combating the drug-trafficking problem, temporarily stopping the training seminars and the associated one-way exchange of intelligence information. From 1970 until 1984, the date of a DEA report to Congress on Bulgaria's lack of cooperation, DEA identified numerous source reports on the *official* involvement of Bulgaria. The reports identified KINTEX and other companies (TEXIM and CORECOM) as State Security front operations which managed drug production and trafficking. Officials of the Communist Party of Bulgaria were involved in organising coordination meetings in Sofia for traffickers. Bulgarian customs (State Security) was also involved in the operation. Nor does this recital take account of additional CIA data on the Bulgarian drug program.

Yet, notwithstanding this continuous and consistent flow of information over fourteen years, the best the DEA could conclude in 1984 was that the Government of Bulgaria *'appears to have established a policy of encouraging and facilitating* the trafficking of narcotics under the corporate veil of KINTEX'[24] [emphasis added]. Moreover, notwithstanding direct source statements and Bulgarian State Security documentation to the effect that **political destabilisation is the objective of narcotics trafficking,** all the DEA could do was to admit that 'the use of drugs as a political weapon may be inferred' and then to state with assurance that more immediate motives were to obtain hard currency and to support dissident groups in the Middle East[25]. To this day, the US Government continues to try to convince the Bulgarians to cooperate with the United States in curtailing drug-trafficking, In 1986, asserted that there were increasing prospects for Bulgarian cooperation[26].

In an apparent attempt to 'have it their way', the State Department's *International Narcotics Control Strategy Report* to Congress (March 1989) denied that traffickers operated openly any longer in Bulgaria and stated that there was 'no indication that either licit or illicit production of opiates is occurring in Bulgaria, nor is there evidence that illicit drugs are refined' and that money-laundering was not a factor [27].

But during the final week in March 1989, the true story became evident – when DEA agent reports, embassy wires, and DEA-CIA correspondence[28] showing that the State Department report was a combination of misrepresentations and lies, were leaked to selected news reporters, who then wrote detailed articles for the *New York Tribune, Newsday* and the *Washington Times*[29]. The reports provided official details on a joint DEA-Swiss action against Turkish money-launderers operating out of Sofia, Bulgaria. They clearly identified the continued production of opiate products in Bulgaria and that official Bulgarian money-laundering assistance was being provided by GLOBUS, described as a successor to KINTEX.

Four days after the reports hit the press, the State Department confirmed that officials of a Bulgarian trading company had been linked to an international narcotics money-laundering operation, but added that 'there is no evidence of complicity of high-ranking Bulgarian Government officials'[30] – which was another misrepresentation. Furthermore, the State Department misrepresented the situation by stating that Bulgaria had clamped down on KINTEX and that Bulgarian involvement in narcotics and money-laundering was a phenomenon that had only surfaced in the 'early 1980s'. This was, of course, not true.

The Bulgarian story was also reported in *Forbes*, which identified the Swiss banks, **Crédit Suisse** and the **Union Bank of Switzerland**, as the primary Swiss facilitators in this money-laundering operation. In Bulgaria, not only was GLOBUS involved, but so were Bulgarian customs, Balkan Air – the Bulgarian national carrier – and Bulgarian officials concerned with handling security and money exchange.

As one of the money dealers in Zürich who has been shipping gold to Sofia for over fifteen years explains: 'Not one suitcase of gold or dollars can move through Bulgaria without the direct involvement of the Bulgarian Government'[31]. Like the Cubans, the Bulgarians secure a cut of everything that moves through their country. It is curious indeed that everyone except the US State Department seems to know about all this.

At one time, it looked as though the head of US Customs, William von Raab, might put an end to this nonsense. In 1986, he refused to attend international narcotics-control meetings with Bulgaria and was reportedly 'furious' when told that the State Department had invited Bulgaria to a meeting in Madrid. 'I have heard of the bias of some in the Department in being soft on Communists, but this is too much', he wrote to Ann Wrobleski, then Acting Assistant Secretary of the Department's Bureau of International Narcotics Matters.

'Has the State Department developed an institutional form of Alzheimer's disease or just plain taken leave of its senses'? he asked[32]. Unfortunately, von Raab appears to have been no more successful in controlling the actions of his own department, which helped to train the Hungarians and Chinese during his tenure.

Nor was this by any means the end of the story. In March 1988, the State Department indicated that cooperative measures with the Soviet Union were brewing[33]. Two months later, immediately prior to the May summit in Moscow, the evening news reported that the United States was planning to share narcotics trafficking intelligence with the Soviet Union and to arrange for US Customs to train Soviet and East European customs (intelligence) agents on US techniques for stopping illegal drug and narcotics trafficking.

Then in July, the DEA Administrator, John C. Lawn, announced that the Soviet Union had proposed to him and to the Assistant Secretary of State for International Narcotics Matters, Ann B. Wrobleski [*see preceding page*] that the Soviets and the DEA should swap intelligence on international narcotics smuggling and suspected drug-traffickers, as well as exchange samples of seized narcotics, which have been used to identify sources (or alternatively could be used to thwart[34] such identification)[35].

In 1989 edition of the *National Drug Control Strategy*, President Bush made it official: 'We must be prepared to share our knowledge and our concern with the Soviet Union and Eastern European nations and be willing to engage them in cooperative counter-drug activities'[36]. **In this strategy document, there was no recognition of the rôle of the Soviet Union and Eastern Europe countries in drug-trafficking and in creating the very sickness the strategy was designed to cure.**

Towards the end of 1989, the DEA made a formal proposal to the Soviets for the DEA to conduct 'advanced narcotics investigations' for about 30 anti-narcotics professionals from Soviet customs, the Ministry of Interior and the KGB. As one DEA official, Paul Higdon, explained: 'We're looking at them as policemen – these guys are cops with a mission similar to ours'. Not to be outdone, US Customs is proposing a formal information-sharing agreement, similar to the ones we have with most of our Western allies'[37].

Another example of US official denial or collective amnesia over the drugs scourge concerns that of Panama. When General Manuel Antonio Noriega was indicted by the US Attorney in Miami in 1988, it rapidly became known that Panamanian officials had a rich tradition of trafficking in drugs and providing arms to revolutionaries. The problems in Panama surfaced in the early 1960s with riots directed against the US presence, most notably attacks on the Canal Zone which had taken place on January 9-14, 1964. In 1968, the Panamanian National Guard deposed the newly-elected President Arnulfo Arias Madrid. Several months later, General Omar Torrijos Herrera took command. Torrijos was credited with having opened Panama to foreign economic penetration by means of a new banking law with favourable bank secrecy provisions, which were reported to have been welcomed by American and other foreign banks[38], and which may have been the *quid pro quo* for the Panama Canal Treaties.

At least some US officials were aware of Panamanian military involvement in drugs and arms deals in the early 1970s. The data extends back at least to 1972 or 1970[39], or possibly earlier insofar as Major Noriega had reportedly been providing the CIA with 'intelligence' at least since late 1967[40]. The arms aspect was confirmed by José de Jesus Martinez, a former professor who became Torrijos's bodyguard: he reported that Torrijos decided at least by 1975 to 'convert our country into a rear base for regional revolution'. Thus, with effect from 1968, Panama has been an active participant in drug-trafficking, providing arms to revolutionaries throughout Latin America, providing a safe haven for drug money-laundering, and serving as a willing host for numerous foreign intelligence operations; for example, technology theft and espionage. It would seem to be no accident that Torrijos was listed as one of the Soviet 'gold reserve' agents (Chapter 7).

Nonetheless, the United States seems to have ignored what was happening, for various 'strategic reasons', until 1988. Not only was Noriega's drug-trafficking ignored, but at the same time the DEA administrators (Peter Bensinger, Francis M. Mullen Jr. and Jack Lawn) and other US Government officials (for example, Attorney General William French Smith) sent letters of commendation to Noriega – praising him for his work to curtail the flow of drugs[41]! All agencies of the US Government were guilty of ignoring what was happening, although the Department of State and the White House were the most active[42].

An attempt to indict Omar's brother, Moises (a.k.a. Monchi) Torrijos in 1972 for heroin trafficking was blocked and the indictment remained sealed until after the Panama Canal Tries had been signed in 1978. State Department officials, including the US Ambassador, William J. Jorden, attempted to pass off reports of the indictment as false rumours, spread in order to dirty Torrijos' name. Torrijos' point of view was recorded by Ambassador Jack Hood Vaughn: 'What bothers me the most', Torrijos told Vaughn, 'is that Monchi is only shipping five kilos a week. Why make a big deal of that'[43]?

One widely advertised factor behind this strange behaviour was indeed the negotiations over the Panama Canal. But this does not seem to explain why complaints to Panamanian military leaders about drugs and arms dealing continued to be conducted only as a charade or why an attempt to indict Noriega in 1980, three years before Noriega was to become military commander, was again stalled by the State Department because of 'administration fears about upsetting Panama'[44]. What really motivated the United States finally to go after Noriega in 1989?

The behind-the-scenes rôle of US banks and other financial institutions, as well as those of the United States' allies and enemies alike, is another aspect of international narcotics trafficking that has led a sheltered life. These centres of power are believed to be among the two primary forces behind *détente*, the other being Soviet strategy[45].

Estimates of the money that US citizens paid for illegal drugs in the early 1980s ranged from $80 to $110 billion per year, with another $60 billion expended on associated health costs. Since those calculations were made, the estimates have doubled; the total annual cost [by 1989] within the United States may have rivalled the $300 billion annual budget of the Department of Defence[46]. The global cost of drug-trafficking may exceed $500 billion per year. Some estimates run as high as $1 trillion per year. [The reader is, however, directed to Chapter 12, completed in December 1998, in which these estimates are revised sharply upwards – *Ed.*].

There have been some modest attempts to track this money, most notably imposition of the requirement for US banks to report on cash withdrawals and deposits in excess of $10,000. In the second half of the 1980s alone, numerous banks and financial institutions in the United States were charged with illegal financial operations – for example, drug-money-laundering – and still more remain under investigation. One bank was charged with 17,000 violations of the federal cash transactions law[47]. Yet few real indictments or serious fines have been assessed; nor has much publicity been focused on drug-money-laundering or on investments of laundered money. Yet what is happening has to be obvious. No $500 billion per year business can exist without the active *and knowledgeable* assistance of many banks and financial institutions[48] [*see also Chapter 12*].

Ramon Milian Rodriguez [*see page 28*], a Certified Public Accountant [CPA] who handled money-laundering and investments for the Medellín Cartel, was arrested in May 1983, while attempting to leave the United States with $5.3 million in cash. In February 1988 he described his activities to Senators John Kerry (D-MA) and Alfonse D'Amato (R-NY). He explained how, with the assistance of Panama's National Defence Forces, he routed enormous amounts of cash through all the banks in Panama and how he was courted by the US banks to handle the Cartel's investments. **'In every instance'**, he testified, **'the banks knew who they were dealing with....** They were dealing with Milian Rodriguez, who represented money from South America, and their corresponding banks in Panama knew where the money came from because we required certain things from them.... We were breaking the laws in a very big manner and you always have to have plausible deniability'.

'And the New York banks are no fools'[49]. The banks implicated by Rodriguez read like a 'who's who' in US finance: **Citibank, Citicorp, Bank of America** and **First National Bank of Boston**[50]. Banks identified in 1983 in an ABC News *'Close up'* on drugs and money-laundering, included **Citibank, Marine Midland, Chase Manhattan, Irving Trust**, the foreign currency exchange house of **Deak-Perera** [since defunct following a drug-related murder and scandal] and **'most of the 250 banks and branches in Miami'**[51].

'Focusing on Florida, James Ring Adams has written that corruption in the banking industry is now endemic. 'The narcotics traffic flourishes not only because of demand, but because of tacit acceptance by elements of the political structure... money-laundering has become an entrenched feature of the state's economy'[52]. Adams describes how banks have been organised specifically for money-laundering. Evidently the Florida banking authorities could not care less.

When one illicit bank goes out of business, another immediately appears, Adams laments: 'Drug dealers flourish and get busted, or murdered, but the morality play never seems to extend to the financial and political infrastructure'[53]. Adams' conclusions were echoed by the US Attorney for South Florida, Dexter Lehtinen: 'I know names of banks that are crooked, public officials who are corrupt, zoning regulations changed for drug dealers, [but] we can't pursue these investigations [due to a lack of manpower]'. Sophisticated drug organisations, which thrive on corrupting officials and using tainted banks to hide their cash, are flourishing, he added[54].

Senator D'Amato's comments on difficulties encountered in obtaining a strict money-laundering bill during the Rodriguez hearings presented the problem from a legislative perspective: **'And let me tell you that we face tremendous, tremendous opposition, and we only explored very superficially some of the violations'**. His frustration is understandable[55]. In 1984 and 1985, the *Boston Globe* published a series of studies on the money-laundering problem, which they turned into a separate report entitled *Money-laundering*.

The *Boston Globe* looked at the banks, money-laundering centres, several money-laundering techniques, the acceptance of cash with no questions asked by car dealers, real estate firms, lawyers, and the failure of the US Government to crack down. The newspaper also identified some of the opposition to improved laws and their enforcement: specifically, the bank lobby and the American Civil Liberties Union [ACLU][56]. Brokerage firms are also involved. Two firms, officials of which were identified in Senate hearings as having assisted in money-laundering operations, were **Merrill Lynch** and **E. F. Hutton**[57].

Rodriguez's testimony also raised questions of a related but somewhat different nature. As he explained, Rodriguez handled money-laundering and investments for the Medellín Cartel in the United States. His financial records were maintained on his personal computer. Apparently the agents who arrested Rodriguez moved his computer as though it were just another piece of furniture, and damaged the hard disk. The information was lost, even though 'they tried their darndest to put it together'[58]. It is indeed unfortunate that the arresting agents were so careless – *if in fact that is what they were*. The financial records would have been invaluable in showing how drug cartel money flowed and in leading US authorities to perhaps many billions of dollars of drug-money investments that could have been seized.

They might have provided data on institutions and individuals who were assisting in money-laundering and drug-money investments. They might also have provided the first detailed accounting of the monetary size of the Medellín Cartel's operation. Based on Rodriguez's testimony, that cartel's share of the cocaine market seemed much less than was being suggested by official US Government reports. If this is true, one possible conclusion is that there were several other Colombian cartels that were considerably larger than the Medellín Cartel, and that were operating in the shadows while the Medellín Cartel received the publicity and the blame[59].

It is hard to believe that the US arresting agents were so careless. It is even harder to believe that the information could not have been reconstructed. According to information routinely provided to individuals in the national security area by intelligence specialists with agencies such as the National Security Agency, even the information on a disk that has been erased can be reconstructed, which is why computers with hard disks that are used to process classified information always have to be locked up when not in use.

The story on Rodriguez's computer records logically originated with US officials. Unbelievable as it sounds, it could be true; *but, is it?* And, if not, *what is the reason for the cover story?* The people who would seem to benefit most if the records really were destroyed are the drug-traffickers and money-launderers, as well as the real estate and financial companies that invest the laundered money.

There have been three highly-publicised operations against money-laundering in recent years [to 1990]. Operation Pisces, which was directed against money-laundering in Panama, a 1988 operation against the Luxembourg-based **Bank of Credit and Commerce International** (BCCI), and operation Polar Cap. José Blandón [*see page 34, Note 11, and page 78*] testified that he did not regard the Pisces operation as a major victory because it captured a mere $18 million[60].

If there was a victory, it was in respect of penetrating secrecy legislation, not in respect of the volume of money seized, as Blandón pointed out. Similarly, in the BCCI case, only $14-$32 million was involved (that was the range mentioned)[61]. If there was any victory, it was only that the case might have represented a start. To place these seizures in perspective, recognise that the amounts are only 'pocket change' to the drug dealers[62]. Recall that the total amounts laundered each year are probably measured in hundreds of billions of dollars. The potential cache available for attachment as drug money is probably in the *trillions* of dollars. The Polar Cap operation resulted in the seizure of bank accounts in Atlanta, Miami, New York and San Francisco, and a lawsuit to recover $433.5 million in drug profits. While much higher than prior operations, this was still small potatoes when compared with the total volume and monetary value of the trafficking.

One of the primary problems in combating money-laundering, as explained by Michele Sindona [*see footnote, page 100*], a professional who knows the inside of the money-laundering business, is that the authorities writing the laws simply do not understand either international banking or money-laundering[63]. Nor, one might add, based on Rodriguez's testimony, does there appear to be any concerted effort to learn. As Senator

D'Amato has explained, there was no attempt by US authorities to utilise Rodriguez's knowledge. 'If it weren't so serious', he remarked, 'it would be laughable'[64]. Sindona† added an especially important perspective. Laundering money, he has explained, allows criminals to use dirty money openly, and then the law has no way of interfering:

'The real evil of money-laundering is its power to allow dirty money – the instrument of crime – to enter the mainstream of economies undisturbed, to consume important sectors of those economies and to transform them into feudi of an international criminal oligarchy beyond the reach of the law – an oligarchy that is to be brought down by men who do not understand money'[65].

The extent to which the US Justice Department is prepared to go after the banks for their rôle in assisting drug-trafficking remains to be seen. In previous years, its efforts appear to have been minuscule. Alternatively, it may have been thought, for a time, that the measures launched against the Bank of Credit and Commerce International may have represented a belated change of approach.

Court documents examined in Tampa, Florida, revealed that 41 banks had their records subpoenaed in a widening money-laundering investigation covering **Manufacturers Hanover Trust Company, Republic National Bank of New York, Security Pacific Corporation, Wells Fargo & Company** and **Bank America Corporation**, German and Israeli banks, and obscure, closely-held banks such as the **Total Bank** in Miami. At least

† Editor's Note: The most revealing account of **Michele Sindona's** own exotic money-laundering 'adventures' is to be found in the early pages of *The Final Conclave*, by Dr Malachi Martin (Stein and Day, New York, 1978). Emerging from Sicily in 1947, with glowing recommendations from the Bishop of Messina, after having operated a lucrative trading business from a truck serving the US forces on the island during the war, he had by 1959 somehow acquired Banca Privata Finanziaria [BPF] and a steel foundry (which he sold to the American Crucible Company); established a Liechtenstein holding company, Fasco AG, through which he had obtained a controlling share in Finabank Geneva; founded a foreign exchange brokerage, Moneyrex; established close relations with the Vatican's Institute for Religious Works [IRW]; become legal adviser to SNIA-Viscoa (textiles), President of Mediterranean Holidays and Philips Carbon Black Italiana, Managing Director of Cheesborough Ponds, and a member of the board of Remington Rand Italiana. After Sindona had raised $2.4 million from Milanese business circles for Archbishop Montini to finance an Old People's Home, Pope Paul VI formally authorised Sindona to become the Vatican's chief money manager. Sindona began by selling the Vatican's controlling interest, worth $350 million, in Societá Generale Immobiliare, then moved $40 million to a Luxembourg bank, Paribas Transcontinental, while IRW took a large block of shares in Sindona's Finabank. After divesting the Vatican of its holdings in Italian companies like Condotte d'Acqua (1969), Pantanella (1970) and Serono, a maker of contraceptive pills (1970), Vatican funds were dispersed all over the place and Sindona himself became President of 7 Italian companies, Vice-President of three banks and majority shareholder in the Vatican-linked Banca Union [BU]. Having forged links with Hambros (25%) and the ill-fated Continental Bank of Illinois (15%), Sindona found himself in close touch with the US Treasury, as that bank's Chairman, David Kennedy, became US Treasury Secretary under President Nixon. Mr Kennedy later became a board member of Fasco AG. After transferring to the United States, Sindona bought a controlling interest in Franklin National Bank. *Il crack Sindona* (the Sindona catastrophe) began to develop when the US Securities and Exchange Commission [SEC] halted all trading in Vetco Offshore Trading Industries, after a Los Angeles investor was found to have acquired 25% of Vetco's outstanding shares in violation of SEC regulations. It transpired that 20% of Vetco's shares and options had been acquired on behalf of IRW through the Liechtenstein-based Fiduciary Investment Services (FIS) which had an office in Sindona's Rome office complex. After the Vatican had been obliged to pay a fine of $320,000 by the SEC for having acquired 454,000 Vetco shares as part of 714,000 Vetco shares sold by FIS, the largest block of shares ever traded to date on the American Stock Exchange, Sindona's BPF sustained foreign exchange losses of $48 million (1973) and of a further $150 million in 1974. It was then discovered that Franklin National Bank had a minimum of $43 million in losses hidden as 'phony profits' in foreign exchange deals with Sindona-controlled Swiss banks. Thereafter, other Sindona-controlled or -linked banks started collapsing, all triggering further Vatican losses. By October 1974, the Italian authorities felt 'ready' to move against Sindona – charging him with falsification of accounts back in 1960! On January 9, 1975, the Swiss authorities closed Sindona's Finabank, after it had sustained foreign exchange losses of $82 million. Malachi Martin adds that 'Sindona made a last fruitless attempt to raise capital (about $300 million) by offering for sale new capital shares in a small holding company, Finambro. But Guido Carli, Governor of the Bank of Italy, scotched that idea…. Swiss banking sources speak of [Vatican losses] in the region of $240 million…. Reports persist that these losses may have gone well over the billion-dollar mark'.

half of the 41 banks were Florida banks or Florida-based branches of foreign banks[66].

In his talk to a drug enforcement conference on April 27, 1989, President Bush referred to the insidious rôles played by Hong Kong bankers and Middle Eastern couriers[67]. To appreciate the unintentional irony of this statement, consider that at least one large US bank, **Marine Midland**, is now owned or controlled by a Hong Kong bank. Similarly, there are US banks that are owned or controlled by Middle Easterners with close ties to Middle East money-launderers, such as the **Republic National Bank of New York**[68].

One puzzling, perhaps damning, dimension of money-laundering was revealed during an *'American Interests'* television special, *Follow the Money*, aired on PBS on July 12, 1989, in Washington. The subject of the programme was Western loans to the Soviet Bloc.

One part of the programme examined how such Western loans were channelled to support terrorist activity[69]. Norman Bailey, a former National Security Council [NSC] official, reported that when he joined the NSC, he first searched the files concerned with financial developments around the world and East-West economic activity, finding next to nothing. There was some information coming in but it was entirely human intelligence. 'It was not based on intercepts', Bailey explained. Then he described how almost all monetary transfers in the Western world of any importance go through three major clearing houses and how it is relatively simple to track certain transfers if you have command of powerful computing mechanisms. Accordingly, through the National Security Agency [NSA], he began a program of following money movements around the world as a means of identifying certain activities the NSC was trying to follow[70].

The activity of interest was a $600 million loan which was lead-managed by **First National Bank of Chicago** to the East German **Aussenhandels Bank**. Bailey explained that:

'[A] loan was cleared in London. The money went to East Berlin, to the Aussenhandels Bank. It was disbursed from there to various front companies and various tax havens around the world. It was then concentrated again in Libya and was sent from Libya to various accounts, which were controlled by terrorist organisations, and was then used by those terrorist organisations in their activities.... Approximately $60 million of the original tranche that was drawn down by the Aussenhandels Bank ended up in the coffers of various terrorist and guerrilla groups around the world'.

'Of these, approximately equal amounts were provided to the Red Brigades in Germany, to the provisional IRA in Northern Ireland, and to the M-19 forces in Colombia, about $20 million each, in other words'[71].

According to other reports, the narrator added, $25 million of the loan was wired directly to an account in Panama held by the Government of Nicaragua.

This information raises several questions. First, why was there no information available in the files when Bailey first joined the NSC? The idea of using the NSA to track the transfer of illicit funds and the CIA to identify account ownership should be obvious, if not automatic. Equally obvious is the need to map the flow of drug money as an integral task in combating drug-trafficking, just as would be done with any other criminal activity.

Following these money transfers would appear to be the single most important step in any attempt to learn who is behind the drug trade, who is facilitating the drug trade, and in attaching the illicit profits. But, evidently, this had not been done.

It is not as though the intelligence community had never been approached about the problem. In October 1969 President Nixon declared war on drugs and formed a White House Task Force on Heroin Suppression[72]. The Director of Central Intelligence, Richard

Helms, was a member of this task force, of the Ad Hoc Cabinet Committee on Narcotics (1970) and of the Cabinet Committee on International Narcotics Control (1971)[73]. Helms established an Office of Narcotics Coordinator within the Deputy Directorate of Plans, which began assembling narcotics intelligence on trafficking in Southeast and Southwest Asia, Europe and Latin America. When one of the analysts suggested that they examine the banks and the money trail, he was given a pat on the head and told: **No**.

In 1970, the Head of BNDD, John E. Ingersoll [*see page 67, and Note 39, page 109*], sent a request to the National Security Agency for assistance.

The BNDD's requirements were listed as follows:

1. The BNDD has a requirement for any and all COMINT [communications intelligence, i.e. electronic eavesdropping] information which reflects illicit traffic in narcotics and dangerous drugs. Our primary interest falls in the following categories:

O Organisations engaged in such activities;
O Individuals engaged in such activities;
O Information on the distribution of narcotics and dangerous drugs;
O Information on cultivation and production centres;
O International agreements and efforts to control the traffic in narcotics and dangerous drugs;
O All violations of the laws of the US concerning narcotics and dangerous drugs[74].

Curiously, information on money-laundering was not included in this list of requirements.

The NSA collection operation against drug-traffickers was run from April 1970 to July 1973, when it was shut down amid concern over the risk of exposure. The CIA also participated, but pulled out over concern that some of the data collection occurred on US soil and was in support of law enforcement rather than of national security. This may be why so many CIA analysts were transferred to the strategic intelligence office in BNDD – to accord with US law[75]. Frank Raven was in charge of the collection of intelligence data at the National Security Agency [NSA]. His assessment of the problem is instructive:

'Before we retired, we did some very nice drug busts.... We demonstrated that we could follow drug transactions and drug dealers. We could do it quite economically – it wasn't even a high-budget item.... NSA could really have cleaned up the drug business, drug-running and such.... But it got so screwed up in American law and American red tape that it wasn't worth the effort'[76].

Tracking drug money is still an essential task today; *is it now being done?* If not, why not? Certainly, the 'legal' problems identified above do not apply to overseas banks, or foreign banks, or even to US banks where national security is an issue; and the President's National Security Decision Directive [NSDD], 'Narcotics and National Security', signed in April 1986, explicitly identified drugs as a national security issue. Moreover, in 1984 the NSA was used to track drug shipments[77].

Why not drug *money*? Alternatively, if the NSA and CIA were collecting such information, **why are not measures in hand to seize all such assets and identify all the people and banks involved?** Why does the US Government focus so much publicity on small multi-million dollar seizures, when the potential is present to capture *trillions of dollars*, as is clearly implicit in Norman Bailey's testimony?

There would seem to be only *one* possible answer – namely, that the war on drugs is really not a serious war within the US Government at all.

The involvement of banks, financial institutions and real estate investment firms in drug-money-laundering is nothing new. It has been going on for decades and has been well-known for decades. Every so often there is a flurry of activity as the US Government appears to be cracking down; but indictments are dropped or small fines assessed and the money-laundering goes on, relatively unencumbered. The Government comes to the aid of banks when billions of dollars of loans to Third World and Communist countries go sour, but then seems to avoid holding the banks responsible for their major rôle in making international drug-trafficking and other crimes profitable. As the outgoing US Customs Commissioner, William von Raab, observed in his resignation letter dated July 31, 1989: **'Maybe it is time for the war on drugs to take its place as our nation's top priority – to interfere with other interests such as banking and Third World debt'**[78].

A statement by Clyde D. Taylor, of the Bureau of International Narcotics Matters, US Department of State, before joint Senate hearings in 1985, revealed the official US analysis of the illicit drug and narcotics challenge and, by implication, US policy designed to combat trafficking. With regard to state-sponsored narcotics trafficking, Taylor recognised that the authorities had seen 'some indications' and that: 'In the few instances, the further indication is that certain of the Communist countries have engaged, to some degree, in facilitating narcotics trafficking'. However, he he went out of his way to stress that '*another fact which we would like to establish before your committees is that narcotics trafficking in Latin America, in Asia, in the Middle East and in Europe, is dominated by narcotics traffickers who are governed only by their greed and whose only ideology – if you can call it one – is the pursuit of profit*' [emphasis added]. That is, according to Taylor, *politics are not involved*. Moreover, Taylor continued, 'Most of these groups cannot be called terrorists, or even political insurgents, *nor do we have evidence of a Communist conspiracy to use drugs to undermine Western democracies or our own society in particular*'[79] [emphasis added].

The dictionary defines conspiracy as the act of planning together to commit a crime or wrongful act. If what has been taking place is not a conspiracy, under this definition, *what is it?*

In the same Senate hearings, the DEA, while appearing equally oblivious to the history of Communist drug-trafficking, at least recognised its political dimension. As the Drug Enforcement Administration official, David L. Westrate, explained:

'The emerging trend of using drug-traffickers to support political aims represents a major change in the historical pattern of drug-trafficking, in which drug-traffickers were only interested in profits. The expanded use of drug-trafficking for political purposes has already had an effect on and could have far-reaching implications for drug enforcement worldwide and US foreign policy'[80]. Quite true. **If the US Government were to recognise the existence of the Soviet drug strategy, not only would US drug policy, but the entire image of Soviet foreign policy which underlies contemporary US policy, would be liable to come tumbling down like a house of cards.**

Over the years, the participation of various Soviet satellite states in drug-trafficking operations has gained a certain measure of public attention. The most notable examples are Bulgaria, Cuba, and most recently, Nicaragua. But the US Government leans over backward to avoid any direct statement that these countries – or Czechoslovakia, Hungary, East Germany, Vietnam, North Korea and China – are officially involved. Indeed, most official energies are devoted to suggesting that such activities are the consequence of the activities of a few corrupt officials. If anyone *does* acknowledge that there have been reports of official government involvement, this is quickly followed by the assertion that there is no confirmation of such reports. The most the US State Department will acknowledge is that certain countries – Bulgaria, Cuba and Nicaragua – facilitate the drug-trafficking of others or, as was indeed confirmed by David L. Westrate, who was then Deputy Assistant Administrator at the Drug Enforcement Administration:

'I would say in relation to Bulgaria, Cuba and Nicaragua we have substantial information that would indicate that the governments, at a minimum, condone this activity in our belief. As I say, we do not have a tape recording or a videotape of a meeting by government officials deciding to and agreeing to'[81].

A notable example of the State Department's approach was its response to the Anti-Drug Abuse Act of 1986. The penalty applicable to any country which encourages the production or distribution of illegal drugs, or whose officials do likewise, or which threatens US drug enforcement officials, or fails to cooperate, is clearly stated in legislation:

'The law requires the President to suspend all United States assistance, and to oppose any loans or other use of multilateral development bank funds for the benefit of any such country'[82].

If a country, especially a Communist country, or its officials, were found to be involved in drug-trafficking, that could have a serious impact on US financial and business transactions with the country concerned. Encouraging exactly such transactions has been a significant Soviet policy objective under Lenin, Stalin, Khrushchev, Brezhnev, and, of course, Gorbachëv. Encouraging such activity has also been a primary objective of US foreign policy since 1969. This is still a high priority thrust of US State and Commerce Department activities[83]. Nor is any change in this policy foreseeable.

Nearly all the industrialised countries are similarly involved, most notably Japan, Great Britain, West Germany, Italy, France and Switzerland, in addition to the United States. This background is important in analysing the State Department's approach to complying with the Anti-Drug Abuse Act. It is also important to recognise that in addition to penalties, there are provisions whereby those penalties can be set aside if the President certifies that the identified countries show signs of cooperating. Unfortunately, the President delegated this certification authority to the Secretary of State.

The State Department's list of countries that produce illicit drugs or facilitating their distribution, published in May 1998, consisted of the following:

Afghanistan, The Bahamas, Belize, Bolivia, Brazil, Burma, Colombia, Ecuador, Hong Kong, India, Iran, Jamaica, Laos, Lebanon, Malaysia, Mexico, Morocco, Nigeria, Pakistan, Panama, Paraguay, Peru, Syria and Thailand[84].

The only overtly Communist country included on the State Department's 1998 list was Laos. Notable by their absence were **Cuba**, **Nicaragua**, **Czechoslovakia**, **Hungary, Poland, Bulgaria, East Germany, Romania, the Soviet Union, North Korea, the People's Republic of China** and **North Vietnam**. Here we had a familiar consequence of *détente*.

Moreover, only two countries on the State Department's list were refused certification: **Syria** and **Iran**. All the remaining countries listed were certified by the Department of State to be not subject to any of the restrictions identified by Congress, because that would be contrary to 'vital national interests', or because it would not encourage cooperation, or because the countries were making *bona fide* efforts. The 'vital national interest' cited by the State Department in not wanting to censure **Laos** was its help in the continuing US search for POW/MIAs [Prisoners of War/ Missing in Action]!

While Cuba was not even mentioned in the report, the State Department's position had been explained in its annual report published three months earlier, in March 1988:

'It is possible that at least some of them [use of Cuban airspace and waters by narcotics smugglers] occur with direct or tacit Cuban government permission'[85].

Attempts to decertify Mexico in 1988 were successfully thwarted by top-level officials in the State Department, Treasury and Congress. They were described in Elaine Shannon's book, *Desperados: Latin Drug Lords, US. Lawmen, And The War America Can't Win*, along with the corruption in Mexico's entire political and police structure, from top to bottom[86]. The book was written around the abduction and murder of a DEA agent, Enrique 'Kiki' Camarena, the subsequent cover-up by Mexican officials, and the attempts by US officials from the State Department, the White House, the Treasury and the Justice Department in *support* of the Mexican officials concerned. The controlling interests were US banks and the business lobby[87].

Deep Cover is a detailed exposé of the Drug Enforcement Administration's incompetence, written by a former DEA undercover agent and group supervisor, Michael Levine. While focused on a particular case involving Bolivian producers and Mexican corruption in a joint DEA-Customs sting operation, Levine also discusses the Camarena case. 'In the aftermath of Kiki's murder, the Mexican Government had stonewalled all efforts – first in finding Camarena's body, second in stopping his killers from escaping, and finally in investigating the event'.

'Many of the Justice Department, DEA and State Department suits [upper management] and politicians – with an interest in projecting an image (no matter how false) of a progressive and honest Mexican Government that was cooperating in our antidrug efforts – wanted to play down and put the Camarena incident out of the front pages as quickly as possible. It had been up to Kiki's street brothers, the DEA street agents, who fought tooth and nail to keep the investigation alive' to keep the heat on the Mexican Government[88].

The story of Camarena's death and the fights DEA agents had to wage against corrupt Mexican officials was dramatised in an NBC television mini-series, '*Drug Wars*', on January 7-9, 1990. Indignant Mexican Government officials complained afterwards, with statements that sounded as though they were taken right from the script[89]. Two weeks later, a Los Angeles grand jury indicted nineteen Mexicans in the torture-murder of Camarena – including the former head of the Mexican Federal Judicial Police, Manuel Ibarra Herrera, and the former head of the Mexican branch of Interpol, Miguel Aldana-Ibarra. Without question, the behaviour of Mexican officials was deplorable.

However, from *their* perspective, the Mexicans may have a valid complaint. What crimes did the Mexican officials commit *that were any worse than the behaviour of their counterpart US officials and business/banking interests over the years* – to wit, those with respect to Panama, Bulgaria, China and Cuba?

Why did US officials not only ignore Noriega's activities *for fifteen years*, but in fact *send him personal letters of commendation?* Why indict Noriega, Vaughan and assorted and sundry Colombian drug-traffickers, and not indict Raúl and Fidel Castro? And why were US business and banking interests more important to US officials than the flow of drugs into the United States, thirty percent of which came through Mexico?

In 1989, the State Department reported on measures taken by the then newly installed President of Mexico, Carlos Salinas de Gortari, to 'curb drug-trafficking'. Yet reports proliferated about continued Mexican corruption and narcotics trafficking. At hearings concerning the State Department's position against decertifying Mexico, the US Customs chief of the day, William von Raab, was prevented from testifying by senior US Treasury officials because of von Raab's critical view of Mexico. As one of von Raab's assistants put it, 'Mr von Raab was particularly anxious to testify' about Mexico: **'He feels that diplomacy seems to have superseded the war on drugs…. There is no evidence of a cooperative effort by Mexico. In many ways the country has become a safe haven for drug dealers, and a huge storage area for drugs'**[90].

In 1990, another graphic illustration of the State Department's perverse behaviour entered the public domain. Kirt Kotula was a program officer for Bolivia in the State Department's Bureau of International Narcotics Matters. In January 1990, he prepared a memorandum which was leaked to the *Washington Post*[91]. The memo was described as highly critical of the then new Bolivian Government under President Jaimé Paz Zamora, noting that Bolivia's performance 'in almost every area indicates a total lack of commitment to the antidrug war'. Not only did the Bolivian Government's eradication of coca fields lag behind the established objectives, but new plantings had resulted in overall production increasing by 9.2 percent.

The US Government uses successful extradition cases as evidence of cooperation. But Kotula pointed out that the Minister of Interior Luíz Arce Gomez, who was subsequently extradited to the United States on drug charges, was 'universally hated' in Bolivia. Another activity highly publicised by Washington was a succession of joint raids on cocaine laboratories in the Bolivian interior. One particular raid, which cost the United States $100,000, was mentioned in Kotula's memo. The raid 'failed to achieve even minimal success', he wrote, probably because the traffickers were tipped off in advance by Bolivians.

But, when the State Department's *Annual Report* was sent to Congress on March 1, 1990, Bolivia was characterised as cooperating fully with the US anti-drug policy[92]. About all that Assistant Secretary Melvyn Levitsky would say when confronted with the memo was that it was part of a 'red team' exercise to give him candid analyses, but that the memo was 'stolen government property' and should not have been made public[93].

With respect to Cuba, even the CIA has been reported to side with the State Department. As Jack Anderson reported, the CIA Deputy Director, Richard Kerr, stated at a meeting of a Cabinet-level board in a February 1987 that it was hard to identify a direct Cuban Government link to drug-trafficking activities[94]. If this is an accurate reflection of US intelligence in action, one has to wonder what they use to reach their conclusions. One embarrassing explanation was provided by Major Aspillaga, the Cuban intelligence official who defected to the United States via Vienna in June 1987 [*see pages 81 and 83*]. **He explained that Cuban Government officials once believed by the CIA to be secretly working for them were actually feeding the CIA with misleading or useless information prepared by the Cuban intelligence service. Several such sources had even passed CIA polygraphs.**

It was the US Attorney's office in Miami which first unleashed court-room evidence on Cuba's involvement. That happened in November 1982. The evidence, however, apparently never made much of an impression on US intelligence or on the State Department. Fortunately, in a subsequent indictment, the US Attorney's office in Miami presented still more evidence – this time, videotapes showing drug smugglers explaining to DEA undercover informants how they shipped drugs from Colombia through Cuba, with the assistance of Cuban officials, air traffic controllers, the DGI, and Cuban Air Force pilots[95]. All such hard details, however, have little impact on the State Department, which still refuses to acknowledge any significant Cuban participation in drug-trafficking[96].

In 1987, as part of the US Senate's advise-and-consent procedures on the nomination of Ambassador Jack F. Matlock, Jr. to be Ambassador to the Soviet Union, several questions on the rôle of the Soviet Union and Czechoslovakia in narcotics trafficking were submitted to the State Department. Concerning Soviet involvement, State Department officials replied: **'The Department of State has no information regarding official Soviet involvement in international narcotics traffic'**. With regard to Czechoslovakia, the State Department replied: **'The Department of State has no information regarding official Czechoslovakian complicity in the international narcotics traffic, nor of any Soviet involvement with the Government of Czechoslovakia in narcotics traffic'**. This statement was made after two articles detailing the involvement of Czechoslovakia and the Soviet Union had been published, and after officials in the two relevant State Department bureaus, International Narcotics Matters and Intelligence and Research, had been informed of Sejna's information. **They expressed no interest in the data whatsoever.**

A particularly interesting film clip was obtained by Jean Michel Cousteau in 1981 during an expedition by his famous father, Jacques Cousteau, to the upper reaches of the Amazon. Deep in the jungle, the younger Cousteau came across an entire village which had been transformed into a centre for cocaine production and research laboratories. The local Indians were used as experimental subjects and in the process many had been transformed into 'zombies'. A segment of the background dialogue in the resultant Cousteau film is worth quoting in detail:

'The secret processing centre seems as well a battle outpost, with planes and a cache of weapons believed imported from Cuba for guerrilla fighters'.

'Some believe that cocaine, once merely a source of illicit profits, now also supports small insurgent armies and is sent northward to the United States by jungle militants as a silent, inexorable, poisonous weapon'.

'The Cousteau team asks: 'Are you worried about the effects of cocaine on other countries such as the United States?"

"No', the trafficker says, 'because a lot of us consider this a way of responding to the attack of imperialism in South America. It's a cultural response. If a lot of people are going to die here because of imperialist policies from the United States, a lot of people there are going to die from cocaine. This is war'"[97].

The original film was reported to have included a passage in which it was mentioned that East German and Bulgarian technicians and chemists were working in the laboratory, together with Cuban and Colombian chemists[98]. While there is no known evidence, it is possible that the highly dangerous 'crack' was developed in this or a similar research facility and then test-marketed in the Caribbean before being introduced into the United States. The US Information Agency was provided with a copy of the original film but has refused to discuss it, even with other agencies, most notably its own Voice of America.

This cooperative assistance by Cuba, East Germany and Bulgaria is not limited to Latin America. Reportedly, these countries have also been active in the Middle East and have helped in the construction of heroin refineries in Syria. The Beka'a Valley in Lebanon is under the control of Syria. The valley has long been noted for the production of marijuana and hashish. But, the shift into poppies and heroin, with the assistance of Cuba, East Germany and Bulgaria, is a relatively new development[99].

The overall situation was summed up in 1988 by the chief assistant US Attorney in Miami, Richard Gregorie, who brought the indictment against Noriega. Gregorie was often critical of the rôle Washington has played, or failed to play, in putting a stop to drug-trafficking. **'If we are publicly fighting a war on drugs, why isn't the State Department involved?'** he asked. **'Prosecutors I have talked with consider the State Department to be working for foreign governments'[100].**

The State Department's own attitude was clearly expressed in its September 1988 *International Narcotics Control Strategy Report*: 'We believe that our international strategy... is working'[101]. If it is working, one is forced to ask: **For whom?** ■

References to Chapter 9:

1. See Anslinger and Tompkins, *The Traffic in Narcotics, op. cit.* and Harry J. Anslinger, 'The Opium of the People's Government', in US Congress, House Committee on Un-American Activities, *Soviet Total War: 'Historic Mission' of Violence and Deceit*, Volume II (Washington, D.C.: US Government Printing Office, September 30, 1956).
2. Stefan T. Possony, *Maoist China and Heroin* (Taipei, Taiwan: China Publishing Company, no date)
3. Candlin, *Psycho-Chemical Warfare: The Chinese Communist Drug Offensive Against the West*, *op. cit.*, page 26.
4. As described in detail by William J. Gill, the new Secretary of State, Dean Rusk, was at least very sympathetic to the interests of the Chinese Communists. Also in 1961, there was an influx into the Departments of State and Justice of individuals who were formerly denied security clearances or whose backgrounds normally would have prevented them from receiving a clearance. *The Ordeal of Otto Otepka* (New Rochelle, N.Y.: Arlington House, 1969).
5. A substantial portion of the CIA's analysis was leaked to and printed by the *New York Times*. Curiously, the printed article does not include any of the data on China, nor is the geography of the original 'Golden Triangle' shown on the included map. See Felix Belair, Jr., 'C.I.A. Identifies 21 Asian Opium Refineries', *New York Times*, June 6, 1971, page A2.
6. Edward Jay Epstein, *Agency of Fear*, (New York: G. P. Putnam's Sons, 1977), page 85.
7. *Ibid.*, pages 149-150.
8. Cabinet Committee on International Narcotics Control, *World Opium Survey -1972*, publisher not identified, released on August 17, 1972 by the Department of State.
9. *Ibid.*, page 26.
10. *Ibid.*, pages A45-A46.
11. Quoted in Hon. Lester L. Wolff, *The Narcotics Situation in Southeast Asia*, Report of a Special Study Mission (Washington, D.C.: US Government Printing Office, 1972), page 12.
12. In reviewing the state of intelligence data, a former counter-intelligence specialist with the Defence Intelligence Agency [DIA] stated that the narcotics intelligence people did not seem to possess any systematic intelligence about narcotics traffic. Epstein, *Agency of Fear, op. cit.*, page 253. Candlin assessed *The World Opium Situation* statements by the BNDD on the rapid decline of mainland Chinese opium production in the 1950s and 1960s as being without 'even the flimsiest basis of support'. *Psycho-Chemical Warfare: The Chinese Communist Drug Offensive Against the West*, *op. cit.*, page 106.
13. US Congress, Senate, *International Terrorism, Insurgency, and drug-trafficking Present Trends in Terrorist Activity*, Joint Hearings Before the Committee on Foreign Relations and the Committee on the Judiciary, May 13,14 and 15,1985 (Washington, D.C.: US Government Office, 1985), page 31.
14. *World Drug Impact*, Part 1, *op. cit.*, page 14.
15. See, for example, US Department of State, Bureau of International Narcotics Matters, *International Narcotics Control Strategy Report* (Washington, D.C.: US Government Printing Office, March 1987).
16. About the only Communist country to be unequivocally identified as trafficking in narcotics 'as a matter of policy' is Laos. See Michael Isikoff, 'US Accuses Laos of drug-trafficking', *Washington Post*, August 30, 1988, page A4.
17. In the interests of *détente'*, US government officials have suppressed data and have knowingly failed to collect and use evidence considered contrary to policy. For example, prior to the Biological and Toxin Weapons arms control treaty signed in 1972, the United States was aware of massive Soviet activity in applying genetic engineering to chemical and biological warfare. As Herbert E. Meyer, the former Vice Chairman, National Intelligence Council, explained, **this data was 'removed at the specific request of Henry Kissinger'.** *The Defence of Western Europe*, London Conference Proceedings (New York: International Security Council, 1988), pages 72-73. This action was most unfortunate. **Had the data been pursued**

at this time, Soviet narcotics trafficking might have been uncovered insofar as it was a component of the Soviet Bloc's chemical warfare strategy. As Ray Cline, then Director of the State Department's Intelligence and Research Bureau, reported, 'crucial intelligence was often suppressed to insure that only Nixon and Kissinger had the full body of information...'. John Ranelagh, *The Agency: The Rise and Decline of the CIA* (New York: Simon and Schuster, 1986), page 518.

Another example of the suppression of data ostensibly in the interests of *détente*, was the handling of the Soviet KGB defector, **Anatoliy Golitsyn**. Golitsyn had been an especially valuable defector, in the opinion of the French and British authorities, and of the CIA's chief of counter-intelligence, James Angleton. Golitsyn had provided important information on Soviet penetrations of several intelligence organisations, most notably the French, British and American, and had provided unique details on Soviet intelligence, the reorganisation of which he had helped to plan, and on Soviet deception. At Angleton's request, Golitsyn was studying the possibility that the Sino-Soviet split was a deliberately orchestrated deception. Edward Jay Epstein, reporting on his extensive discussions with Angleton, stated that **in 1969 the Director of the CIA, Richard Helms, told Angleton that it was now the policy of the Nixon White House to accept the Sino-Soviet split as genuine** – that is, drop the investigation. Edward Jay Epstein, *Deception*, (New York: Simon & Schuster, 1989), page 98.

18. Jack Anderson, 'Kennedy May Help in California', *Washington Post*, May 26, 1972, page D19.

19. Edward Jay Epstein, *Agency of Fear* (New York: G. P. Putnam's Sons, 1977).

20. *Ibid.*

21. US Congress, Senate, *Drugs and Terrorism, 1984*, Hearing Before the Subcommittee on Alcoholism and Drug Abuse of the Committee on Labour and Human Resources, August 2, 1984 (Washington, D.C.: US Government Printing Office, 1984).

22. Assuming they did not have advance notice.

23. It would be only prudent to assume that many of the 'Bulgarian' officials were actually Soviet and East European intelligence service officials acting under Bulgarian cover.

24. *Drugs and Terrorism, 1984, op. cit.*, page 55.

25. *Ibid.*, page 60.

26. *Ibid.*, pages 59, 66.

27. US Department of State, Bureau of International Narcotics Matters, *International Narcotics Control Strategy Report* (Washington, D.C.: US Department of State, 1989), pages 19, 159.

28. The key report was *Shakarchi Trading Company*, File No. UN-89-0002, January 3, 1989.

29. See Peter Samuel, 'Senior Bulgarian Aides Linked to a Booming Trade in Heroin', *New York City Tribune*, March 30, 1989, page A1,;'Druglords Seen Moving Into Havens in Communist Bloc', *New York City Tribune*, March 31, 1989, page A1; 'In 1986, Bulgarian Connection Surfaced in Big Seizure in L.A. of Drug Money', *New York City Tribune*, April 4, 1989, page A1; and 'State Dept. Said to Slight Drug Enforcement to Preserve *Détente*', *New York City Tribune*, April 7, 1989, page A1; Knut Royce, 'Heroin Labs in Bulgaria', *Newsday*, April 1,1989, page 7; 'Dirty Money: Drugs to Gold', *Newsday*, April 2, 1989; and Bill Gertz, 'Bulgarian Front Linked to Drugs', *Washington Times*, April 3, 1989, page A1.

30. Bill Gertz, 'State Confirms Bulgarian Company's Drug Ties', *Washington Times*, April 7,1989, A6.

31. Peter Fuhrman, 'The Bulgarian Connection', *Forbes*, April 17,1989, pages 40-44.

32. Robert S. Greenberger, 'Customs Chief's Feud on Drug Conference Typifies Appointee-Bureaucrat Conflict', *Wall Street Journal*, May 19, 1986, page 66.

33. US Department of State, Bureau of International Narcotics Matters, *International Narcotics Control Strategy Report* (Washington, D.C.: US Government Printing Office, March 1988), pages 14, 35.

34. Chemical analysis can be used to help determine the manufacturing origins of drug samples, especially if certain trace elements that are characteristic of the particular production process are present. This information also could be used by knowledgeable authorities to thwart proper identification by deliberately introducing indicator chemicals during the manufacturing process that would cause incorrect conclusions to be drawn following such chemical analysis.

35. Michael Isikoff, 'Soviets Suggest Trading Facts on drug-traffic', *Washington Post*, July 20, 1988. Also, the *Boston Globe* reported on September 13, 1988 that Great Britain and the Soviet Union agreed to 'unite in the fight against drug smuggling by sharing intelligence,training and operations'.

36. *National Drug Control Strategy, op. cit.*, p.67.

37. Michael Isikoff, 'DEA Proposes to Train KGB to Combat Drugs'. *Washington Post*, December 15, 1989, page A23.

38. Larry Rohter, 'America's Blind Eye', *New York Times Magazine*, May 29, 1988, pages 26, 29.

39. 1972 is the year given in Jim McGee and David Hoffman, 'Rivals Hint Bush Understates Knowledge of Noriega Ties', *Washington Post*, May 8,1988, page A16, citing access to Justice Department files. According to Michael Isikoff, a DEA official stated that the DEA's knowledge of Noriega's ties to illicit drug-trafficking dated from 1970. 'DEA Fights to Keep Office in Panama', *Washington Post*, October 4, 1988, page A27. As John E. Ingersoll, then Director of the Bureau of Narcotics and Dangerous Drugs, confirmed in 1972, there was sufficient evidence that one of the options considered as a solution to Panama's drug problem was Noriega's assassination. Seymour M. Hersch, 'US Aides in '72 Weighed Killing Officer Who Now Leads Panama', *New York Times*, June 13, 1986, page 1.

40. Rohter, 'America's Blind Eye', *op. cit.*, page 26. According to a *Washington Times* report, Noriega was recruited in 1966 by the CIA case officer Nester Sanchez. Bill Gertz, 'Noriega Was a Spy for Nearly Everyone', *Washington Times*, January 8, 1990, page A1.

41. Michael Hedges, 'To Gen. Noriega with Love: Letters from America's Top Drug Enforcers', *Washington Times*, January 17, 1990, page A1.

42. With respect to developments surrounding the finalisation of the Panama Canal Treaties under President Carter, see Warren Brooks, 'How Canal Drug Ties Were Hidden: Carter Wanted His Treaty', *Washington Times*, July 28, 1988, page F1. See also G. Russell Evans, *The Panama Canal Treaties Swindle: Consent to Disaster* (Carrboro, North Carolina: Signal Books, 1986).

43. This incident and others where Panama's involvement in drug-trafficking is denied are identified by Rohter in 'America's Blind Eye', *op. cit.*

44. Jim McGee and Bob Woodward, 'Noriega Arms Indictment Stalled in '80', *Washington Post*, March 20, 1988, page A22.

45. *'Détente'* was first identified in a secret Soviet dispatch from Moscow Novosti KGB headquarters in 1968 by KGB-International Department operative **Yuri Bezmenov**. In 1969, the new *détente* project was explained to a gathering of Novosti-KGB staff including Bezmenov by Nikolai Agayantz, the son of the KGB disinformation specialist General-Major Ivan Agayantz. The meeting took place in Ambassador Pegov's office at the USSR Embassy in India. *Détente* was not mere propaganda, Agayantz lectured. Rather, it was part of a new strategy, based on the theory and practice of the ideological offensive as formulated in various texts, such as *The Art of War* by Sun Tzu. See Joseph D. Douglass, Jr., *Why The Soviets Violate Arms Control Treaties* (Washington, D.C.: Pergamon-Brassey's, 1988), pages 9-10.

46. Street costs of drug-trafficking in America were estimated at $140 to S200 billion in 1990. The costs in lost labour, prisons and health treatment are estimated at $60 to $100 billion. This totals $200 to $300 billion. To this total must be added the cost of street crimes as well as blue and white collar crimes, which are not known to have been totalled. See US General Accounting Office, *Controlling Drug Abuse*: A *Status Report* (Washington, D.C.: US Government Printing Office, 1988).

47. Howard Kurtz, 'Bank of America Officer Indicted in Drug Probe', *Washington Post*, March 19, 1986, page A3.

48. As explained by Ramon Milian Rodriguez, a CPA who handled money-laundering and investments for the Medellín Cartel: **'In every instance, the banks knew who they were dealing with....** They were dealing with Milian Rodriguez who represented money from South America, and their corresponding banks in Panama knew where the money came from because we required certain things from them.... We were breaking the laws in a very big manner and you always have to have plausible deniability. And the New York banks are no fools'. US Congress, Senate, *Drugs, Law Enforcement and Foreign Policy: Panama*, Hearings Before the Subcommittee on Terrorism, Narcotics and International Relations of the Committee on Foreign Relations, February 11, 1988, (Washington, D.C.: unpublished stenographic transcript, 1988) pages 66-67, 92-93.

49. *Ibid.*

50. *Ibid.*, page 65. See also Howard Kurtz, 'Bank of America Officer Indicted in Drug Probe', *Washington Post*, March 19, 1986, page A3.

51. *'Cocaine'*, ABC News *'Close-up'*, August 20, 1983, Mediascan Transcript ABC-COCAINE 082083, pages 5, 7.

52. James Ring Adams, 'Losing the Drug War: Drugs, Banks, and Florida Politics', *American Spectator*, September 1988, page 20.

53. *Ibid.*, page 24.

54. Michael Hedges, 'Lack of Prosecutors Forces US to Blink at Florida Drug Crimes', *Washington Times*, November 18, 1988, page A1.

55. *Drugs, Law Enforcement and Foreign Policy: Panama*, February 11, 1988, *op. cit.*, page 94.

56. *Boston Globe* Spotlight Team, 'Critics Say Cash Probes Violate Rights of Privacy'. Part 7 in *Money-laundering*, published by the *Boston Globe*, no date or page numbers given.

57. US Congress, Senate, *National and International Security Threat of Narcotics Trafficking*, Hearing Before the Caucus on International Narcotics Control, June 8, 1987 (Washington, D.C.: US Government Printing Office, 1987), page 36.

58. *Hearing to Receive Testimony on Drugs, Law Enforcement and Foreign Policy: Panama*, February 11, 1988, *op. cit.*, page 79.

59. Another Colombian cartel from Cali received publicity as a result of drug wars in New York for control of the cocaine and crack markets. Michael Isikoff, 'DEA Official Guarded After Death Threat', *Washington Post*, August 28, 1988, page A9.

60. US Congress, Senate, *Hearing to Receive Testimony on Drugs, Law Enforcement and Foreign Policy: Panama*, February 10, 1988, stenographic transcript, pages 65-66.

61. Michael Isikoff, 'US Links Bank to Drug Cartel', *Washington Post*, October 12, 1988, page A1; and 'Indicted Banker Testified to Noriega Links', *Washington Post*, October 13, 1988, page A3.

62. Ramon Rodriguez was caught taking $5.4 million in cash out of the country to Panama. This was mainly expense money – bribes and so forth. Rodriguez testified that he made $2-4 million a month and that he paid Noriega about $10 million a month. Most of the real money he shipped to Panama in commercial shipping containers. The $14-32 million involved in the Bank of Credit and Commerce International [BCCI] indictment was a trivial amount when compared with the overall size of money-laundering operations. See US Congress, Senate, *Hearing to Receive Testimony on Drugs, Law Enforcement and Foreign Policy: Panama*, February 11, 1988, stenographic transcript, page 59.

63. Nick Tosches, *Power on Earth* (New York: Arbor House, 1986), pages 81-107.

64. US Senate, *Hearing to Receive Testimony on Drugs, Law Enforcement, and Foreign Policy: Panama*, February 11, 1988, *op. cit.* page 95.

65. *Power on Earth, op. cit.*, page 89.

66. Charles McCoy, 'Records from 41 Banks Are Subpoenaed in Widening money-laundering Inquiry', *Wall Street Journal*, October 31, 1988, page B12. Other banks allegedly used by the money-laundering ring and identified in the article were: **Atico Savings Bank; Banco Central S.A.; Banco de Bogotà; Banco Granadero de Colombia; Bank Real Miami S.A.; Barnett Banks; Capital Bank; Consolidated Bank N.A.; Dadeland Bank; Deutsch Sudamerikanische Bank; Eagle National Bank; Eastern National Bank; First Federal Savings of Palm Beach; First Nationwide Bank; Florida International Bank; Florida National Bank of Miami; Israel Discount Bank; Marine Midland International Bank; Miami National Bank; NCNB National Bank of Florida; Northern Trust Bank of Florida; Peoples First National Bank; Professional Savings Bank; Southeast Banking Corporation; United National Bank; Westchester Bank; Banco Atlantico; Banco Leumi Trust Co. of New York; Philadelphia International Bank; Lorain County Bank; California First Bank; Philadelphia National Bank;** and **Sun Bank N.A.**.

67. The White House, Office of the Press Secretary, *Remarks by the President to International Drug Enforcement Conference*, April 27, 1989, page 2.

68. See Peter Samuel, 'Senior Bulgarian Aides Linked to a Booming Trade in Heroin', *New York City Tribune*, March 30, 1989, page A1; 'Druglords Seen Moving Into Havens in Communist Bloc', *New York City Tribune*, March 31, 1939, page A1; 'In 1986, Bulgarian Connection Surfaced in Big Seizure in L.A. of Drug Money', *New York City Tribune*, April 4, 1989, page Al; Knut Royce, 'Heroin Labs in Bulgaria', *Newsday*, April 1, 1989, page 7; and 'Dirty Money: Drugs to Gold', *Newsday*, April 2, 1989; and DEA Investigation Report *Shakarchi Trading Company*, File No. UN-89-0002, January 3, 1989, pages 3-5. The Republic Bank of New York, its deposits of $760 million with the San Francisco Reserve Bank in 1984 – almost all of it from correspondent banks in Hong Kong – and the bank Treasurer's desire not to advertise or talk about this business,were discussed in 'West Coast Cash Surge Linked to Drug Dollars', *Money-laundering, op. cit.*

69. For a general description of the program, see 'US Loans to E. Germany Sent on to Terrorists', *Free Press International Report*, July 14, 1989.

70. *American Interests Special 'Follow the Money'* (Federal News Service, 1989), page 13-1.

71. *Ibid.*, pages 14-2, 15-1.

72. James Bamford, *The Puzzle Palace* (New York: Penguin Books, 1982), page 325.

73. Edward Jay Epstein, *Agency of Fear* (New York: G. P. Putnam's Sons, 1977), pages 85, 158.

74. Bamford, *The Puzzle Palace, op. cit.*, page 327.

75. For a good description of this abortive beginning of the use of intelligence in fighting the war on drugs, see Bamford, *The Puzzle Palace, op. cit.*, pages 314, 325-337, 369-370, and 381.

76. Bamford, *The Puzzle Palace, op. cit.*, page 336.

77. Guy Gugliotta and Jeff Leen, *Kings of Cocaine* (New York: Simon & Schuster, 1989), page 126.

78. Associated Press, 'Customs Chief Vents Anger As He Resigns', *Atlanta Journal*, August 1, 1989. His remarks are supported in *Drug money-laundering, Banks and Foreign Policy*, A Report on anti-money-laundering law enforcement and policy based on oversight hearings before the Senate Foreign Relations Committee on September 27 and October 4 and hearings before the Senate Banking Committee on November 1 submitted to the Foreign Relations Committee by the Subcommittee on Narcotics and Terrorism, undated but *circa* February 1990.

79. US Congress, Senate, *International Terrorism, Insurgency, and drug-trafficking Present Trends in Terrorist Activity*, Joint Hearings Before the Committee on Foreign Relations and the Committee on the Judiciary, May 13, 14 and 15,1985 (Washington, D.C.: US Government Printing Office, 1985), page 114.

80. *Ibid.*, page 141.

81. Senate, *International Terrorism, Insurgency, and drug-trafficking, op. cit.*, page 168.

82. Department of State, *Report to Congress, op. cit.*, page 2.

83. See William E. Simon, 'Should We Bail Out Gorbachëv?' *Reader's Digest*, September 1988.

84. US Department of State, *Report to Congress*, Section 2013, P.L. 99-570, Reports and Restrictions Concerning Certain Countries, May 1, 1988, page 2.

85. *International Narcotics Control Strategy Report*, March 1988, *op. cit.*, page 35.

86. Elaine Shannon, *Desperados* (New York: Viking, 1988), pages 393, 432-433.

87. *Ibid.*

88. Michael Levine, *Deep Cover* (New York: Delacorte Press, 1990), page 229.

89. Michael Isikoff, 'Mexico Says NBC Reports Distorted', *Washington Post*, January 11, 1990, E1.

90. Michael Hedges, 'Helms: Von Raab Shushed on Mexican Drugs', *Washington Times*, April 6, 1989, page A6.

91. Michael Isikoff, 'Blunt Assessment of Bolivia Ignored', *Washington Post*, March 1, 1990, A4.

92. US Department of State, Bureau of International Narcotics Matters, *International Narcotics Control Strategy Report* (Washington, D.C.: US Department of State, March 1990). See also Michael Isikoff, 'World Output of Narcotics Soars, Congress Told', *Washington Post*, March 2, 1990, page A24.

93. 'World Output of Narcotics Soars, Congress Told', *op. cit.*

94. Jack Anderson and Dale Van Atta, 'CIA Breaks Ranks on Cuba, Nicaragua', *Washington Post*, June 3, 1987, page E19.

95. Michael Hedges, 'Drug Money Ends Up in 'Drawer of Fidel'', *Washington Times*, March 10, 1989, page A5.

96. See US Department of State, *Report to Congress, op. cit.*; and US Department of State, Bureau of International Narcotics Matters, *International Narcotics Control Strategy Report: Mid-Year Update* (Washington, D.C.: US Government Printing Office, September 1988).

97. Brian Crozier, 'Drogue: la Filière Sovietique', *L'Express*, December 25, 1986, page 104. For a partial English translation, see 'The Soviet Drug War Against the West', *The Free Nation*, February 1987, pages 1-2.

98. *Ibid.*, page 104. Also see Brian Crozier, *The Gorbachëv Phenomenon* (London and Lexington, Georgia: The Claridge Press, 1990), pages 147-170.

99. Rachel Ehrenfeld and Peter Samuel, 'Drugs, the DEA and Damascus', *Australia/Israel Review*, August 25 - September 7, 1987; and Jack Anderson, 'Syrians Aiding Heroin Traffic in Beka'a Valley', *Washington Post*, February 1, 1984, page F10.

100. Michael Hedges, 'Federal Scourge of Drug Kingpins', *Insight*, June 6, 1988, page 24.

101. US Department of State, *International Narcotics Control Strategy Report: Mid-Year Update*, *op. cit.*, page 1.

QUESTIONS
OF INTELLIGENCE

How could a massive global Soviet Bloc intelligence operation, such as the Soviet narcotics offensive, have been underway for so long without the United States knowing
what was happening? This is a most important and potentially explosive question.
Implicit in it are a number of additional questions; for example, what else are we
unaware of and how else might we have been misled?

To a degree, the question, 'Why haven't we known'? is answered in the previous
chapter. Part of the answer involves the political and private interests that have stood in
the way of comprehension. A second element of the answer concerns the inner workings
of US intelligence. Two aspects are particularly relevant. The first involves the collection
and evaluation of intelligence; specifically, in this case, the detailed handling of General
Major Jan Sejna's debriefing. The second aspect concerns understanding how Soviet Bloc
intelligence operations work and the communication of this understanding. Let us consider, first of all, the debriefing.

General Sejna defected to the United States in Trieste on February 25, 1968. The usual
procedure is that preliminary debriefings of defectors in Europe are conducted at a special
debriefing facility near Frankfurt, Germany[1]. In Sejna's case, this was not done. Rather, he
was immediately flown to Washington. This might have been because of Sejna's rank or
unusual importance – if it were not for the fact that his subsequent debriefing and handling was more à propos a low-level defector of inconsequential importance. Nevertheless,
his rapid transportation to Washington does suggest that someone somewhere may have
wanted to exercise strict and immediate control over his debriefing.

The news of Sejna's defection to the United States, along with a brief description of
the circumstances, were published in the *Washington Post* and the *New York Times* in the
week following his defection. The description of Sejna in the articles was rather vague. He
was described as the chief of the Communist Party at the Ministry of Defence, a member of
the General Staff and of the Presidium of the National Assembly. Those were the only particulars to be published. While acknowledging that Sejna was 'one of the highest-ranking
Communists ever to defect', the *Washington Post* instantly played down his importance by
noting that Sejna was simply of higher rank than either of the previous year's defectors,
Svetlana Stalin and Lt. Col. Renge. The only hints of his importance were statements that
he had top secret information on his country's defence and on Warsaw Pact operations.

Aside from the foregoing, there was no information or even speculation in the *Washington Post* or the *New York Times* concerning the full spectrum of Sejna's positions, responsibilities, or knowledge. Rather, both papers focused attention on material designed to defame Sejna which had been published in the Communist press. There was no indication of any attempt to learn more or in any respect to challenge the descriptions of Sejna that had appeared in the Communist press specifically in order to discredit him[2].

General Sejna was certainly not presented as an official of even moderate importance – notwithstanding the fact that he was probably one of the five most knowledgeable Czechoslovak officials as regards Soviet and Soviet Bloc political, military and intelligence strategy and objectives[3]. Rather, he was described as an embezzler, a Stalinist, a public school dropout, an individual who had been promoted through favours and against the recommendations of his peers, one who had organised an abortive coup against the new liberal Czechoslovak leadership, and who had defected with his son and a young woman 'who', as the *Washington Post* wrote, 'is being described officially here [Washington] as the General's 22 year-old mistress'. The young woman was, in fact, his son's fiancée; they were later married in the United States. These characterisations of Sejna are all false[4] and constitute a pertinent example of a Communist character assassination and disinformation being picked up and echoed by leading US newspapers.

The importance of this type of shallow reporting, and the failure of the US Government to correct the record, should not be underestimated. These reports, in effect, told people that Sejna was not a credible source nor an individual of any value. The reports materially damaged his opportunities to use his background as the basis for a new career; for example, teaching, speaking engagements, writing and consulting. They also, in effect, discouraged anyone in the intelligence or national security communities from seeking him out or from listening to what he had to say. How could anyone trust an individual with such a reputation? It should also not go unnoticed that when the charges were made, Sejna did not speak or read English and was not aware of how his credibility, and thus his future, were being undermined. He was unable to defend himself.

The image of Sejna portrayed in the *Washington Post* and the *New York Times* was perhaps best summarised by the description published in *Newsweek* a week and a half later. 'Up until now Americans could always fall back on one sure test: if an East European defected to the West, he was *ipso facto* a good guy. Last week, however, Washington unveiled its latest defector – only to discover that he was the heavy [that is, villain] in the case'[5]. To make certain the message had been adequately communicated, *Newsweek* printed a picture of Sejna with the caption, 'Sejna: The heavy in the case'.

From the news reports, one can infer that US officials confirmed the Communist reports on Sejna's defection and acknowledged that Sejna was now in the United States. They apparently did not provide any information beyond that contained in the Communist press, or any elaboration or clarification. Moreover, according to the news reports, as illustrated in the preceding excerpt from the *Washington Post*, US officials evidently directly supported at least one of the slanderous statements printed in the Communist press to discredit Sejna; namely, that Sejna was running away with his 22 year-old mistress, which was a lie, as indicated above.

To a degree, the official US handling of Sejna was understandable. It does not seem that even within the CIA or the US State Department, there was anyone equipped to clarify the record who had possessed any real appreciation of how important a defector Sejna actually was. For example, Sejna was a political officer, a commissar. Political commissars are generally regarded in the United States as thugs or watchdogs who report on their friends and acquaintances to authorities. They are not held in high regard or seriously considered, in any sense of the word[6]. Accordingly, just this one aspect of Sejna's background is sufficient to have caused most people to discount his value.

Additionally, there was little knowledge of (and thus, little attention focused on) the organisations that Sejna was a member of, or of the positions he held. US officials throughout the intelligence and diplomatic communities are not known to have appreciated the rôle of the *Kolegium*, which functioned almost as a mini-Defence Council and served, within the Ministry of Defence, to review and critique plans and issues prior to their being sent forward to the Defence Council; or of the Party Group at the Presidium, which exercised Party control over the National Assembly (parliament); or of the bureau which provided direction to the Main Political Administration, which in turn was responsible for maintaining ideological watch over the military; or of the powerful Administrative Organs Department, which ruled over the military, civilian intelligence and justice[7]. These were just some of the organisations in which Sejna had held leadership positions.

US officials evidently did not know what it meant to be the chief of the Communist Party (that is, First Secretary) at the Ministry of Defence, in which capacity Sejna monitored all top-level Czechoslovak decisions and communications to and from other countries, including the Soviet Union, and exercised *nomenklatura* (position appointment power) over all mid-level military officers. Most Soviet Bloc intelligence experts did not even know a Defence Council existed, let alone what its function[8] was or what it meant for Sejna to be its secretary and in charge of the Defence Council agenda, the preparation of decisions, and the dissemination of implementing directives.

Thus, it is entirely possible that there was no US official in a position to know and take appropriate action, who understood how truly important a defector General Sejna was. At the same time, there were several glaring inconsistencies and departures from normal practice, such as: **(1)** The lack of an initial debriefing in Europe; **(2)** the manner in which Sejna's CIA debriefing was terminated, which will be described later; **(3)** what appears to have been an immediate decision to exercise strict control over his debriefings, keeping them focused on tactical military matters and away from topics of possible strategic significance; and, **(4)** at the same time, a decision to discredit Sejna so that no-one would actively seek him out or listen to what he had to say.

While these decisions were made within the US Government, **it seems more probable than not that the decisions were not based upon bureaucratic self-interest or policy considerations, but were orchestrated, on the contrary, by Soviet intelligence or agents of influence**. The logic behind this hypothesis will become more evident during the following description of what happened, and, more particularly, *what did not happen*.

Sejna's debriefing began in the normal manner. First, the debriefings focused on questions of tactical warning: the possibility of an imminent attack, security codes, alert measures and conditions – items of immediate military significance. Following these potentially time-sensitive questions, the debriefings shifted to questions of a personal and professional nature. This was the establishment of the *bona fides* phase, which had its problems because the people conducting the CIA debriefings did not understand the Communist system[9], had many misperceptions, and hence often did not like Sejna's responses to their questions.

After General Sejna's *bona fides* had been established, the debriefings finally settled down to probe his knowledge of Czechoslovak and Warsaw Pact military organisation and operations. This is where serious questions about the nature of General Sejna's debriefings arise. The debriefings, which lasted for roughly ten months, were confined to questions relating to matters of tactical military significance[10]. And, while Sejna's knowledge in these matters was unquestionably extensive, these subjects were at the same time the least important ones of which Sejna had detailed knowledge. Moreover, some of these debriefings were so trivial that they properly should be regarded as strictly ways to pass the time and maintain the image of being busy. (Sejna was asked, for example, to sketch the different Czechoslovak military insignia, which, as he told his debriefers, were freely available in the library across the street from the US Embassy in Prague)[11].

General Sejna had also turned over to the CIA secret and top secret documentation he had brought with him, carefully selected by him for its wide-ranging importance[12]. He was never asked one question about these documents or the material they contained. While the documents were translated, the translations were never made available to the intelligence community[13]. It was also about this time that the decision was made to actively discredit Sejna, cast aspersions on his character and on the reliability of his testimony, and thus dampen any interest in what he had to say. As described by a former CIA official, the word was spread throughout the middle and upper echelons that Sejna was a 'heavy'. It was important to recognise that this was inconsistent with the distribution of the CIA intelligence reports on Sejna's debriefings, all of which identified the material as having come from a reliable source'.

The failure to debrief Sejna cannot be excused on the ground that the CIA debriefers did not know that Sejna possessed information of prime strategic significance. Often, following the sessions, he would chat with his debriefers and tell them that they were not asking the right questions. Also, one of the first things Sejna told his debriefers was that in his opinion the most important information he brought with him was his detailed knowledge of the Soviet 'Long-Range Plan for the Next Ten to Fifteen Years and Beyond'; but, that he would not discuss this plan, which detailed the Soviet Bloc's coordinated strategy and tactics around the world[14], until the decision to grant him political asylum had been made. But, after that decision was made, and continuing to the present, there was no effort to debrief Sejna on the contents of the Soviet plan[15] 'to bury us'. This was, and continues to be, a most serious error.

In 1975 the importance of Sejna's knowledge of the Soviet long-range plan was made public by Lord Chalfont in a series of three articles in *The Times* of London[16]. Even so, no attempt to debrief Sejna was made, nor subsequently in 1983 after Walter Hahn, the editor of *Strategic Review*, wrote about Sejna's knowledge[17]. He has still [1990] not been debriefed on the long-range plan; and, given the nature of Soviet intentions, goals and strategy[18], which had not materially changed in over seventy years, most of the objectives, strategies and operational concepts set forth in the long-range plan probably remain valid.

In the late spring of 1968, General Sejna was made available to a Defence Intelligence Agency (DIA) debriefing team, which consisted of two warrant officers, a major and on a few occasions, two colonels, none of whom seemed to Sejna to have any background or interest in political, military, or intelligence strategy, policy or objectives. Their debriefings were also confined to matters of tactical military significance; for example, Tables of Organisation and Equipment (TOE) for small units, such as companies and battalions and unit locations. As a further indication of the CIA's attitude towards Sejna, during the Defense Intelligence Agency debriefings the DIA officers always addressed Sejna as 'General Sejna' out of military courtesy and respect. Then one day, in Sejna's presence, the CIA handler directed the DIA officers not to refer to Sejna as General Sejna any longer because the Czechoslovak Politburo had 'taken away his rank'[19].

During Sejna's debriefing throughout 1968, and for many years thereafter, there was (and still is) no indication of any serious top-level US intelligence or national security interest in what he had to say[20]. He was not taken to meet any high CIA officials, such as Richard Helms, who was then the CIA director, or his deputies, or any key officials within the Operations Directorate, such as James Angleton, whose counter-intelligence office exercised cognisance over General Sejna from 1970 until the office was broken up in 1974. Nor, for that matter, was he taken to see any of Angleton's deputies, not even the one who was directly responsible for Sejna from 1970 to 1975. And while Sejna was scheduled to visit Congress on four or five different occasions, each time the visit was cancelled; why and by whom has not been divulged, but these are important questions.

Perhaps the most important inconsistency during Sejna's debriefing occurred in May 1968, when the former US Ambassador to the Soviet Union, Llewellyn Thompson, then a senior State Department adviser on Soviet affairs, came to visit him. Why such a high-ranking US State Department official would want to visit Sejna, given the way in which he was described and officially debriefed, is curious, to say the least. Did he visit Sejna on his own initiative, or in response to another person's request or suggestion? Thompson began the conversation by asking Sejna if he thought Communism was changing[21]. Sejna answered no. **The strategy, the objectives remain as set forth by Lenin. There had been no change in these objectives, and neither was any change likely, Sejna said.** Thompson responded sharply, advising Sejna that he, Sejna, was wrong. The conversation went downhill and soon ended.

Thompson was the only high-ranking official whom Sejna recalls came to see him. At the mid-level, things were no better. Only two individuals of moderate rank visited Sejna, the deputy head and the Czechoslovak desk officer of the CIA's Soviet Bloc division. Presumably, Sejna's debriefings would have been controlled by this division. But these two people apparently did not come to question Sejna, they came only to visit informally. Both spoke Czech, one having emigrated[22] from Czechoslovakia prior to World War II, the other having served as a military attaché in the US Embassy in Prague. Both were introduced to Sejna under false names, which Sejna immediately recognised because both individuals were among those that Sejna and other Czechoslovak officials had been warned about on numerous occasions during KGB counter-intelligence briefings that were a regular part of Czechoslovak and Soviet internal security practices.

Sejna, who had an extremely well-disciplined memory, recalled with ease their pictures, correct names and backgrounds as previously provided by the KGB. What these CIA officials were after or why they did not show any apparent interest in what Sejna really had to say, is not known. However, it is almost inconceivable that anyone in such a position would fail to recognise that Sejna was no ordinary defector and that his main value lay not in what he had to contribute to our understanding of Warsaw Pact *tactical* military matters but, rather, in his first-hand knowledge of matters of *strategic* importance; for example, Soviet political, military, and intelligence strategy and decision-making.

Indeed, that this was recognised by someone, would seem to explain a second visit by Ambassador Thompson. When the Soviets invaded Czechoslovakia in late August 1968, Sejna asked that he be allowed to speak out and explain to the American public and to statesmen around the globe what was happening in Czechoslovakia, including detailed background information on Soviet preparations for the invasion, which Sejna had recognised well in advance would probably take place. Sejna was most insistent, which was the reason behind Thompson's second visit. In this case, Thompson's visit was certainly not self-initiated. Thompson was summoned to discourage Sejna from telling his story to the public. He quickly explained to Sejna that it was not in the interests of the US Government to publish and describe what was happening. Sejna disagreed. Then Thompson communicated a clear threat. He told Sejna that Czechoslovakia had requested Sejna's return and that Prague's request might be honoured if Sejna were to make trouble. Sejna told Thompson that this was not possible because under the United Nations charter, the United States could not return him to Czechoslovakia or any other Soviet Bloc country. Again, the conversation deteriorated rapidly. When it was clear that he was not about to change Sejna's mind, Thompson advised Sejna that he should not tell the United States what we can do and abruptly terminated the meeting.

At this point, additional questions arise. Who called Thompson and requested his assistance, and why? Why was it not in the US interest to have the invasion explained to the US public and the rest of the world? Most importantly, *who was pulling the strings?*

In deference to Sejna's request, he was placed in contact with a reporter from the *New York Times*, Richard Eder, and offered the opportunity to go up to New York, at his (Sejna's) own expense and tell what he wanted to say. This he did, and then was shocked at the manner in which the interview was written up[23]. As Sejna described the articles, Eder did not use any of the most important facts behind the invasion, for example the seven months' advance preparation, twisted much of what Sejna had to say to compromise him, and lied about the interview in a manner that made Sejna look like a 'primitive'. He called Eder in New York and complained bitterly. Eder's reply was that it was not his fault. His editors were responsible for the final form of the article, he told Sejna.

Notwithstanding the nature of the reporting, a moderately informed reader would still have to wonder what else Sejna had to say about politically important events in which the Soviets had participated. Nor were the Eder articles the sole reason that someone should have reached (or clearly did reach) this conclusion. Neither does it seem credible that Sejna's information on the Long-Range Plan was overlooked merely by accident.

In the summer of 1968, one of Sejna's CIA handlers advised him to write his story, which could be published and provide him with a good income. Sejna set to work in the evenings writing his story. His son's fiancée typed the manuscript, which the CIA had translated into English as it was being produced. The manuscript, which ran to over 300 pages, was completed shortly before Christmas that year.

It did not deal with tactical military matters. It set forth Sejna's background, including the various positions he held, his steady interaction with the highest level Communist leaders from all countries, and, of special importance, the nature and dimensionality of Soviet long-range strategy and the world revolutionary process. Again, it is inconsistent with the nature of the intelligence process to believe that this material was not reviewed within the CIA division responsible for Sejna[24]. Nor does it seem likely that anyone with responsibilities for intelligence on Soviet Bloc operations could have read the document and not understood that here was a source of immense value (or danger, depending on one's perspective), and a defector who was being totally mis-debriefed.

When Sejna's first draft had been completed, in mid-December 1968, he gave a copy to the *Readers Digest*. Earlier, the CIA had allowed a *Readers Digest* editor to meet and interview Sejna. During their conversation, Sejna mentioned the book he was writing. The editor had asked to see a copy when it was finished[25]. Evidently they liked what they saw, because they prepared a contract to publish the book and five short articles, which Sejna signed.

What happened next is of paramount significance. As a senior member of James Jesus Angleton's counter-intelligence staff explained, almost immediately after President Nixon's inauguration in January 1969 a directive was sent from the White House to the CIA, ordering them to cease debriefing Sejna immediately and, in the process of getting rid of him, not to give him a job in the US Government. Even more amazing than this White House interest in a Czechoslovak defector *who had been so unimportant that he had only been worth debriefing about tactical military matters*, were the lengths to which the CIA went to implement the White House directive as fast as was humanly possible.

Sejna was told that the debriefings had been terminated and the next day he was moved out of the safe house. Without arranging for a new identity for Sejna, or paying any evident attention to Sejna's personal security, the CIA proceeded to help Sejna find a house to rent in Maryland. On almost his first day in the new house, the US Postal Service delivered an envelope addressed to 'General Sejna' from the real estate agent. It was his copy of the rental agreement. The actual rent, he learned, was more than the stipend he was receiving from the CIA. He next learned that his neighbour was a Bulgarian diplomat. Finally, in the process of locating a school for his son's fiancée's brother, who had defected in August 1968 and after several months had been reunited with his sister, he had asked the CIA to see if a local school was safe. He was told that they had checked it out and it was – only to learn later that the children of ten Czechoslovak diplomats were then attending the school. Can all this be excused as oversight, or as an unfortunate string of coincidences? Was he being taught a lesson? Or was the object to let the Soviets know where to find Sejna? Then he was told that there was no job for him in Washington – notwithstanding the initial agreement he had reached with the CIA which included productive employment, schooling for his son, and the stipulation that his son should not be drafted to serve in Vietnam (his son had a fused disc in his back), as conditions for Sejna's cooperation. The CIA reneged on all three provisions.

The whole manner in which Sejna's debriefings were first carefully controlled and restricted to the tactical military area, notwithstanding Sejna's suggestions of more important areas for inquiry, and then precipitously terminated, raises serious questions. It would seem that someone with control mechanisms deep within the CIA and with access to the White House knew that Sejna was an explosive time bomb that needed to be defused.

Clearly, Sejna's knowledge placed in jeopardy numerous Soviet Bloc operations, methods, agents and plans. The problem was certainly recognised by the controlling powers the instant his defection became known. It also seems that his importance was unlikely to have been known by CIA or White House officials because of limitations in their own background knowledge, as previously described. The debriefing process kept Sejna out of the way for a year; but the emergence of his manuscript could well have underscored the need to seek a more permanent solution. Whatever the cause, the same powers that controlled the process may have recognised that additional measures were required. Timing is the essence of success in intelligence work. The confusion within the (new) Nixon Administration provided an ideal cover for displacing the threat that Sejna represented; hence, the White House directive following the inauguration.

The question is, who took that decision? It seems reasonable to conclude that more than one person was involved, just as more than one person would have been needed to control the debriefing process so completely and effectively for ten months. The operation appears to have enjoyed advance CIA-White House coordination. That is, the skids appear to have been well greased. Otherwise, implementation by the CIA would not have proceeded so expeditiously, if at all. Might there have been a linkage between the completion of Sejna's manuscript and its submission to the *Reader's Digest*, or was everything planned months in advance, only waiting for the turmoil associated with the arrival of the new administration for its implementation?

As part of his book contract with the *Reader's Digest*, Sejna was to work with the *Digest* in writing five articles. The first was placed in motion in April 1969. It dealt with the seizure of the US intelligence collection ship, *Pueblo*, by the North Koreans on January 23, 1968. In the article[26]Sejna, set forth the time, place, and circumstances when he was informed by Marshal Andrei Grechko, the Soviet Minister of Defence, of the Soviet strategy to humble the US intelligence collection program.

Sejna described the entire Soviet strategy, including the logic underlying the use of the North Koreans and the Soviet excitement over the volume of intelligence they obtained when they briefed the top Czechoslovak leadership a few days before Sejna's departure for the West.

What was particularly unfortunate about the failure of US intelligence to have obtained the information about Soviet objectives and their use of North Korean intelligence is the possibility that the information, if obtained earlier, might have been used to avoid the shooting down of the US EC-121 reconnaissance plane which occurred over the Sea of Japan in April 1969.

Alternatively, it is also easy to understand why the US strategic leadership might not have liked what Sejna had to say. For example, in the article, he described the situation the day after the *Pueblo* was seized, when Soviet Colonel General Aleksandr Kushchev, the principal Soviet military adviser in Prague, explained to the most senior members of the Czechoslovak leadership what had happened:

'The entire operation went off smoothly – incredibly smoothly. The *Pueblo* crew, to a man, capitulated. They did not fire a shot. Frankly, we thought it would be much more complicated. The Americans were so bewildered that they failed to destroy thousands of documents. It will take our experts quite a while to analyse them. We've all heard about what a great communications and command system the Americans have, how they use computers, how they can respond instantly to an attack'.

'Well, yesterday it took Washington literally hours to pull itself together and even begin to react. This is a precise example of how the most advanced military technology cannot compensate for a lack of will and leadership'[27].

The *Preface* to the article by Jan Sejna was particularly interesting. After introducing the author, the editor acknowledged that the article had been excerpted from Sejna's forthcoming book and then stated: 'Much of what he reports here cannot be confirmed because of the rarefied circles in which he moved. But he has been interviewed at length by *Digest* editors, and specific references that could be cross-checked have been painstakingly investigated. No contradictions have been discovered'.

Similar findings were reported by Lord Chalfont in 1975, when he wrote the series of three articles for *The Times* of London, previously cited, based on interviews with Sejna. No-one, to my knowledge, including top US and British intelligence and counter-intelligence specialists who worked with Sejna, has ever found any honest reason to question

Sejna's *bona fides*. The *Reader's Digest* article also carried a concluding paragraph which the editor (possibly a different editor) added to Sejna's article. That paragraph read as follows:

'General Sejna's assertions were made available to the *Reader's Digest* last April 13, just two days before North Korean MIGs shot down a US Navy EC-121 reconnaissance plane in the Sea of Japan. No evidence exists at this writing that the Soviet Union had a hand in this second act of piracy perpetrated by the North Koreans within 15 months'.

Why did the *Reader's Digest* editor *suddenly call into question* Sejna's intelligence by now referring to what Sejna had to say as 'assertions'? Why did the editor further suggest that both acts of piracy were perpetrated by the North Koreans when Sejna had just finished explaining that the *Pueblo* affair was a Soviet-conceived and directed operation? And why did the editor suddenly and gratuitously suggest that there was no evidence that the Soviet Union was involved in the second act of piracy? If anything, the presumption should have been that the second act of piracy had merely been a continuation designed to capitalise on the success of the first act.

It was established as early as 1946 that Soviet intelligence set up, trained and directed North Korean intelligence. This Soviet direction continued with little diminution of control well beyond the *Pueblo* and EC-121 incidents. Moreover, the CIA had determined that the Soviets routinely passed data on the location of American ships in North Korean waters to North Korean intelligence[28].

Sejna confirms Soviet control of North Korean intelligence, and adds that North Korea was often used as a transfer country for bringing people covertly into Soviet Bloc countries[29]. Additionally, it may be relevant to recall that Soviet pilots are known to have flown North Korean planes in combat with the United States during the Korean War, although this fact was kept secret for many years.

One has to wonder: what was going on. Why would the *Digest* have wanted to undercut its own article?

All three Washington newspapers carried stories about Sejna's article and both the *Associated Press* and *United Press International* despatched stories on the international and domestic wires. Interestingly, the *New York Times* printed nothing. As the *Digest* editor who worked with Sejna in preparing the article wrote to him following publication of the article, 'Why [the *New York Times* ignored the article], I cannot imagine'.

As indicated earlier, after Sejna's debriefings were abruptly terminated, he was told that there was no job for him in the government. Soon thereafter, the CIA persuaded Sejna to accept a small lump-sum payoff and then arranged to have him relocated to Lake George, New York. The CIA also helped him obtain a restaurant, which he would then manage as his 'new life'. Who made the decision to move a former high-ranking Communist with no capitalist experience into a business in what has to be regarded as a particularly capitalistic region of New York State is another important unanswered question. Needless to say, Sejna's business failed, and within nine months he was destitute.

Repeated calls to the CIA for assistance went unanswered. Finally, in desperation and with his son's help, Sejna wrote a short letter to the director of the CIA, Richard Helms, explaining the tragic nature of his situation and offering his advice on how the CIA could change their approach to handling defectors so that this type of situation would be avoided in the future. The letter did generate action. The Czechoslovak-speaking member of the Soviet Bloc division of the CIA went up to Lake George and brought Sejna and his family back to Washington.

Before examining what happened after his return, it is important to recognise one positive accomplishment of Sejna's while he struggled to survive, capitalist style, in upstate New York. He redid the manuscript for his book in accordance with instructions from the *Reader's Digest* editor. The second draft was finished about the same time that Sejna had reached the end of his financial rope, in November 1969.

Subsequently, after his return to Washington, while he was trying to repair his own self-esteem, the *Reader's Digest* arranged to have an emigré Czech professor translate the new manuscript and also hired a full-time editor, whom they set up in the Sheraton Hotel in Washington for six months, at no small expense, to edit the translated manuscript.

By early summer, the manuscript had been completed and the New York *Reader's Digest* editor told Sejna that the manuscript was fine and needed no further editing. They would be back in touch with him in Washington in a few weeks. A few weeks went by with no word received. He telephoned to learn what was happening, and was told to go to the Washington office, where he was informed by the Washington editor that the *Readers' Digest* had decided not to publish the book for economic reasons. Sejna recalls the editor's simple explanation: 'It was not our decision'.

General Sejna's attempts to find a US publisher for the manuscript proved to be fruitless†. It was not until British intelligence offered to help that a publisher was found – a British publisher. Sejna's book, *We Will Bury You*, was finally published in 1982 by the London firm of Sidgwick & Jackson. Of course, by that time many people in the West regarded what Sejna had to say as ancient history.

When General Sejna was brought back to Washington at the end of 1969, his control was transferred to counter-intelligence under James Angleton. While there were some indications of a broader range of interest in Sejna's knowledge on the part of his handlers in counter-intelligence, he was, if anything, treated worse than he was in 1968 – when at least the debriefings were professional if not well-directed. At one point in time, he was asked to write several papers, and a CIA retiree who was a Czechoslovak defector was brought in to help translate and write down what Sejna had to say.

Among the information contained in those short papers were the first revelations on the Soviet Bloc's training of international terrorists; the penetration by Soviet Bloc intelligence services of organised crime; the Soviet use of sports organisations in connection with military intelligence operations; the formal agreement concerning Soviet direction and control of the satellite countries' intelligence services signed at a meeting in Moscow of the heads of the Soviet Bloc intelligence services in October 1964; deception and *maskirovka*; and recommendations on the use of narcotics against the United States' forces in Korea[30]. The reaction of Sejna's handler to all this information was:

'You are writing too much. I do not have time to read it. Stop it'[31].

During his 'tenure' in the counter-intelligence office, as another counter-intelligence officer explained, General Sejna was employed almost exclusively to read through count-

---

† *Editor's Note:* The same sterile and pointless game was played with a manuscript prepared by the genuine Soviet defector **Anatoliy Golitsyn**. After a fruitless search for a US publisher, a British publisher, Edward Harle Limited, who have produced the present work, was found; and *'The Perestroika Deception'* duly appeared [1995 and 1998]. Initially, this Editor also, misguidedly, sought a US publisher on behalf of Mr Golitsyn. On one occasion, a US organisation known to have intelligence community connections wrote a warm letter of commendation about the new Golitsyn work to a publisher in the Washington area, based upon the provisional contents list for the book which had been provided by the Editor. In a separate sentence, though, the writer added that 'personally I don't agree with it'. The lesson appears to be that genuine (as opposed to controlled) defectors to the United States who are dissatisfied with their treatment at the hands of US intelligence, and seek to publish the fruits of their labours and experience in the interests of truth and integrity, would be best advised to approach publishers in London from the outset, without wasting time doing the rounds in Washington.

less Soviet and East European newspapers and to write down on index cards the names of any US citizens appearing in the articles. As a secondary activity, he was sent to numerous foreign countries to brief their officials on Soviet strategy. On these visits General Sejna encountered receptive and appreciative audiences.

Other than this, and the abortive attempt to draft the papers described above, the only attempts to tap Sejna's vast knowledge were the debriefings undertaken by British counter-intelligence, substantial elements of which were ultimately incorporated into his manuscript. There were no detailed debriefings by the CIA counter-intelligence staff.

It is also relevant in reviewing this matter to recognise that General Sejna is not a unique example of US failure to debrief and handle a key defector properly. The failure of the CIA to make good use of defectors became sufficiently well-known that Congressional hearings were held on the subject, and in 1985 the President's Foreign Intelligence Advisory Board began to look into the matter.

The handling of Yuri Nosenko and of Anatoliy Golitsyn[32] are two of the best-known cases, but difficult to deal with because of the serious counter-intelligence implications. Suffice it to say that the CIA failed seriously to debrief a defector whom British intelligence considered to be the most important defector of the time. Vladimir Sakharov[33], who was one of the first defectors to 'go public' with his story of mishandling and CIA tradecraft incompetence, played an important rôle in drawing attention to the mishandling issue.

Lt. General Ion Pacepa[34] is another interesting example which bears certain similarities to Sejna's case. Pacepa was a high-ranking Romanian intelligence official. David B. Funderburk was US Ambassador to Romania from 1981 to 1985. In his book about his tenure as Ambassador[35], Funderburk described his attempts to curtail Romania's policy of stealing technology from the West. Evidence on these transfers dated back to the mid-1960s, consistently with Romania's increased ties with the West.

Funderburk explained: 'While I am not at liberty to present the intelligence information which documents case after case, I can say that Pacepa has publicly reported on many of them. Also, I was told at a CIA briefing during the summer of 1984 that Pacepa was never asked questions about tech transfer by US intelligence when he came out in 1978. This seems like a strange omission'. Strange, because technology theft was one of Pacepa's principal responsibilities. Funderburk also indicated that when Pacepa began reporting on Romania's technology theft operations, the State Department initiated a discrediting operation. However, 'the State Department can continue using minute discrepancies to discredit all of Pacepa's revelations, but it will not erase reports he has made which ditto other evidence US intelligence already has'[36].

While most of these cases can be dismissed as mishandling or examples of an anti-defector bias, Sejna's case stands apart because of his extensive knowledge and experience at the highest levels throughout the Communist system. My conclusion is that it is totally unreasonable to attempt to excuse what happened to Sejna (and continued happening until his death in 1997 – Ed.) as simply poor tradecraft, sloppy technique, the results of distrust of defectors within US intelligence, or mere incompetence.

On the contrary, it seems clear that Sejna was handled, at least during his formal debriefing in 1968, in an extremely professional manner, albeit not in accordance with the United States' interests. It seems equally clear that what Sejna had to say was contrary to *détente* and could have done great damage to Soviet strategy and Soviet intelligence operations – if only someone had listened to him and acted on this vital information.

This is the critical point. Certainly in the beginning, and continuing up to the time that the CIA terminated their relationship with Sejna in the mid-1970s, the only people who really knew how important Sejna's knowledge was, would seem to have been the Czechoslovak and Soviet Defence Councils.

The detailed nature of General Sejna's knowledge can be deduced from the forego-ing chapters. Nor does this material represent the limit of Sejna's knowledge of Soviet Bloc drug operations. I have left out considerable material which was not essential to this story; for example, names of specific individuals who were directing and running differ-ent phases of the operations, details on many of the drug-related meetings and plans, and Soviet Bloc operations in Africa, the Middle East, Europe, South Asia and the Far East.

Furthermore, the Soviet Bloc's drugs strategy was not the only area where Sejna could offer detailed knowledge. On the contrary, as a result of his position, Sejna's overall knowledge was known to be encyclopaedic. The narcotics data represented but a small sampling. His knowledge covered a wide variety of Communist military, intelligence, political plans, operations, strategies and tactics[37].

It is also important to recognise that what General Sejna had to say has been con-firmed time after time – the material on Soviet training, supply and financing of interna-tional terrorists being a typical example.

Another enlightening instance of the accuracy of Sejna's revelations in the public domain was the Czech defector's report on the successful Soviet use of West European news media to discredit Franz Josef Strauss. The details of that operation and the success-ful efforts of Sir James Goldsmith to confirm Sejna's information are presented in Chap-man Pincher's book, *Secret Offensive*[38]. Moreover, in discussions with various intelligence officials *who have worked with Sejna and studied his data*, I have not uncovered a shred of evidence that any of these officials know of any data provided by Sejna that had been shown to be suspect, deliberately misleading or false [*see also page 120*].

There has been a continuing attempt by CIA professionals over the years to discredit General Sejna. The campaign began almost as soon as his debriefings started and has never really ceased. Among the more important instances were attempts in the early 1980s to discredit Sejna's testimony on the Soviet involvement in international terrorism. A more typical example was the statement by a CIA mid-level official in 1986 to some researchers at the Fletcher School of Law and Diplomacy who were taking Sejna's testi-mony in an oral history project. The official referred to Sejna as only a 'two-bit whore'; in effect, advising them not to pay any attention to what General Sejna had to say.

As Sejna's expertise in various areas of strategic importance has surfaced over the years, intelligence specialists ask why he did not tell us about something before – or other-wise discredit the information by suggesting that he became smarter with age. It was clear that, as a general rule, neither the intelligence nor the national security policy community liked what Sejna had to say. He was viewed, not as an expert from whom to learn, but as a threat to entrenched policies and institutional misperceptions about how the Communist system works. But most of all, he was **a threat to Communist political subversion strategy**.

Thus, the question is not, why did he not tell us these things before? The answer to that question is that **no-one asked, no-one wanted to know, and many wanted not to know**. The real questions are, why do people not want to know; why was there no attempt to debrief him seriously or even to learn the total spectrum of his knowledge? Why were false rumours spread in a campaign to prevent others from listening to what he had to say? Who was behind the concerted campaign to bury Sejna's knowledge? And, why does this process continue even today?

I repeat: How on earth could a major global Soviet Bloc intelligence offensive, such as the Soviet drugs operation, have been underway for so long without the United States knowing what was happening? This crucial question has a simple answer. No-one in the US Government with the authority or responsibility to take action evidently wanted to know, or wants to know. Indeed, they wanted **not** to know. This is still true today and knowledge of this reality provides one of my motivations for writing this book.

Are there other important examples where Sejna's knowledge is ignored? Yes, numerous ones: for example, Soviet decision-making; Soviet long-range strategy; Soviet strategic deception practices; Soviet Bloc intelligence operations; Soviet revolutionary war strategy; Soviet penetration and use of organised crime; Soviet penetration and subversion of political parties, especially the Social Democrats; and Soviet sponsorship of international terrorism, to mention just a few areas of the defector's expertise. General Sejna's knowledge about these (and other) subjects was not unprecedented in the sense that there are other sources with considerable detailed information about them.

What *was* unique however, and virtually unprecedented in the case of Sejna, was his high-level perspective. He was able to explain the overall operations and strategy, which then enables the analyst to understand how the various details from other sources and from seemingly independent subject areas relate and fit together. That is, he provided the overall picture which gives meaning to the individual pieces of information provided by the many lower-level sources.

While Sejna defected in 1968, his broad knowledge is especially important now in understanding the cataclysmic changes that are taking place. **His high-level understanding of how the Communist system handled previous changes and of how organisations are split apart and reconstituted in different forms, specifically to deceive the West about the nature of the changes, should be most valuable today.** One context would be in understanding the alleged 'dismantling' of the various secret intelligence agencies and the mechanisms by which various government agencies in satellite countries are 'controlled' by Moscow.

These disturbing errors of omission bring to mind additional insights provided during a colloquium on intelligence in 1987 by Ken de Graffenreid. De Graffenreid was responsible for intelligence on the National Security Council staff from 1981 to 1987. He identified what was in his view a significant US counter-intelligence problem; namely, that **many US officials oppose activities aimed at combating Soviet intelligence operations**. 'When I was at the NSC' he explained, 'one example was the insistence of many State Department colleagues that little serious effort, diplomatic or otherwise, should be directed at the KGB threat within the United States. They argued that doing so would 'upset US-Soviet relations''.

Still further, de Graffenreid explained that 'whatever the policy during my years at the White House (1981-1987), the State Department, to my knowledge, opposed at least initially every one of the hundreds of recommendations for dealing with the hostile intelligence threat presented within the government'[39]. This opposition to action against Soviet Bloc intelligence agents, particularly the KGB and GRU, was a source of contention long before 1981. The FBI continually encountered problems obtaining PNG (*persona non grata*) action approval. The same is true in the drug business. In his letter of resignation dated July 31, 1989, the outgoing US Customs Commissioner William von Raab wrote: 'For the past eight years, the State Department has objected to every effort to control foreign drug production, thus earning the title the 'conscientious objectors' in the war on drugs'[40].

The second characteristic of US intelligence which helps explain the evident lack of attention directed to Soviet drug-trafficking strategy concerns the perceptions among US decision-makers and advisers about how the Communist system operates – especially the coordination that takes place between Soviet intelligence operations and those of its satellites, and the mechanisms by which the satellite operations are initiated and controlled. There are two important questions. The first concerns internal control. When several officials of a Communist country are involved in drug-trafficking, is the government of the country involved? The second concerns external control and the degree to which the Soviet Union is responsible for the actions of its satellites.

Communist systems are noted for their effective internal control mechanisms. This is one of the primary functions of the notorious secret police. People are required to spy on their associates, even on their parents. Additionally there are important organisations the function of which is the organisation of spying on the nation's own citizens. Organisations that keep watch over their own citizens include the secret police or civilian counter-intelligence and, in the case of the military, military counter-intelligence, and the Main Political Administration. There are also a variety of lesser-known Party organs, especially with respect to keeping watch over the watchers; that is, a counter-counter-intelligence agency. As Sejna described the situation, every person is watched three ways. So it is inconceivable that any individual would be engaged in significant narcotics trafficking without the knowledge, approval, and participation of the State.

It is quite true that there are corruption and illegal operations in Communist countries. But it is not true that they are not known. Rather, they are known and are tolerated. Indeed, toleration of certain illegal activities is the only way the Communist system is able to survive. Additionally, corruption is, in a sense, *desired* because people who are corrupted can usually be blackmailed or intimidated, and as such are easier to direct and control. The question of what is tolerated revolves around the furtherance of State policy. Many vices are accepted. The black market is generally tolerated. Indiscriminate use of women by high-ranking officials is tolerated. But corruption that would negatively impinge on State policy, corruption that is regarded as treasonous, is not tolerated. Certainly the large-scale trafficking in drugs and associated money-laundering would not be tolerated because it would place State policy at risk.

To the extent that it is tolerated, it is absorbed into a parent intelligence operation where it can be carefully monitored and controlled. The idea of Cuban officials being involved as they are, or the Bulgarians, or Nicaraguans, or Vietnamese, or North Koreans and so forth, without official direction and control, is *simply not a reasonable proposition.* These countries do not simply 'facilitate' or 'condone' the trafficking. **They authorise, direct and control the trafficking as an official State activity.**

Fixing the responsibility for satellite intelligence operations is a more difficult but an equally important task. Indeed, it is essential, and not just because of the drug business. The Soviets habitually use satellites and surrogates as agents in implementing Soviet intelligence operations. This has been pointed out to US officials by numerous defectors from Soviet and Soviet Bloc intelligence services. There are several reasons; some are obvious, some not so obvious. The obvious reason, and one most often provided by defectors in trying to explain what is happening, is to afford the Soviet Union *distance and deniability* in potentially embarrassing operations. Certainly, drug-trafficking is an excellent example of such a deniable operation. Assassinations with a high risk of disclosure is another good example. Minimising the associated political risk is also a reason for using Third World country surrogates – as was explained by Janos Kadar, First Secretary of the Hungarian Communist Party, in the proposal he made at the 1962 Moscow meeting (Chapter 4).

Less obvious factors are that in many ways the Soviet satellite services are more imaginative and competent than the Soviet intelligence services themselves. Satellite countries often have skills and knowledge that are lacking or scarce in the Soviet Union. The satellite services also have better ethnic ties into many countries, for example into the Middle East or Latin America. These ties are exploited in setting up intelligence operations. And finally, most countries are inherently suspicious of the Soviets, but not of satellite citizens, who tend to be regarded as victims, not co-conspirators. All these factors led to the development of effective and operationally utilised satellite intelligence services, of which the Czechoslovak intelligence service was an especially good example. This underscores the importance of Sejna's knowledge. As secretary of the Defence Council, Sejna participated in the annual review and approval of the one-year intelligence plans and during the Party Congresses, in the five-year and fifteen-year intelligence plans.

The critical question, then, is, to what extent are these satellite services independent? If the Bulgarians or Cubans are trafficking in drugs, as they are, are the Soviets tied in or responsible? This type of question had bothered US intelligence early on. As explained by the late James Angleton, the legendary head of US counter-intelligence until his organisation was broken up in December 1974: 'Since 1948, we [the CIA and its sister services in Britain, France and West Germany] found sufficient evidence of coordination [among Soviet, Bulgarian, East German, Libyan, Cuban, Hungarian, Romanian and Polish intelligence] over extended periods to satisfy even the sceptics'[41].

Angleton then identified the two critical aspects of the continued reluctance of US officials to make the connection. 'It may be *politically convenient* to assume that Soviet bloc intelligence services act independently of the Soviet Union, especially when it concerns an assassination, but what we don't really know, or perhaps want to know, is what is the nature of the relationship between the KGB and the other Communist intelligence services?'[42]. 'Politically convenient' is an understatement. Many policymakers simply did not (do not) want to know or admit the relationships between the Soviet and the satellite intelligence services. Admission would restrict policy options, particularly the release of strategically important materials and technology.

The actual nature of the relationship is another significant element of information that has been supplied by Sejna. Soviet control over satellite intelligence organisations was formally established, he explained to me, when the satellite intelligence service chiefs met in secret in Moscow on October 3rd, 1964, and signed an agreement establishing a Warsaw Pact 'integrated intelligence system'. **Under the terms of the agreement, all satellite intelligence activities would be coordinated by Moscow.** All operational plans – the long-range fifteen-year plans, the five-year plans that were coordinated with the five-year funding budget, and the one-year plans – would be approved by the Soviets. The Soviets would determine when satellite services would cooperate on operations and would also coordinate all the activities of the satellite Departments of Special Propaganda. All collected intelligence was to be passed immediately to Moscow and the Soviets would then determine all subsequent distribution. Of special importance for drug and narcotics trafficking, in addition to the requirement for all plans to be approved by the Soviets, was the stipulation that strategic intelligence agents would be trained in the USSR.

These arrangements provide an illustration of a few of the mechanisms by which the Soviets maintain control of their satellites. Operations such as drug-trafficking, assassinations, and strategic espionage are not undertaken except by Soviet direction. Formulation of the one-, five- and 15-year plans is, overall, among the most important control mechanisms, insofar as all activities are planned well in advance, and even new, 'emergency' actions need to be approved in the same manner as the regular plans before they can be implemented[43].

Cuban intelligence, which had worked closely with Czechoslovak and other Soviet satellite intelligence services since the early 1960s, was *de facto* incorporated into the integrated intelligence system in 1967, Sejna reported. The one-year intelligence plans were formulated and approved in the fall. It was during this review process in November 1967 that Sejna recognised that the Cuban intelligence plan was not independent but had been incorporated into the Warsaw Pact integrated intelligence system.

As such, then, Cuban operations were coordinated and controlled by the Soviets. Previously, control had been more indirect, provided by the presence of advisers and spies. These are the informal controls that are present within all Marxist-Leninist control structures – the combinations of Soviet advisers and both intelligence and counter-intelligence agents who are covertly positioned at critical places in satellite and surrogate organisations. These people provide both an advisory control and a covert reporting mechanism employed to keep the Soviets informed.

The mechanisms described by Sejna can be seen in operation in the testimony of numerous defectors and other intelligence sources. For example, former Cuban intelligence agents have testified that since about 1970, the Cuban intelligence service has been under the direct control of the Soviets. They have also testified that all plans are sent to the Soviet Union for approval. Cubans and Nicaraguans described the controls over Nicaraguan intelligence in similar terms. Cuban advisers hold key positions and wear uniforms indistinguishable from the Nicaraguans.

There are also some 100 Soviet military security advisers, along with 25 Bulgarians, 40-50 East Germans, 25 PLO specialists and a few Libyans within the Nicaraguan service[44]. Similar controls with respect to the PLO have also been reported. According to the Defense Intelligence Agency [DIA], the Kuwaiti News Agency published a long interview with the PLO's Moscow representative, who said: **'We have a signed a treaty that requires that before we take any kind of serious action, we sit down and discuss it with the Russians and coordinate our activities'**[45]. Senator Alfonse D'Amato (R-NY) cites other US intelligence studies showing that 'the KGB controls most of the operating sections of the DS, which is the Bulgarian secret police. The Soviets have used the Bulgarians as surrogates'. He also cites DEA estimates that 25 percent of the heroin reaching the United States comes through Bulgaria[46].

These are but a few of the many relevant instances of Soviet control, especially with respect to the East European satellites, but including quasi-satellites and surrogates as well[47]. In some countries where autonomy still exists, for example, Vietnam, Laos and Suriname, there are uncertainties. But insofar as Cuba, Nicaragua, North Korea, Bulgaria, Hungary, Poland, East Germany and Czechoslovakia are concerned, the presumption should be that the Soviets are not only involved, but at least until recently were fully responsible.

The only serious question, then, is why, when the activities of these key Soviet satellite intelligence services are brought out into the open, the behind-the-scenes rôle of the Soviets is rarely discussed? The answer to that question is implicit in the preceding chapter and in the preceding discussion of General Sejna's debriefing process. People simply do not want to know – as Angleton explained, for reasons of 'political convenience'. It would perhaps be reassuring if this were the *only* reason. Unfortunately, that does not appear to be the case. While 'political convenience' is certainly a factor, there also seem to be much more sinister and deadly possibilities at work – possibilities that suggest the need for a detailed investigation into the reasons why General Major Jan Sejna was never debriefed. **But who would conduct the investigation?** ■

References to Chapter 10:

1. See for example, the initial debriefings of Golitsyn and Nosenko at the Frankfurt facility, notwithstanding the very important nature of both defectors, in Epstein, *Deception, op. cit.*, pages 59, 67. The facility, which is referred to as Westport Station, is described in William R. Corson, Susan B. Trento, and Joseph J. Trento, *Widows* (New York: Crown Publishers, Inc., 1989), pages 167, 415-416.

2. Even the Czechoslovak emigré press, including so-called CIA proprietary operations, was utilised in this smear campaign, which continued for many years.

3. Rank in Communist countries can be misleading. What is important is *position*, not rank. Sejna's rank was General Major, equivalent to a US Brigadier General. In terms of the positions Sejna held, he outranked most four-star generals. In his position as Secretary of the Defence Council, Sejna participated in the annual reviews of all the most sensitive plans: the operations plan, the technical espionage plan, the weapons systems development and acquisition plan, the training program and schedule, the special (secret) budget, the intelligence plan, the materiel and supply plan and the mobilisation plan. He also participated in the review, evaluation, and future planning of deception operations. All these plans were coordinated with Soviet and other Warsaw Pact force planning which gave General Sejna substantial insights into the Soviet counterpart plans. See also *endnote 7*.

4. For example, Sejna was not a Stalinist. Indeed, he was the first Czechoslovak leader openly to denounce Stalinist practices at a meeting of the Central Committee in 1954. His impromptu speech led to the removal of the Minister of Defence, Alexei Cepicka, who was widely feared because of his Stalinist tactics. Sejna was not a public school dropout; the public school was closed when the Germans invaded Czechoslovakia. Sejna did not lead a coup against the new 'Liberal' leadership; he was working against Soviet interference with the developments inside Czechoslovakia.

Indeed, this is what led to his defection. The KGB had learned that Sejna was warning Dubcek about Soviet plans to tighten up (a process that peaked with the invasion in mid-August). His Party committee was denounced in the newspaper *Obrana Lidu* (Defence of the People), the official party newspaper, in a manner that was tantamount to a charge of treason. Sejna recognised immediately that a web intended to trap him was being woven. Later in the morning, a friend warned him that his immunity as a member of the Presidium was to be lifted on Monday, two days hence, so that he could be taken into custody and implicated in black market fraud charges that had been brought against one of Sejna's staff five weeks earlier. From his knowledge of police operations and their ability to manufacture evidence, Sejna knew that if the Secret Police had been told to bring charges and obtain a confession, they would succeed. He defected the next day, Sunday, when he reasoned that the border guards would be least alert. Sejna was not promoted through favouritism. The military units of which he was deputy commander as political commissar consistently achieved the highest merit ratings. Nor was he not liked by his colleagues, who applauded the informal announcement of his promotion to General.

5. 'Czechoslovakia: Tip of the Iceberg', *Newsweek*, March 18, 1968.

6. The commissar is an official of the Communist Party within the military. Consider, for example Henry Kissinger's description of the Party: 'The small group of votaries who arrogate to themselves superior insight into the processes of history derive from this conviction the monomaniacal intensity required to make revolution. But once they are firmly established in power, what is their function? They are not needed to run the government or the economy or the military'.

'They are guardians of a political legitimacy that has long since lost its moral standing as well as its revolutionary élan. They specialise in solving internal crises that their centralised system has created and external crises into which their rigidity tempts them. The Party apparatus duplicates every existing hierarchy without performing any function. Its members are watchdogs lacking criteria, an incubus to enforce order, a smug bastion of privilege inviting corruption and cynicism'. *Years of Upheaval* (New York: Little, Brown and Company, 1982), page 244.

7. Colonel Penkovskiy, who spied for the CIA from April 1961 until his arrest during the Cuban Missile Crisis, referred to the head of the Administrative Organs, General Major Nikolai Mironov, as 'an all powerful tsar and god over the GRU and KGB, one before whom even General Serov [then head of the GRU] stood at attention'. John J. Dziak, *Chekisty: A History of the KGB* (Lexington, Massachusetts: Lexington Books, 1988), page 151.

8. The Defence Council is the highest decision-making party body with authority over defence, national security, intelligence, counter-intelligence, foreign policy, and the economy. It is a far more important organisation than the Politburo.

9. For example, Sejna's debriefers did not understand how socialism worked, as evidenced by their asking him for the names of his family lawyer and family doctor, which do not exist as such in the Communist system.

Nor did they believe that the high quality suit he wore when he defected could have been purchased in Prague. Evidently they were unaware of the special stores available to high-ranking officials. They had only vague knowledge about the existence of the Defence Council and no appreciation of its true function or importance, and no knowledge of how promotions are organised through the system known as nomenclature. Additionally, they had many false impressions of how the system operated – for example, the idea that promotions and positions were generally the result of nepotism and that selection and training were of little importance, a mis-impression that still characterises the Western perception of the Soviet system.

10. This point was also recognised by Claire Sterling in *The Terror Network: The Secret War of International Terrorism* (New York: Holt, Rinehart and Winston, 1981), page 290. 'Debriefed at length in Washington, he [General Sejna] had been questioned only about military matters regarding the Soviet and Warsaw Pact armies; terrorism was not a Western worry in 1968, and nobody even asked him about it'. Sejna had identified the rôle of the Soviet Union in international terrorism in roughly 1971 when he was under the control of Angleton's counter-intelligence division, but was not debriefed on the subject. He provided the first detailed information on the subject, in an interview conducted by Michael Ledeen in 1980, and was subsequently debriefed in detail by Defense Intelligence Agency [DIA] analysts. Throughout this process, the CIA officials with responsibility in the area continued attempts to discredit Sejna and his information – which was confirmed by their own most sensitive sources in nearly all respects, and by court testimony taken in Italy.

11. Similar frustrations (debriefings by the Soviet Bloc Division related to trivia rather than to items of importance) are reported by Epstein to be the reason **Major Anatoliy Golitsyn** requested resettlement in Great Britain. Epstein, *Deception, op. cit.*

12. General Sejna brought with him detailed analyses which had been conducted by the Czechoslovak Ministry of Defence of the Czech Air Force, ground forces, personnel management, mobilisation system and Military Intelligence; an analysis of developments in the world and the Warsaw Pact in the future, by the Main Political Administration and Science Administration and, based on these analyses, military policy after the 13th Party Congress; and Presidium analyses of the Czechoslovak economy.

13. The failure to make such information available is, in reality, not unusual. Important material is often not made available to intelligence analysts, and the reason is not security – examples being **Golitsyn** and **Pacepa**. Even worse, false information is often distributed, without the knowledge of the analytical side of the intelligence community, **Penkovskiy** being a case in point.

14. This Soviet plan was transmitted to the East European satellites in 1967 for them to use as the basis for their development of their own coordinated long-range plans. Distribution was tightly controlled. Only two copies were available within Czechoslovakia. Sejna had one copy. It was his responsibility to ensure that the Ministry of Defence's planners received proper instruction and that their work fully complied with the requirements of the Soviet plan.

15. There has been a continuing effort, especially within US policymaking circles, to ridicule the notion of Soviet planning or grand strategy, an awareness and understanding of which is a *sine qua non* for meaningful and relevant strategic analysis. For example, as Henry Kissinger explained: '**I sent the President an analysis of Soviet policy at the end of 1969, which I prepared with the help of Hal Sonnenfeldt and Bill Hyland of my staff. It began by rejecting the proposition that Soviet policy necessarily followed a master plan'.** Henry Kissinger, *White House Years* (Boston, Massachusetts: Little, Brown & Company, 1979), page 161. Hyland was previously a senior CIA analyst. John Ranelagh, *The Agency: The Rise and Decline of the CIA* (New York: Simon and Schuster, 1986), page 509. While what is meant by a 'master plan' is not explained here by Kissinger, the detailed lay-out of Soviet revolutionary objectives, strategy, tactics and assignments was contained in the 'Long-Range Plan for the Next Ten to Fifteen Years and Beyond' that General Sejna identified to his debriefers.

British counter-intelligence officials debriefed Sejna in 1970 on Soviet strategy in various regions of the world, especially Europe. *One of the areas they concentrated on was the ease with which Czechoslovak and Soviet intelligence services had penetrated the British Labour Party and UK Government structures – particularly the Foreign Office, the Colonial Office and the intelligence services*. A copy of their write-up of Sejna's data was provided to US counter-intelligence. The regions that received the least attention in the British debriefings were the United States and Latin America. Yet there was no CIA counter-intelligence attempt to follow up and extend this work for the United States and Latin America. This was the only analysis that dealt with the Soviet long-range plan, but it did not begin to cover the important objective and policy objectives element of the plan. A project to debrief General Sejna on the whole plan was begun in 1978 under Dr Gene Durbin, in the US Defense Department's Office of Net Assessment. Dr Durbin left the office shortly after the project was started. After the first section of the plan, the political objectives element, had been completed, the funding was cut off and the project terminated.

Editor's Note: A detailed summary of the long-range plan as described by General Sejna diverges, but is nevertheless paradoxically dialectically complementary to, the long-range plan as unfolded by Anatoliy Golitsyn in his two books, *New Lies for Old* and *The Perestroika Deception* [*op. cit.*]. However Golitsyn's analysis focused primarily upon strategic deception, identified as the core of the plan, and on long-term preparations for the dismantling of the Stalinist model of control ahead of its replacement, following Gorbachëv's *perestroika* (meaning *reformation*, as in *a military formation*), by an upgraded and revitalised Leninist model of global revolution. By contrast, Sejna's long-range strategy was plainly formulated within a neo-Stalinist framework, even though Sejna himself denounced Stalinism. This suggests that – as would be expected among Leninists, for whom the dialectical *modus operandi*, or dualism, is routine practice – the coexistence of two or more long-range strategic plans. They would not have been intended to be, nor would they have been conceived as being, mutually exclusive. While General Sejna's version has been superseded, the 'general line' (strategy) remains unchanged.

16. Lord Chalfont's articles in *The Times* (London) were: 'Moscow's Brutal Reality' (July 28, 1975); 'How Israel Fits into the Jigsaw of Soviet Power' (August 4, 1975); and 'How Britain's Economic Difficulties Help the Soviet Grand Strategy' (September 1, 1975).

17. Walter Hahn, 'A Soviet Game-Plan?', *Strategic Review*, Spring 1983.

18. As explained by Aleksandr Yakovlev, chairman of the Foreign Commission of the Central Committee of the CPSU and a top adviser to President Gorbachëv, on November 18, 1988, with reference to *glasnost*, **there was to be no change in the basic values and strategic aims and intentions of Soviet foreign policy. Only the tactics were to be changed.** 'USSR's Yakovlev Answers Questions in Prague', FBIS-EEU-88224, November 21, 1988, page 11.

19. In 1988, the Politburo must have reversed their decision, insofar as the Czechoslovak Party newspaper began referring to him as General Sejna once again.

20. The United States is unique in this respect. During the early 1970s, Sejna was permitted to travel abroad to discuss his knowledge of Soviet strategy with officials of friendly foreign countries, where he met and exchanged views with many high-ranking officials. In all instances, where there was operational knowledge, it confirmed what General Sejna had to say.

21. After every change in the Soviet leadership, there is a attempt in the West to identify change in the Soviet Union/'former' Soviet Union. As Harriet Fast Scott and William F. Scott explained in *Soviet Military Doctrine: Continuity, Formulation and Dissemination* (Boulder, Colorado: Westview Press, 1988), page 47: 'Khrushchev's ouster in 1964 had been greeted with a sigh of relief. It was felt that Brezhnev was more sensible and reasonable. Therefore, when the third edition of *Military Strategy* appeared in 1968, very little changed from earlier editions, this was not welcomed abroad by those seeking an arms control agreement with Moscow'. As an example of how this book was handled, consider the following passage in a letter dated September 11, 1968 from CIA deputy director Vice Admiral Rufus L. Taylor to the Commander of the Air Force Foreign Technology Headquarters: 'I have browsed through it [the book] and found parts of it to be of some interest. Our people, as do I, have mixed feelings about the validity and influence of him [Marshal V. D. Sokolovskiy] in Soviet military circles'. At the time, Ambassador Thompson was one of the leading proponents of the changes taking place in the Soviet Union. He was also, on directions received earlier from Secretary of Defence McNamara, engaged in arms control talks with the Soviets on ballistic missile defence in an attempt to head off US deployment of an anti-ballistic missile defence system. Phyllis Schlafly and Chester Ward, *Kissinger on the Couch* (New Rochelle, New York: Arlington House, 1975), page 315. Thompson died on 6th February 1972.

22. It is startling, to an outsider, how many Czechoslovak emigrés or defectors (at least four, according to my count) were enabled by the CIA to interact with Sejna and assist him in various phases of his debriefings and relocations. My concern is the difficulty in establishing *bona fides* beyond a doubt, especially given the evident ease with which trained Communist agents can pass the CIA polygraph. In general, defectors are reluctant to interact with other defectors for this very reason. In the late 1970s the FBI identified a Czechoslovak defector, Karl F. Koecher, as a Czechoslovak intelligence service officer who had penetrated the CIA.

Koecher passed the CIA polygraph, was hired by the CIA, and assigned to the Operations Directorate to translate cables from agents, an extremely sensitive assignment. Another example of a defector with an extremely sensitive assignment was Paul Bellin – a Soviet defector, who became a CIA polygraph examiner! Corson, Trento and Trento, *Widows, op. cit.*, pages 48-49, 125. See also Ronald Kessler, *Moscow Station* (New York: Charles Scribner's Sons, 1989, page 195). While the CIA is notorious for its mishandling of defectors (that is, treating them like dirt), it is clear that this is not a consistent policy and, indeed, that some defectors are given inside jobs of the highest sensitivity.

23. Richard Eder, 'Anti-Dubcek Rôle Denied by General Who Fled Prague', *New York Times*, August 26,1968, and 'Sejna Says Novotny's Errors Led to Liberalisation in Prague', *New York Times*, August 28, 1968. It was a Defence Intelligence Agency (DIA) employee, not the CIA, who brought the articles to Sejna's attention, translated them for him, and then helped Sejna call Eder and complain about the articles.

24. At the same time, if one wanted to perform a general debriefing outside the normal debriefing process, that is, without any follow-up questions and without the material finding its way into the Intelligence Reports that are produced during the debriefing process, this might be an excellent approach. The basic concept of having a defector write down a detailed history of his activities as an integral part of the debriefing process is a normal and excellent technique, but this does not appear to have been the approach in the case of Sejna.

25. The *Reader's Digest* was also used by the CIA to provide a mechanism for the Soviet defector Yuri Nosenko to 'tell his story' about Lee Harvey Oswald and the Kennedy assassination. In this case, the *Reader's Digest* proposed the book idea to Edward Jay Epstein, and offered to put him in contact with Nosenko in 1976. Nosenko had been the focus of a major dispute within the CIA. His *bona fides* were not established, at least not until *after* Angleton's counter-intelligence organisation was broken up. As Epstein described the situation, almost every intelligence official involved with the Nosenko case had his career wrecked. Epstein, *Deception, op. cit.*, page 62.

26. General Jan Sejna, 'Russia Plotted the Pueblo Affair', *Reader's Digest*, July 1969.

27. *Ibid.*, page 75.

28. Epstein, *Deception, op. cit.*, page 282.

29. In roughly 1962, Czechoslovakia signed an agreement with North Korea to provide North Korea with technology and intelligence in return for North Korea serving as a transit point for the covert movement of people to Eastern Europe.

30. The individual identified as making the suggestion was Colonel Karel Borsky, who, as identified in Chapter 2, was the Zs chief in charge of the drug-trafficking training centres. See pages 27 and 31.

31. He also asked Sejna to misrepresent certain aspects concerning Soviet deception planning so that

Angleton would find the information more acceptable. Sejna refused to compromise his integrity in this and other similar episodes.

32. See, for example, Epstein, *Deception, op. cit.*, pages 70-74.

33. Vladimir Sakharov, *High Treason* (New York: Ballantine Books, 1980).

34. Lt. General Ion Mihai Pacepa, *Red Horizons: Chronicles of a Communist Spy Chief* (Washington, D.C.: Regnery Gateway, 1987).

35. David B. Funderburk, *Pinstripes and Reds: An American Ambassador Caught Between the State Department and the Romanian Communists, 1981-85* (Washington, D.C.: Selous Foundation Press, 1987).

36. *Ibid.*, page 46.

37. For example, areas on which General Sejna had detailed knowledge that I am personally aware of and on which, with a few notable exceptions, there was no systematic effort to debrief him include:

● Organisation, rôle, and function of the Defence Council.
● Penetration of foreign governments and bourgeois political parties, notably the Social Democrats.
● Soviet interests in hiding missile development/deployment .
● Methods of covert military research and development .
● Mobilisation mechanisms and planning.
● Use of terrorism in revolutionary war strategy.
● Training of international terrorists.
● Soviet Bloc strategy for penetrating/using organised crime.
● Details of Soviet long-range strategy.
● Mechanism for development and use of 1-, 5- and 15-year plans.
● Peaceful coexistence deception strategy.
● Military technology requirements and acquisition process.
● Details on intelligence planning and plans.
● Soviet Bloc infiltration and use of Western news media.
● Soviet Defence Council policy and directives on use of news media.
● Intelligence penetration of religions and financial institutions.
● Training, organisation and use of special operations forces.
● Soviet Bloc sabotage networks in Europe and war plans.
● Principles for the recruitment of the Western élite.
● Intelligence penetration of the French Government.
● Intelligence penetration of NATO structures.
● Rôle and importance of operational ideology.
● Communist control and discipline process.
● Secrecy in economic planning and the nature of the budget process.
● Soviet narcotics trafficking strategy.
● Special propaganda employed against military and civilians.
● Special analytical teams within departments and ministries.
● Coordination of civilian and military intelligence operations.
● Deception and *maskirovka* organisation and oversight.
● Organisation and operations of strategic intelligence agents.
● Organisation and rôle of Special Propaganda organs.
● Rôle and function of key Central Committee Departments.
● Errors in clandestinely obtained 'Soviet' documents.
● Hierarchical organisation of deception and its oversight.
● Formulation of deception and management of constituent parts.
● Operations of foreign intelligence services (both Communist and non-Communist).
● Maintenance of smuggling routes and preparations for sabotage.

38. Chapman Pincher, *The Secret Offensive* (New York: St. Martin's Press, 1985), pages 32-55.

39. Roy Godson, editor, *Intelligence Requirement for the 1990s* (Lexington, Massachusetts: Lexington Books, 1988), page 153. For an especially revealing account of the extent of security problems throughout the US Government, particularly the Department of State, see William J. Gill, *The Ordeal of Otto Otepka* (New Rochelle, New York: Arlington House, 1969).

40. Michael Hedges, 'Customs Chief Blasts Just About Everybody', *Washington Times*, July 28, 1989, page A10.

41. Epstein, *Deception, op. cit.*, page 290.

42. *Ibid.*, page 282.

43. For a more extensive discussion of planning and emergency decisions, see Jan Sejna and Joseph D. Douglass, Jr., *Decision-Making in Communist Countries: An Inside View* (Cambridge, Massachusetts and Washington, D.C.: Institute for Foreign Policy Analyses and Pergamon-Brassey's, 1986).

44. *Writers and Speakers for Freedom*, Nov/Dec. 1987, page 5, citing interview with Miguel Bolanos, a former official from Nicaraguan intelligence, at the Heritage Foundation, June 16-17, 1986.

45. Workman, *International Drug-trafficking, op. cit.*, page C3, citing a DIA report, *The International Terrorist Network, op. cit.*

46. Peter Samuel, 'State Dept. Said to Slight Drug Enforcement to Preserve *Détente*', *New York City Tribune*, April 7, 1989, page A3.

47. See, for example, Chapman Pincher, *The Secret Offensive* (New York: St. Martin's Press, 1985). Also, with respect to Poland, see Corson, Trento and Trento, *Widows, op. cit.*, page 172.

FIXING THE RESPONSIBILITY

The US drug scourge has been blamed on social unrest, unemployment, capitalist decadence, and the traffickers' lust for profits, which are most readily available in the United States. The drug plague is a demand problem, officials from the producing nations claim[1]. If it were not for demand, there would be no plague. But, is this correct, or is the supply side of the equation equally, if not more, to blame? Consider a few 'coincidences'.

Two sources of data assembled during the early 1970s show the growth in narcotics-related deaths and addiction in New York and San Francisco. *Figure 4* below summarises recorded deaths from drug abuse in New York City in successive years between 1930 and 1969. *Figure 5* on page 135 gives details of addicts in the Haight-Ashbury subculture in San Francisco covering the years 1935-68. The consequences of the controlled launch of the narcotics war against the West are immediately apparent.

Both series show a precipitous jump in 1949-50, which is precisely when the Communist Chinese international narcotics trafficking strategy was organised and launched.

YEAR	Reported deaths	YEAR	Reported deaths
1930	23	1950	56
1931	29	1951	77
1932	22	1952	82
1933	25	1953	75
1934	23	1954	86
1935	12	1955	82
1936	13	1956	109
1937	30	1957	86
1938	17	1958	84
1939	26	1959	76
1940	27	1960	126
1941	16	1961	275
1942	24	1962	236
1943	12	1963	342
1944	17	1964	264
1945	0	1965	195
1946	11	1966	262
1947	19	1967	490
1948	18	1968	519
1949	32	1969	689

Figure 4: Historical data on drug-dependent deaths in New York City, 1930-69[2].

Which is the cause – supply or demand – and which is the effect? Both data also show a massive exponential rise beginning in about 1960, which is when the Chinese operation was intensified and when the Soviet narcotics trafficking operation commenced. This massive rise is not a unique US phenomenon. In Great Britain, heroin addicts were few in number between 1930 and 1960. Then after 1960, the situation suddenly became unmanageable[3]. Nor are these growth rates due to the alienation of youth during the Vietnam War. They *preceded* the Vietnam War reaction. The surge began during the Kennedy Administration, which, if anything, was an uplifting period in American politics. The sharp rise cannot be explained as simply the result of increased demand. It appears to have been more the result of increased supply, as well as of the associated Soviet and Chinese marketing techniques that were designed to **create demand**.

As noted earlier, what has been happening is also remarkably evident in data from Southeast Asia and Europe in the early 1970s. In both cases there was a surge in drug addiction among US servicemen. The reaction of the American military was at first to deny that there was a problem, and then to blame the drug crisis on the poor quality of recruits. But there is little question what caused the increase. It was due to a mammoth increase in the **supply** of drugs, high-pressure marketing techniques, and ultra-low prices.

The prices were artificially depressed and the availability of drugs was maximised. Prostitutes were used to push drugs on unsuspecting servicemen. Addiction was covertly increased by mixing opium and heroin in with drugs that were not considered addictive, such as marijuana. Cartons of cigarettes and 'reefers' laced with narcotics were given away free to American troops. Heroin was sold as cocaine, which at the time was not considered addictive.

This represented blatant political warfare directed against the youth of the United States. The source of the problem was not weak-willed American youth, dissatisfaction with society, or some other muddled explanation. There may have been some of that, there always is. But that was not **the cause**. The cause was a massive supply of cheap drugs and a system dedicated to pushing these drugs among the American military. These Soviet and Chinese operations were immensely successful.

This historical evidence is exceedingly important. What has been happening in America has been explained as the result of American social decay, a growing decadence. America was to blame. This was just one dimension of an important propaganda and disinformation campaign designed to cause Americans, and the rest of the world, to lose faith in America and in the American way of life. These propaganda campaigns are part of a massive influence operation on which the Soviets have been spending over $3 billion per year since the late 1950s[4]. There is no question that American society is far from perfect. It has many faults, but it is much better than any existing alternatives. This is why the Soviets work so hard to tear it down. It is time for Americans and our friends and neighbours to recognise what is happening. The massive growth in drug use in the various free societies is not the result of internal decay in those societies. Nothing could be further from the truth, and until we face the truth, an effective strategy to combat the drug offensive is unlikely to be developed.

It is also possible to relate what has been taking place in the United States with the historical data presented above. There has been a steady increase in US drug interdiction activity and an ever-increasing quantity of drug seizures, especially of cocaine. Yet simultaneously, the flow of cocaine has increased, the quality has improved, and the price has decreased. Is this effect just the result of an oversupply and trafficking competition? Or, might the tempo of the political war against the United States have been accelerated, speeded up in part, perhaps, to cause the United States to believe the war on drugs is a lost cause?

Perhaps the greatest 'coincidences' are the manner in which the trafficking has grown almost precisely as identified in the Soviet studies, and in accordance with Soviet strategy. Are the Soviets merely tremendously prescient, or has the trafficking that the United States and many other countries have been subjected to been heavily influenced by Soviet Bloc intelligence operations, assisted and abetted by coordinated propaganda and disinformation activity[5]?

Consider the fact that the primary countries involved in trafficking in the 1980s were the initial Latin American and Caribbean targets in the Soviet drug strategy of the early 1960s: Cuba, Panama, Colombia, Mexico, Haiti, Jamaica, and most recently, Argentina. Or consider the fact that the vast majority of the drug dealers operating in the United States are minorities – Haitians, Jamaicans, Cubans, Colombians and Black people – most of whom General Sejna identified as having been priority Soviet revolutionary war targets –

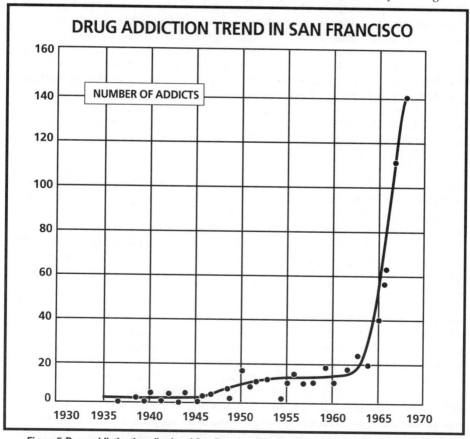

Figure 5: **Drug addiction in a district of San Francisco:** The number of addicts in the Haight-Ashbury subculture who first used heroin, as a function of the year [6].

and, to a lesser extent, organised crime, also a high-priority Soviet Bloc target since 1956.

The three top Soviet political targets in South and Central America that have been identified by defectors and are singled out in Soviet literature are Mexico, Argentina and Brazil. Mexico is now in deep trouble, and the drug trade is a critical factor. Argentina is a growing source of drugs and Brazil, according to Diego Cordoba, a lawyer for the Medellín Cartel, will replace Colombia as the largest exporter of drugs within the next three years[7].

Mexico has become one of the most fragile Latin American countries because of its drug-associated destabilisation potential. Might this development reflect the Cuban-Czechoslovak **'Rhine'** and Soviet-Czechoslovak **'Full Moon'** operations? And what about the operational tactics observed with respect to the Cuban, Haitian, Colombian and Jamaican operations in the United States, and which seem to mirror-image the push-pull tactics of the **'Full Moon'** operation. Is all this strictly coincidence?

Jamaica is an especially interesting case. When Michael Manley was Prime Minister of Jamaica, from 1972 to 1980, Jamaica almost became a client state of Cuba. By 1973, Manley was recruiting Jamaicans to go to Cuba for training in guerrilla warfare[8] and Jamaica was being openly used for drug-trafficking into the United States. The appearance of Jamaican gangs (known as *'posses'*) is thought to have evolved around 1974. The well-organised Jamaican gangs like the Raetown Boys and the Dunkirk Boys are believed to have arrived in New York City in 1976. Originally organised for violence and terror, the *posses* switched from being 'hitmen' and extortionists to traffickers in crack cocaine in 1986[9]. Is it strictly coincidence that Jamaicans and Haitians are so prominent in the crack distribution and marketing networks today? Is it just coincidence that Marxist Mexican guerrillas are heavily involved in the guns-for-drugs trade?

As discussed in Chapter 3, Guadeloupe was the centre of a Caribbean drug operation conceived by the Second Secretary of the French Communist Party and the First Secretary of the Communist Party of Guadeloupe. With their assistance, it was placed in operation in the mid-1960s – and run by two French-speaking Czechoslovak intelligence agents.

In 1987, a private US security specialist was hired by several Europeans who had significant investments in St. Vincent, south of Guadeloupe in the Grenadines, to eliminate problems caused by local terrorists that their staff in St. Vincent had been experiencing. The security specialist soon learned that drugs were plentiful throughout the Grenadines. Marijuana was a major crop on St. Vincent, and production there was controlled by the Rastafarians, Communist guerrillas, and local businessmen. The local police were totally corrupted. The islands' marijuana production was sold to the 'French' who dominated the inter-island sea transportation. Also in prominent were representatives of the Grenada-based New Jewel Movement, subsequently 'decapitated' by invading US forces.

The Communist guerrillas were the terrorists. Their objective seemed to be to drive local businessmen off the island. They were supplied with guns and ammunition by inter-island steamers. One night the specialist, who was operating under cover, infiltrated a group of twenty-five 'merchantmen' from a ship who came ashore for dinner and entertainment. Most of them were young Cubans; about ten percent were older Soviets.

The ship travelled from island to island supplying terrorists. Guns and ammunition were sealed in plastic and then placed in crab traps. This was also the method used to deliver a propaganda magazine, *Oclae*, which was printed in English in Cuba. The terrorists, masquerading as fishermen, would travel out to the various buoys and retrieve their supplies from the crab traps. Marijuana and other drugs were used to finance their operations. As the security specialist learned shortly before his departure, 'French' control of distribution was not recent, but extended back into the 1960s. Another coincidence?

Is it mere coincidence that the language used by many of the drug operators from Colombia, Cuba, Mexico, Nicaragua and Panama – for example, that drugs are 'a revolutionary means of struggle against imperialism'[10] – is impregnated with Marxist-Leninist phrases and concepts? And who deserves the responsibility for the non-Communist criminals who were trained at drug-trafficking 'academies' in the Soviet Union, Czechoslovakia, Bulgaria, East Germany and other Soviet surrogate states? The output of those schools – trained criminals – based on the Czechoslovak model and assuming no expansion or contraction, would be over 600 per year between 1970 and 1990. That adds up to over 12,000 non-Communist 'graduates', and another 12,000 non-Soviet Bloc Communist 'graduates. Those totals do not include the Cuban and East European intelligence services' operations throughout Latin America and the rest of the world which were not connected with the drug-trafficking training centres.

Is it only paranoia that led Ramon Rodriguez to be concerned about DGI infiltration of the Medellín Cartel and to respond 'Absolutely!' when asked if Cuba had infiltrated the drug community[11]? During the campaign by Colombia to crack down on drug dealers following the assassination of a presidential candidate, Luís Carlos Galan, on August 19, 1989, thousands of suspected traffickers were arrested. In one sweep of Medellín, 27 Cubans were seized. They carried forged Costa Rican passports[12]. What were they doing in Colombia's drug capital? Were they on vacation?

Or consider the manner in which numerous sources have reported statements made to them by high-level Communist officials on the deliberate use of drugs against the United States by the Communist countries. Some of the many such statements which appear at various places in this text are assembled in *Figure 6*, on page 138.

The rationale and strategy associated with drug-trafficking operations are logical and consistent with the first principles of Marxist-Leninist doctrine. The operations conform with informal statements made by many high-echelon officials who were involved and who come from a wide variety of countries – Colombia, Nicaragua, Panama, Cuba, Czechoslovakia, China, Romania and Bulgaria.

It should be clear that Chinese and Soviet drug-trafficking strategies have been primary forces behind the US (and of course the global) drug offensive. **In 1967, Sejna reported, the Soviets estimated that they (that is, they or their satellites) were in control of 37 percent of drug output then being supplied to the United States and Canada, and that this figure would be expanded by up to 13 percent each year. In terms of distribution and sales within the United States and Canada, the figure was lower – at 31 percent.** By 'control' was meant that the people they had trained had a hand in running the operation and the Soviets were receiving a cut of the profits.

Just as the original edition of this book was going to press, fresh intelligence surfaced that North Korean officials had directed farmers in a central province to grow marijuana [in the summer of 1989][13]. North Korean intelligence, with its strong links to Soviet intelligence as set forth in Chapter 10, is certainly involved. But even more interestingly, the arrest of the former East German Communist leader, Erich Honecker, has led to information concerning vast amounts of 'illegal' money earned through bribes, gun-running and drugs. East German State Security, well known to have been directly controlled from Moscow, was implicated. The few details that have leaked out have simply identified cocaine transshipments from Latin America through Rostock Harbour in East Germany

**OVERT COMMUNIST WORLD REVOLUTIONARY STATEMENTS
ON THE SUBVERSIVE VALUE OF THE GLOBAL NARCOTICS OFFENSIVE**

Opium should be regarded as a powerful weapon. It has been employed by imperialists against us, and now we should use it against them. Such warfare can be called chemical warfare by indigenous methods.
MAO TSE-TUNG, *1935.*

We will disarm the capitalists with the things they like to taste.
CHOU EN-LAI , *1958.*

Anything that speeds the destruction of capitalism is moral.
NIKITA KHRUSHCHEV, *1962.*

Deception and drugs are our first two strategic echelons in the war with capitalism.
NIKITA KHRUSHCHEV, *1963.*

The United States is the main target because they are our worst enemy; it is simple to move drugs into the United States; and, there is an unlimited supply of money there. **TODOR ZHIVKOV, First Secretary, Communist Party of Bulgaria,** *1964*

We are growing the very best poppies for the US servicemen.
CHOU EN-LAI , *1965*

Drugs will be a decisive weapon in disrupting the fabric of Western democracies.
RAUL CASTRO, *Late 1960s*

The goal is to hurt the United States full with drugs.
FERNANDO RAVELO-RENEDO, Cuban Ambassador to Colombia *1978.*

I was ordered to load up the United States with drugs.
MARIO ESTEVEZ GONZALEZ, Cuban intelligence agent *1981.*

Drugs were used as political weapons.
The target was the youth of the United States.
ANTONIO FARACH, High-level Nicaraguan official *1984.*

Drugs are the best way to destroy the United States.
GENERAL BARREIRO, Chief of Cuban Intelligence 1987.

The trafficking is a way of waging war on the United States.
It also provides a profit.
HUMBERTO ORTEGA, Nicaraguan Minister of Defence *1987.*

Drugs are considered to be the best way to destroy the United States...
by undermining the will of American youth, the enemy is destroyed without firing one bullet.
MAJOR JUAN RODRIGUEZ, Cuban intelligence officer *1988.*

Figure 6: **Representative statements by top overt Communists on narcotics trafficking.**

to East Berlin and thence by courier to West Germany[14]. Earlier data had linked East Germany to a heroin smuggling operation that ran through Mexico into the United States[15]. How much of the East German operation will have surfaced as a result of ongoing debriefings of former high-ranking officials believed to have been involved, remains to be seen. But the politics of reunification took precedence over all other matters, including exposing the details on another Moscow-directed drug-trafficking operation.

But what direct evidence is there? People continue to ask. Are the Soviets still involved today? Perhaps the critical question is: what amount of 'evidence' is adequate? What volume of 'evidence' would it take to change the behaviour and attitudes of US Government officials towards the drug offensive and its sponsors?

What is happening is best described by resorting to a fictional scenario. Suppose, for example, that tomorrow the Soviet General Secretary appeared before the Supreme Soviet in a special open session. He states with obvious displeasure that he has just learned about Soviet intelligence involvement in international drug-trafficking. The operation, he explains, was a carryover from the days of Khrushchev and Brezhnev which continued on its own momentum. Then, after severe criticism of both Khrushchev and Brezhnev, he states that as soon as he had become aware of this operation, he had ordered the activity to be halted and everyone responsible to be identified and disciplined.

What would be the American response? While many variants are possible, I submit that the most likely response of the US leadership would be to breathe a sigh of relief and praise the Soviet leadership for their courage in bringing this matter to the attention of all the peoples of the world and for Moscow's rapid response in curtailing such activities. The news media would probably use the announcement to further bolster the General Secretary's image as a statesman. A new round of articles on the significant changes taking place in the Soviet Union would follow.

Now, this is precisely what *did* happen in 1956 following Khrushchev's famous February denouncement of the crimes of Stalin. That partial public confession was part of a larger deception the purpose of which was to convince the West that the Soviets were changing their ways. Through a controlled revelation of Stalin's crimes, the blame for the past could be left on Stalin's shoulders. Of special relevance here was the fact that the information on Stalin's crimes was nothing new. Indeed, a book which had presented even more detail on Stalin's crimes than revealed by Khrushchev, who of course had participated in them, had been published in the United States two years earlier; but no-one in the news media or in the US Government had paid the slightest attention to this anti-Stalin slander until Khrushchev proclaimed it from the pulpit. Then, all of a sudden, the attention of the press was directed towards the new, reformed Soviet Union – exactly as planned.

Or, to suggest a further possibility, suppose another defector with detailed knowledge of Soviet and Chinese drug-trafficking operations were to seek political asylum in the United States. What would happen?

It is unlikely that the defector would ever be debriefed on Soviet and Chinese drug-trafficking, at least not for several months. If and when such debriefing did take place, what would happen to the data? More likely than not it would end up in one of the thousands of classified IRs (intelligence reports) and never see the light of day. Should the information somehow emerge, the most likely response of US officials would be to ask the Communist leaders for an explanation. Naturally, they would be told that the information was false – a provocation by an unreliable defector who could not be trusted – and they would be reassured that no such activities had ever been sanctioned.

To the extent there was any such activity, the Soviets or Chinese would probably indicate that rogue intelligence activities were always possible, as the United States learned during the Vietnam period (when a veiled threat had emerged concerning reported CIA drug-trafficking activities), and that they would check to make certain that no such independent endeavours were in place. US officials would then explain, in response to questions raised about the defector's testimony, that they had queried the heads of the accused countries and had been reassured that there were no such activities as described by the defector. Again, this is not completely hypothetical. That was exactly what took place following reports on the involvement of such countries as Cuba, Nicaragua, China and Bulgaria[16].

Also relevant here is the situation prevailing 1968. A source of the highest credibility, Jan Sejna, has described in detail the major involvement of the Soviets and Chinese in drug-trafficking, right up until the day he left Czechoslovakia in February 1968. Yet we had no 'evidence' of the Soviet operation at that time, or of the involvement of Moscow's East European satellites, aside from Bulgaria. **That is, the absence of information, which is the current US Government response to questions about Soviet or Chinese involvement, only indicates that Chinese or Soviet operational security is very good, or that US intelligence is deficient, or that data are not being examined, or are being suppressed, or some combination of the foregoing.**

While Sejna is an especially unique source, it is clear that he is not the *only* source. During the five years to 1990, for instance, data and other source testimony were forthcoming linking almost every Communist country to drug-trafficking. These data generally indicate official involvement of governments, rather than the independent dealings of a few corrupt public officials. In the case of Cuba, for example, it is not just one or two officials. Ten or more high-level officials have been identified, and there is the active assistance of military units of all three services, the involvement of the Cuban intelligence service, and the involvement of Cuban counter-intelligence. To suggest that Cuba merely 'facilitates' the trafficking or 'condones' it, is blatantly to close one's eyes to what is happening. To accept Cuba's arrest, trial and execution on July 14, 1989 of General Arnaldo Ochoa Sanchez [*see page 1*], Colonel Antonio de la Guardia Font, Major Amado Pardon Trujillo and Captain Jorge Martinez Valdes – and the jailing of other Cuban officials for drug-trafficking[17] – as indicative of Cuba's non-involvement with drug-trafficking, or interest in curtailing drug operations, is the height of gullibility.

By contrast, in the case of the non-Communist countries that play host to various drug-trafficking activities – for example, the Bahamas, Colombia, Bolivia and Peru – the data generally indicate official corruption, but drug-trafficking organisations that are non-governmental. The one country that seems to be 'in between' is Mexico, which is so corrupt that it is difficult to imagine that the Government is not involved. Recall Senator Alfonse D'Amato's (R-NY) observation: 'That country is seething with revolution and has been really totally captured, whether we want to admit it or not, totally by the drug forces'[18]. In the past year or two, there has been an increase in Mexican anti-drug-trafficking activities. However, given the continuing lack of cooperation[19] and continuing production[20] in, and flow of drugs through, Mexico, it would seem that certain highly publicised activities may well be just another example of efforts undertaken and publicised mainly for the 'benefit' of the United States: To conclude that there is any real effort by Mexican officials to curtail the illegal drug trade is, at the time of writing, at best premature.

Soviet, Marxist and Maoist terrorist revolutionaries are involved in drug-trafficking in all regions of the globe. Certainly, there are numerous non-Communist drug-traffickers. Even some apparently non-Marxist 'freedom-fighter' resistance movements, notably the Contras in Nicaragua, were evidently tempted to use drugs as a weapon or source of money, as well. There is no denying that; but this seems to be a rather minor element of the problem and should not be allowed to detract attention from the rôle of China, the Soviet Bloc countries, and the Marxist and Maoist guerrillas and terrorists. On the contrary, the participation of such groups serves the Communists just fine, since it confuses the overall picture, enhances 'deniability' and helps to divert attention from their far more intensive activities, while providing a ready source of propaganda ammunition for disinformation purposes.

An interesting example of one Soviet recruitment technique using drugs was contained in an affidavit by Nelson Mantilla-Rey, filed in support of his application for political asylum. Mantilla is a Colombian who was awarded a scholarship to study medicine in the Soviet Union. He described how he and a classmate, Rafay Mehdi, gradually came under the watchful eye of a counsellor, who introduced them to black market activities to earn extra money, and who also used them to collect information on various individuals and situations during vacations. The counsellor further displayed considerable power when Mantilla or Mehdi got into trouble with the police or college authorities – a revelation which led Mantilla and Mehdi to give him the nickname 'Angel'. They eventually concluded that Angel was in reality a KGB officer and that they were being recruited. One of the paragraphs in the affidavit is significant:

'32. In the summer of 1982, Rafay came with me to Colombia. Angel suggested that we should buy drugs in Colombia, telling us that he had contacts in the Colombian airport and could set something up. He suggested that we could sell the drugs to the American soldiers we had seen on the bases in West Germany and that we could make a lot of money for ourselves. This was the first time we refused to do what Angel asked of us. We said selling jeans was commerce, but selling drugs was causing harm, and that we were doctors and could not participate in such a thing. He did not get angry and dropped the subject. He then asked us to contact some of the former Colombian students who had studied in the Soviet Union, to find out what they were doing and to check on their addresses, explaining that it would be interesting to know what had happened to all these students after they left the Soviet Union. We agreed to do that'[21].

He also reported on his attempts to interest the US Embassy in the way in which Third World students were brainwashed and recruited, and was told that US officials were not interested in what he had to say. They were only interested in military secrets, not in long-term indoctrination [recruitment] programs. Upon his return to Colombia after graduation, he began receiving phone calls from other students who had studied in the Soviet Union and who encouraged him to join their political group.

One advised him not to worry about the trouble he was having finding a job; 'former students who were Soviet sympathisers were getting into positions of power and the network was spreading', he was told.

The purpose of this book is not, of course, to go to the extreme of placing 100% of the blame for the global drugs pandemic upon the Chinese or Soviet Bloc intelligence services. Nor can anyone say how effective their operation has been. If those services controlled 31 to 37 percent of the North American market in 1967, which was what the Soviet estimate of their market share was at that time, what percentage might they control today?

The problem of assigning responsibility is especially difficult in the case of 'crack'. Crack is a highly potent form of cocaine which is smoked. It enters the blood-stream through the lungs and proceeds immediately to the brain. It can be almost instantly addictive, gives the user a sense of self-confidence and superiority, and is closely linked with violent behaviour. At the start of 1985, crack usage was virtually unheard of. Exactly when crack first appeared is not precisely known; but it seems to have made its primary *début* in late 1985, just in time for the holidays. By January 1986, crack use was reported in California, New York, Iowa, Maryland, Michigan, Florida, Alabama and Washington State. By June 1986, it was reported throughout the United States[22] and by September it had been reported in Canada, United Kingdom, Finland, Hong Kong, Spain, South Africa, Egypt, India, Mexico, Belize and Brazil[23].

The spread of crack seems best explained as a consequence of coordinated mass marketing. So, too, is its design. As analysed by M. M. Kirsch[24], crack was designed for the consumer with $5 to $15 to spend. It was designed for the user who is wholly unaware of its devastating effects: 'The market push has been directed at the young and the ignorant'[25]. As the Drug Enforcement Administration reported in 1989, almost four years after crack began its rapid spread, the interstate networks, manufacture and distribution were dominated by Jamaicans, Haitians and US Blacks, and the primary targets were the ethnic minorities in the inner cities, principally the Black people and Hispanics[26].

Where did crack come from? Who orchestrated its development and its marketing? The drug was priced to match perfectly an unexploited marketing opportunity – people who could not afford an expensive cocaine or heroin habit. It is also interesting to recognise that the characteristics of crack correspond *in all important respects* to the objectives of the Soviet Bloc's drug development program as it existed in the 1960s (described in Chapter 7). The rapid spread of its use did **not** match the 'normal' pattern associated with the introduction of a 'new' drug, such as the California designer drugs of the early 1980s.

Even more significantly, however, the marketing of the drug by Caribbean and US Black people to the inner-city poor, particularly Black people and Hispanics, matches identically the Soviet marketing and distribution strategy developed in the mid-1960s and then placed in operation. Following the development of crack, which evidently took place in the late 1970s or early 1980s, it would then have been a simple task clandestinely to insert instructions for its manufacture into the Latin American trafficking networks over which the Soviets exercise influence, to ensure that there would be nothing linking the new drug with the Soviets. The operation would have been 100 percent effective but with no apparent links (from a US perspective) to the Soviet Union or even to any of its satellite intelligence services, most notably Cuba's intelligence services.

Or, consider the rôle of the majority of the Latin American and North American traffickers. To suggest that they are all Communists, or obeying Communist orders, would be silly. It is a fair assumption that most of the traffickers and their collaborators are not Communists. For the most part, they are only pursuing profits without any regard for the consequences of their actions. But, how many of them were trained in a drug-trafficking camp located in the Soviet Bloc? Is there a connection between these training schools and the drug-trafficking schools in Colombia[27]? And how many of the traffickers are simply pawns in a larger game whose dimensions they do not understand? In drug-trafficking, many people are used – and being used *without asking questions* is accepted as part of the cost of doing business. Curiosity is known to be a fatal disease.

How they are being used and by whom, most of the traffickers do not know, nor necessarily care. Very few people really know, as few as possible, which is very few. This is the whole objective of narcotics operational security as developed by the Soviets in the late 1950s, and as described in Chapters 3 and 4 of this book. This is also why the testimony of the few people who did know what was happening is so important.

The bottom line is that there is no way to measure the extent or effectiveness of the Soviet and Chinese drug operations, nor is any method of measurement about to be concocted. But, as indicated earlier, the actual extent of the Soviet or Chinese involvement in drug-trafficking is not a primary issue.

The real issue is: **Why is the US Government ignoring this dimension of the drug problem?** Why, especially when it could turn out to be the most important dimension, for the reasons which have been described in previous chapters? Why is the US Government unable or unwilling to recognise political warfare or the continuing duplicity of the Soviet Union? Why is the US Government unable to face up to the rôle of Cuba, Nicaragua and Bulgaria? Why have **all** Western governments avoided the mass of multi-source data on the Soviet operations to train, equip and finance international terrorists – and then, to make matters worse, have perversely adopted projects to join forces with the worst criminal régime of all, the Soviet Union, to fight terrorism and share intelligence data on terrorism in the process[28]? Why join forces with a nation which organised training camps for terrorists in half a dozen different countries? The issue goes well beyond the Soviet and Chinese involvement in drug-trafficking chronicled in this book.

'Why'? is a hard question to answer with any degree of confidence. Part of the problem may be the manner in which US intelligence is organised, or rather divided; and part may relate to the manner in which the Soviet Union is viewed from Washington. Overseas intelligence generally falls within the purview of the CIA, the State Department and the Department of Defense – and US domestic intelligence, within that of the FBI.

Most Soviet Bloc and Chinese drug operations are located *overseas*, while the US drug problem is perceived as a *domestic* issue. Also, overseas drug production and trafficking organisations are not an *obvious* threat against the United States, so why should the CIA concern itself with drug operations in Haiti, Indonesia, or North Vietnam, or with the TIR customs-facilitating operation in Europe? Drugs are the DEA's responsibility, not the CIA's. Nor could the CIA be anxious to share sensitive source information with the State Department, the DEA, or Customs, when these agencies are negotiating arrangements for sharing intelligence information with the Soviets.

More basic, however, is the fact that the CIA does not collect data for law enforcement; that is, data that can be used as evidence in a court of law. Its rôle is national security, but drug-trafficking is viewed as a *law enforcement* problem. Moreover, as previously explained, Soviet drug operations are handled mainly by surrogates, which further complicates the situation. Law enforcement agencies often do not understand or have access to the data describing the relationships that exist between foreign intelligence services. Nor has it been at all evident, until recently, what has been happening.

Yet, while these considerations are all valid, they are not satisfying because they *still* do not answer why intelligence priorities and drug-trafficking data collection did not change when data on the Soviet Bloc operations began appearing in the open literature, beginning in December 1986[29]. None of the above factors explains the failure to debrief Jan Sejna and the efforts, which continue today [and continued until his death in August 1997 - *Ed.*], to discredit him and what he had to say. *Why do the US authorities not want to know?*

Another part of the problem is Washington's '*détente* view' of the Soviet Union and the world Communist system as a whole. The prevailing [1989 – *Ed.*] view of the 'threat' is that which supports *détente* politics. Only minor recognition is given to the nature of Communism, its goals and objectives, and especially its strategy. At times it almost seems as though the US Government has a death wish[30]. There has been tremendous reluctance to face the nature of the Soviet military threat. People who have described this threat as it is – **a war-planning, war-fighting and war-winning capability** – have been subjected to ridicule and derision. There has been and still is an official reluctance to face the threat of international terrorism and its primary sponsor, the Soviet Union. The intelligence community has avoided the whole concept of a long-range Soviet strategic plan for world domination, even to the extent of not collecting known data that describes the plan, its strategy, tactics and the responsibilities of the various Soviet satellite nations within it.

An especially perceptive description of the general problem Westerners have in understanding the Soviets comes from one of the most famous US-UK spies who provided information on Soviet military activities in the early 1960s, Colonel Oleg Penkovskiy. As explained in *The Penkovskiy Papers*, a work prepared by the CIA based on his information and debriefings:

'One thing must be clearly understood. If someone were to hand to an American general, an English general and a Soviet general the same set of objective facts and scientific data, with instructions that these facts and data must be accepted as unimpeachable, and an analysis made and conclusions drawn on the basis of them, it is possible that the American and the Englishman would reach similar conclusions – I don't know. But the Soviet general would arrive at conclusions which would be radically different from the other two. This is because, first of all, he begins from a completely different set of basic premises and preconceived ideas, namely, the Marxian concepts of the structure of society and the course of history. Second, the logical process in his mind is totally unlike that of his Western counterparts, because he uses Marxist dialectics, whereas they will use some form of deductive reasoning. Third, a different set of moral laws governs and restricts the behaviour of the Soviets. Fourth, the Soviet general's aims will be radically different from those of the American and the Englishman'[31].

Westerners have an immensely difficult time in coming to grips with Soviet logic and morality, which, being based on the Leninist dialectic, are totally different from and inconsistent with, counterpart pragmatic Western concepts.

A critical example of the operational problem is the field of deception, disinformation and propaganda, which is one of the primary Soviet weapons used against the West – their first strategic echelon, as Khrushchev himself referred to it. **Deception is as natural a Russian national characteristic as is freedom in the United States**[32]. The Soviets were spending over $3 billion each year in the late 1970s on deception, disinformation and propaganda, according to CIA estimates[33]. Yet the best that a US interagency study could conclude in 1982 was: 'The fact that the Soviet leadership continues to use active measures [which includes disinformation and political influence operations] on a large scale and apparently funds them generously, suggests a positive assessment of their value as a foreign policy instrument'[34].

The FBI carried this bland assessment still further: 'We do not see Soviet active measures in the United States as having a significant impact on US decisionmakers....

The American media is sophisticated and generally recognises Soviet influence attempts…. The FBI has uncovered no evidence that suggests American policymakers have been induced to adopt policies against America's interests through KGB influence operations in the United States'[35]. This is contrary to the view of numerous defectors with expertise in that area[36]. It is also contrary to the view of many non-government experts†[37].

Nor does it explain the uncommonly high number of assumptions regarding the Soviet Union that serve as the basis for US policy and that correlate well with the assumptions promoted by Soviet deception operations. Needless to say, the CIA and FBI positions involve a measure of self-interest: to the extent that there is a severe deception and disinformation problem, that would reflect badly on US counter-intelligence capabilities, which are centred in the FBI and CIA.

The FBI wrote a follow-up report on Soviet active measures which was placed in the *Congressional Record* by Representative C. W. 'Bill' Young (R-FL). The report covered the 1986-87 time period and was considerably less bland. It concluded:

'Although it is often difficult to judge the effectiveness of specific active measures operations, the Soviets believe these operations have a cumulative effect and are detrimental to US foreign policy and national security interests. Furthermore, the Soviets believe that their active measures operations in the United States do contribute to their overall strategy to advance Soviet foreign policy interests, influence US Government policies, and in general discredit the United States'[38].

While the report still failed to reach any conclusion concerning the US assessment of the effectiveness of Soviet active measures, it did represent a step in the right direction.

In 1987, the Leadership Foundation sponsored a book on Soviet deception[39]. Independent analyses in different functional areas by seventeen experts were commissioned. One of the principal findings that emerged in nearly every analysis was that the United States' views do not correspond with reality and, indeed, were to a disturbing degree aligned with Soviet deception objectives[40]. Mere coincidence?

To what extent might our perception of the drug-trafficking problem have been influenced by the Soviet Bloc's deception, disinformation and propaganda apparatus? As reported by Jan Sejna[41], the Soviet Bloc's disinformation and propaganda apparatus has been working hard for over twenty-five years to mould US perceptions of the drug problem. To what extent has the possibility of finding Soviet and Chinese involvement in international drug-trafficking simply been contrary to US policy? And why?

Might the Soviets have just 'primed' their drug-trafficking operations and then let them continue as independent, self-sustaining activities? Naturally, anything is possible. But this course of action would seem to be an unlikely possibility. The Soviets sustain a long-range revolutionary view. Their activities are governed, in general, by long-range strategy and by plans that extend for decades, and beyond.

† *Editor's Note:* For instance, it flies in the face of the fact that for many years, a known Communist occupied a senior management position on the staff of one of the leading US newspapers. It also disregards the continuing dissemination of mis- and disinformation over the years by agents of influence in features and reports in newspapers throughout the West, designed to pull the wool over the eyes of policymakers and the public. A case in point at this Edition's press date was a spate of articles which appeared in the United Kingdom and the United States that were clearly intended to sustain and reinforce the illusion, intended by Moscow, that the explosion of global drug-related criminality is just an unfortunate circumstance of modern life – rather than a consequence of a long-term intelligence offensive, as explained here.

Is what has been happening evidence of a change of tactics, or a strategic adjustment? While there have been domestic 'upheavals' throughout Eastern Europe, control mechanisms still appear to be in place, and intelligence operations are not known to have been seriously affected, at least not as of March 1990. Why would the Soviets walk away from such an eminently successful, long-term strategic offensive?

One reason might be to avoid getting caught. But the Soviet approach to sensitive strategic operations is to build into the operation good secrecy, counter-intelligence controls, and, from the beginning, a strategy that is ready to be implemented if there is a breach in the secrecy, and the enemy begins to recognise what is happening. The groundwork is laid, right from the beginning, to deny any responsibility and to place the blame on someone else. They even have a name for this strategy. It is called **'offensive denial'**[42].

As their narcotics trafficking strategy developed, the Soviets were careful to watch for any signs of Western awareness. By way of example, in 1964 British and Canadian delegations visited Czechoslovakia on separate occasions. Czechoslovakia was instructed to query the delegations to learn if British or Canadian counter-intelligence had connected drug-trafficking with the Soviet or East Bloc intelligence services. The purpose was to ready their counterattack in case something surfaced. The Czechoslovak approach was to indicate casually during informal one-on-one conversations that they had heard that the opposition party in the United Kingdom (or Canada) was linking the party of the person in the conversation to drug-trafficking and then see where the conversation went.

This Soviet strategy is also reflected in Moscow's decision, with effect from 1964, to publicise the drug-trafficking rôle of Communist China. Advertising China's rôle would draw attention away from the Soviet operation and provide a convenient culprit for the West to blame for the escalating drugs scourge. The 1964 article by Ovchinnikov[43] (*see page 41*) tied the opium, morphine, and heroin problem in Japan, the United States and Southeast Asia to China. Yunnan Province was identified as the main producing area feeding Southeast Asia. The article also discussed the coordination meeting held in Peking in 1952 and the decision to expand production which formed part of the 'Great Leap Forward'. This theme was repeated and expanded in 1969, in *Literaturnaya Gazeta*. More details were now provided with the important elaboration that the CIA was also identified as a participant in the trafficking in Southeast Asia. The article linked the CIA to the transportation of 100-kilogram bars of opium from the remote regions of Laos to bases in Thailand and to secret factories on an island in the Mekong River, where the opium was processed. 'From that factory, the heroin goes to the United States, Japan and Western Europe'[44].

Reports of foreign nationals trafficking from Bulgaria are especially curious. As indicated earlier, in a 1984 report to Congress[45], the Drug Enforcement Administration indicated that it had knowledge of numerous foreign nationals who were using Bulgaria as their base of operations. The DEA provided Bulgaria with lists of names of such people on at least four different occasions. Some 56 names were apparently provided to Sofia[46]. What is interesting is that none of the lists identified Bulgarian citizens. Why?

Did the United States have *any* names of Bulgarians who were involved, but which for some reason were not disclosed, or did the United States actually *only* have the names of non-Bulgarians, as was implied in the DEA report? It is distinctly possible that the latter situation is the case, and that the process by which the United States obtained the names was *not* the result of poor Bulgarian security – but that the United States was intended to learn *only* the names of non-Bulgarian traffickers.

KINTEX is reported to have been set up in 1968, although there are indications that it was in operation several years earlier and was tied into the provision of morphine base to Italian and French laboratories during the 'French Connection' era – the mid-1960s[47]. In 1969, 200 kilograms of heroin were seized in West Germany. Through sophisticated chemical analysis of the drug, the German authorities determined that the heroin had been manufactured in Bulgaria, thus directly linking Bulgaria with the manufacture of heroin used in illicit trafficking. It was after this determination was made that a DEA source disclosed the Bulgarian plan for enabling foreign nationals to use Bulgaria as a base for drug manufacturing and trafficking operations.

This disclosure materialised in June 1970[48]. It would also appear, based on the DEA report, that the names of the non-Bulgarian nationals conducting heroin manufacture and trafficking first started appearing in December 1970[49]. It does not require much imagination to hypothesise the Bulgarian use of KINTEX to manage foreign nationals as part of an operation deliberately designed so that if information were leaked to the United States, presumably due to lack of appropriate care by one of the foreign nationals, there would be a non-Bulgarian explanation for the manufacture and movement of drugs to the West from and through Bulgaria. Such an operation could also be designed as a cover for Bulgarian operations conducted without the participation of any foreign nationals[50].

When Cuba's rôle in drug-trafficking was disclosed in the US courts in 1982, the linkages to the Soviet Union were implicit. It was only a matter of time before questions would be raised about Soviet participation. This event, which was widely publicised in the news media, must have set off discrete alarms in the Soviet offices responsible for 'Druzhba Narodov'. Some type of protective response was now urgently needed.

In thinking back over the events of the early 1980s and the Soviet need for a diversion, it is interesting to recall the manner in which reports that the Soviets had a drug problem of their own, began surfacing. For years the Soviets had claimed that they had no drug problem because of their social conditions – full employment, no homelessness, and ample opportunities for young people to obtain a good education or learn a trade. Then, suddenly in 1986, a drug problem emerged in Soviet literature[51]. Much of the blame was placed upon Afghanistan 'Freedom Fighters' who were selling drugs to the Soviet soldiers. But another report from the Soviet Union was particularly odd. It concerned the theft of poppy seeds, which was portrayed as *another* indication of the growing drug problem. This should have raised a red flag. Throughout the Soviet Union there is widespread cultivation of poppies. Poppies are grown for medicinal purposes and for the seeds. Children often drink the nectar in the buds of the ripening flowers. Poppy-seed cake is a national desert in the Ukraine and poppy seeds are widely available. So concern over theft of poppy seeds is hardly worth reporting.

According to an analysis by Dr James Inciardi, Professor and Director, Department of Criminal Justice, University of Delaware, the sudden emergence of a Soviet addiction problem in 1986 was *inconsistent with the facts*, which included the easy availability of poppies and hashish and a population known for its alcoholism. Moreover, as he explained, an important Soviet research study on drug addition published in February 1987 was not suggestive of a recent problem. Inciardi then pointed out that most of the work on this new research article was actually done in the late 1960s, and referenced source material dating as far back as 1955. He showed that the Soviets most probably had extensive clinical exposure to drug abusers as far back as the 1950s[52] (which, coincidentally, is precisely when the Soviet analyses of the use of drugs as strategic weapons were intensified). The obvious question, of course, was: why did the Soviets decide to start publicising their drug problem in 1986?

Two possibilities are worth considering. First, in 1985 the Soviets were in the process of *modifying their tactics towards the West*. As part of this process, they sent numerous emissaries to the United States to talk to prominent 'hardliners', inquiring of them what it was that the Soviet Union had to do to show that it was changing. In the past, it had been a common practice for the Soviets to adopt a strategy designed to portray this image of change as part of a programme to obtain increased financial and technical assistance from the West[53]. This could very well explain many of the 'changes' that were to appear in the latter half of the 1980s. It could also help to explain, in part, the sudden publicity the Soviets gave to their drug problems, beginning in 1986.

Additionally, it must have been evident, with effect from at least mid-1983, that measures were needed to offset the growing focus of attention on the rôle of Soviet surrogates in drug-trafficking. In 1986-87, descriptions of Sejna's knowledge of the Soviet narcotics strategy first began to emerge – initially in a private newsletter in the late summer of 1986, and publicly in France in December 1986[54] and in America in January 1987[55].

The Soviets could easily have been aware, as early as 1985, that this material was being developed. Also, in 1986 and 1987j149
, further indications of Soviet activities surfaced, with reports of seizures of narcotics being transported on Soviet ships. In 1986, Dutch police seized 220 kilos of heroin aboard the Soviet freighter, the *Kapitan Tomson*. Belgian and Canadian officials seized Soviet containers stashed with illegal drugs in 1987. Also in 1987, Italian customs police seized 880 pounds of hashish concealed in the bottom of a container[56]. The cat was definitely out of the bag.

While these events were unfolding, news about internal Soviet drug problems continued to grow. This provided an understandable basis for the new Soviet interest in 'working with the West', specifically the British and Americans, to 'stop drug-trafficking't. In February 1988 the Soviets and British signed a memorandum of understanding on cooperation over drug-trafficking. Three months later, the Soviets tipped off the British about some drugs that were about to be smuggled into Britain. On April 29, 1988, *Tass* announced that a joint operation, code named 'Diplomat', conducted by Soviet and British customs agents, had led to the seizure of three-and-a-half tons of hashish with a street value of £10,000,000. The drugs were in transit from Afghanistan via Leningrad to Tilbury. The Soviets reported that the source of the hashish was Pakistan. One wonders why the Soviets did not seize the drug shipments in Afghanistan, or the Soviet Union, as would have been logical if the object of the exercise had really been to combat drug smuggling. Rather, the *Tass* announcement noted that Operation 'Diplomat' was *another example of broadening international cooperation*. The particular broadening referred to were agreements which were then being negotiated with France and the United States.

Is what the Soviets had in mind 'cooperation'? **Or is this 'cooperation' in reality a carefully orchestrated Soviet protection, deception, and penetration operation?**

Incidentally, a rather simple test of the Soviets' sincerity on this score comes to mind. Let the authorities in Moscow provide a detailed description of the drug operations that

---

† *Editor's Note:* It also provided the necessary false impression of 'equivalence' between of the drug problems in the USSR and the West, which was a prerequisite for East-West 'cooperation' in the 'fight against drugs'. Moscow sought such 'equivalence' in order to be able to neutralise Western anti-drug operations effectively, while obtaining a constant stream of Western drug-related intelligence from inside sources. This 'Bold Bolshevik' approach is typical of Leninist activist revolutionary methodology, to which Western Governments are tragically blind.

they have had a 'hand' in running from 1955 to the present, complete with the names, details and photographs of everyone they trained and everyone who has assisted them over the years; let them provide copies of all Soviet Bloc intelligence files on non-Soviet narcotics trafficking operations; and let them channel back to the countries of origin, all drug-related profits realised by the Soviet Bloc's intelligence services.

Would the Soviets simply have walked away from their drug operation? Possible, but hardly likely. '*Druzhba Narodov*' was eminently successful. It was also a long-term operation involving a substantial commitment of resources. **Why would the Soviets suddenly trash the operation, especially considering the reluctance of the West to focus serious attention on either the drug-trafficking problem or on the rôle of Soviet surrogates in drug-trafficking?** While one cannot deny that such a response would have been possible, it certainly would have been inconsistent with Soviet strategy and with Moscow's operational doctrine, one of the central principles of which is **control**. The Soviets go to great lengths to ensure **control**. The last situation they want is the emergence of economically independent and uncontrolled splinter operations[57].

Notwithstanding the changes which impressed the whole world under Gorbachëv there have been few indications of any favourable changes in Soviet strategic capabilities or intelligence operations. As William H. Webster, the CIA's Director of Central Intelligence at the time, observed in February, 1990, the intelligence services in Eastern Europe were likely to remain at work notwithstanding the sweeping changes taking place in those countries; and, they would continue cooperating with the Soviets[58]. Additionally, Soviet military support continues to flow into various besieged countries, and the Soviet Union's propaganda apparatus continues to spread lies about the United States around the globe[59].

The offer extended by the Drug Enforcement Administration and US Customs back in 1971 to work with the Bulgarian intelligence services to help them arrest drug-traffickers provided the Soviets with an almost heaven-sent mechanism for taking the pulse of US narcotics-trafficking intelligence. This 'cooperation' is now being expanded to include sharing drug-trafficking intelligence directly with the Soviets. Naturally, this provides the Soviets with what might be the ultimate *feedback mechanism* with which to keep track of US data and concerns. And, in the light of such 'cooperation', how could US Government officials, or officials from other countries similarly involved, ever suspect – let alone publicly charge – the Soviets with masterminding a comprehensive Soviet Bloc intelligence drug-trafficking operation? Even if Western suspicions were to be aroused on this score, as they have been from time to time, any conclusion along those lines would be pigeon-holed indefinitely on the basis that it conflicted with 'accepted' US policy.

Data provided by the former Secretary of the Czechoslovak Defence Council are extensive and have far-reaching consequences. Drug-trafficking by the Soviet Bloc countries and China is just one of the monstrosities revealed in his disclosures. Yet notwithstanding the apparent importance of the data, it continues to be ignored, swept aside, or damned with faint praise. Is the problem one of *confirmation*? **Or, do people in Washington simply not want to know?** Is the force of Soviet disinformation, deception and infiltration *too strong to combat*; is current propaganda on the new and 'reformed' Soviet policy of *glasnost* so powerful that all the preceding '*glasnosts*'[60] and failed promises of reform are now **ignored or cast aside as ancient history**[61]? Are the data not given serious attention because they are not believed, or because the instant one gives them serious attention, **it becomes clear at once that the United States has serious problems, requiring urgent attention?** ∎

References to Chapter 11:

1. 'Without demand there is no supply'. Advertisement paid for by the Government of Colombia, *Washington Post*, October 14, 1988, page A22. For a more sophisticated statement, consider the words of President Julio Maria Sanguinetti of Uruguay at the opening of a meeting of seven Latin American Presidents. 'The key factor of consumption of drugs', he said as reported in the *Washington Post*, 'springs from deep-seated societal issues that will not easily be resolved'. Eugene Robinson, *Washington Post*, October 12, 1989, page A35.

2. Data taken from 'Drug Dependent Deaths Reported in New York City from 1923 to 1984', Communication from the Department of Health, New York City, September 14, 1988.

3. Gabriel G. Nahas, 'The Decline of Drugged Nations', *Wall Street Journal*, July 11, 1988.

4. This is a US intelligence estimate of Soviet active measures expenditures *circa* 1979. However, given the limited knowledge by US intelligence of Soviet active measures, for example, narcotics operations, the $3 billion figure is probably a gross underestimate.

5. One of the most pernicious political movements – supported, if not created, by Soviet-directed propaganda and active measures – is the drug (particularly marijuana) legalisation movement. As reported by Candlin, a meeting was organised by the Comintern in New York in 1934 to disseminate information on the use of marijuana as a conditioning medium for riots and revolutionary activity. The principal speaker explained the virtues of marijuana as a 'valued weapon in the Red arsenal' and described its experimental use in Mexico and the need for valuable revolutionary cadres to avoid excessive use of the drug. At that meeting, speakers rose and 'propounded a long-range campaign to arrange legal acceptance of marijuana and other similar drugs, using as an argument the right to freedom of individual choice. Some elements present – left-wing doctors, lawyers, news media representatives, and even clergy – were urged to get a coordinated campaign running in which the public would be urged to accept and legalise the drug'. *Psycho-Chemical Warfare: The Chinese Communist Drug Offensive Against the West*, *op. cit.*, pages 45-48. See also the quotation from the 1966 secret resolution on page 28 (Chapter 3).

6. C. W. Sheppard, G. R. Gay and D. E. Smith, 'The Changing Patterns of Heroin Addiction in the Haight-Ashbury Subculture', *Journal of Psychedelic Drugs*, Spring 1971, page 23. Copyright 1971 by the *Journal of Psychedelic Drugs*. Reprinted with permission. Data for 1969 and 1970 is omitted because of their proximity to the collection date.

7. 'Brazil May Become No. I Drug Exporter', *Insight*, July 25, 1988, page 37, citing *O Globo*, June 26,1988.

8. Earlston Spencer, 'Subverting Jamaica', National Committee To Restore Internal Security, *Houston Hearing*, September 29, 1980, pages 29-34.

9. *Crack Cocaine Overview 1989*, *op. cit.*, page 7.

10. Interview with Carlos Lehder, Uri Ra'anan *et al.*, *Hydra of Carnage* (Lexington, Massachusetts: Lexington Books, 1986). page 434.

11. *Hearing to Receive Testimony on Drugs, Law Enforcement and Foreign Policy: Panama*, February 11, 1988, *op. cit.*, pages 88, 97.

12. James M. Dorsey, '12 Killed in Medellín by Bomb, Despite Curfew', *Washington Times*, September 1, 1989, page A1.

13. 'US Official Says North Korean Farmers Ordered to Grow Drugs', *New York City Tribune*, February 21, 1990, page 6.

14. ''Western Intelligence' Links Honecker to Drugs', Hamburg *BILD*, reported in *Foreign Broadcast Information Service*, FBIS-EEU-89-233, December 6, 1989, page 40.

15. In one of the largest heroin smuggling cases on record, Manuel Dominguez Suarez, a one-time head of the Mexican Federal Judicial Police, was arrested on May 7,1970 in San Antonio, Texas. He had made nine trips to East Berlin, each time returning to Mexico with fifty kilograms of heroin, which were then moved across the border into the United States. Suarez received special treatment when he entered East Berlin – his passport was never stamped. He had been recruited by a Pole with East German connections. *World drug-traffic and Its Impact on U S. Security*, *op. cit.*, Part 4, page 157.

16. After DEA information was leaked to the press in March 1989 on the active involvement of Bulgaria in drug refining, trafficking and money-laundering, all in contradiction to the State Department's report to Congress on March 1, the State Department confirmed the DEA's data and said: 'It is the intention of the US Government to present the facts to the Bulgarian Government for whatever remedial action appears warranted', which is probably as far as the matter will have gone. After all, an 'intention' need never be realised in practice. Bill Gertz, 'State Confirms Bulgarian Company's Drug Ties', *Washington Times*, April 7, 1989, page A6.

17. Bill Gertz, 'Cuban Officers' Arrests Linked to Drugs', *Washington Times*, June 19, 1989, page A3; Gilles Trequesser, 'Cuban General Arrested for Treason Could Face Firing Squad', *Washington Times*, June 20, 1989, page A11; Giles Trequesser, 'Cuban Officials Pledge Crackdown on Drugs', *Washington Times*, June 23,1989, page A11; Julia Preston, 'Cuba Details Drug Deals', *Washington Times*, June 23, 1989, page A27; Michael Hedges, 'Drug Trial Testimony Forced Castro's Hand, Officials Believe', *Washington Times*, June 26, 1989, page A7; Mark A. Uhlig, 'Raúl Castro Adds Sparks to Cuban Trial', *New York Times*, June 27, 1989, page A3; Alfredo Munoz-Unsain, 'Firing Squad Likely for Cuban General in Drug-trafficking', *Washington Times*, June 27, 1989, page A9; Julia Preston, 'Castro Fires Top Official For Security', *Washington Post*, June 30, 1989, page A25; Julia Preston, 'Cuba Sentences Officers to Death for Corruption', *Washington Post*, July 8, 1989, page A1; and 'Cuba Executes Convicted Officers', *Washington Post*, July 14,1989, page A24.

18. *Hearing to Receive Testimony on Drugs, Law Enforcement and Foreign Policy: Panama*, Hearings Before the Subcommittee on Terrorism, Narcotics and International Operations of the Committee on Foreign Relations, February 10, 1988, unpublished stenographic transcript, page 70.

19. When the US Coast Guard attempted to board and search a cargo ship chartered by Cuban interests for evidence of drugs, the ship fled and sought refuge in Mexican waters. The United States had information that indicated the Cuban cargo was suspect. The ship was registered in Panama and the US had permission from Panama to board and search the vessel. The Mexicans then refused a US request to conduct a joint search of the vessel, and said they would conduct the search by themselves. Patrick E. Tyler, 'Coast Guard Fires Upon Cuban Ship', *Washington Post*, February 1, 1990, page A1.

20. The estimate on marijuana grown in Mexico, for example, rose during 1989 by a factor of ten. Michael Isikoff, 'World Output of Narcotics Soars, Congress Told', *Washington Post*, March 2, 1990, A24.

21. *Affidavit of Nelson Mantilla-Rey* (A 28-279-438) in Support of Political Asylum Application, Sworn to and subscribed to Gial Valentino, Notary Public, May 19, 1989, Suffolk County, Massachusetts.

22. M. M. Kirsch, *Designer Drugs* (Minneapolis, Minnesota: CompCare Publications, 1986), page 56.

23. James A. Inciardi, 'Beyond cocaine: basuco, crack, and other coca products', *Contemporary Drug Problems*, Fall 1987, page 471.

24. *Designer Drugs, op. cit.*

25. *Ibid.*, pages 46-47.

26. *Crack Cocaine* (Washington, D.C.: US Department of Justice, 1989), page 13 and appendices.

27. 'Today, Federal officials estimate there are as many as 10,000 Colombian traffickers operating in the United States, most of them in four key distribution centres – Miami, New York, Los Angeles and Houston. Trained at special drug-trafficking schools in Colombia and paid up to $20,000 a week, the cartel traffickers are rotated among the four cities, compartmentalised into small 10 to 20 member 'cells". Michael Isikoff and Nancy Lewis, 'Making the California Connection to the Cali Cartel', *Washington Post*, September 3, 1989, page A18.

28. Thomas L. Friedman, 'US and Soviets May Swap Secrets', *New York Times*, April 21, 1989.

29. Crozier, 'Drogue: la Filière Sovietique', *L'Express*, December 25, 1986, *op. cit.* This was immediately followed by Rachel Ehrenfeld, 'Narco-Terrorism: The Kremlin Connection', *Heritage Lectures No. 89* (Washington, D.C., The Heritage Foundation, 1987), and Joseph D. Douglass, Jr. and Jan Sejna, 'International Narcotics Trafficking: The Soviet Connection', *Journal of Defence and Diplomacy*, December, 1986.

30. For an excellent analysis of the overall problem, see Jean-François Revel, *How Democracies Perish* (Garden City, New York: Doubleday & Company, Inc., 1984).

31. Oleg Penkovskiy, *The Penkovskiy Papers* (Garden City, New York: Doubleday & Company Inc., 1965), pages 243-244.

32. See Hedrick Smith, *The Russians* (New York: Quadrangle/The New York Times Book Co., 1976), page 17; and *Journey for Our Time*, the journals of the Marquis de Custine, edited and translated by Phyllis Penn Kohler (London: Arthur Barker, Ltd., 1951).

33. The French analyst Mme. Suzanne Labin estimated the Soviet propaganda effort at $2 billion *per annum* back in 1960, which would suggest a much larger size today. US Senate, *The Technique of Soviet Propaganda*, A Study Presented to the Subcommittee to Investigate the Administration of the Internal Security Act and Other Internal Security Laws of the Committee on the Judiciary (Washington, D.C.: US Government Printing Office, 1960), page iii.

34. US House, *Soviet Active Measures*, Hearings Before the Permanent Select Committee on Intelligence, July 13, 14, 1982 (Washington, D.C.: US Government Printing Office 1982), page 49, emphasis added.

35. *Ibid.*, pages 226-227.

36. See, for example, **Anatoliy Golitsyn**, *New Lies for Old* (New York: Dodd, Mead & Company, 1984); John Barron, *KGB Today: The Hidden Hand* (New York: Reader's Digest Press, 1983); Chapman Pincher, *The Secret Offensive* (London: Sidgwick & Jackson, 1985); Richard H. Shultz and Roy Godson, *Dezinformatsia* (Washington, D.C.: Pergamon-Brassey's, 1984); Ladislav Bittman, *The KGB and Soviet Disinformation* (Washington, D.C.: Pergamon-Brassey's, 1985), and Edward Jay Epstein, *Deception* (New York: Simon & Schuster, 1989).

37. See Raymond S. Sleeper, editor, *Mesmerized by the Bear* (New York: Dodd, Mead & Company, 1987); and Brian D. Dailey and Patrick J. Parker, editors, *Soviet Strategic Deception* (Lexington, Massachusetts: Lexington Books, 1987).

38. US Federal Bureau of Investigation, *Soviet Active Measures in the United States 1986-1987*. Reprinted by the Security and Intelligence Foundation, Arlington, Virginia, 1988, page 20.

39. For several case studies in Soviet deception, see Raymond Sleeper, editor, *Mesmerized by the Bear, op. cit.*, and Brian D. Dailey and Patrick J. Parker, editors, *Soviet Strategic Deception, op. cit.* Regarding Soviet deception and assumptions underlying United States policy; see *Mesmerized by the Bear, op. cit.*, pages 223-224. See also **Anatoliy Golitsyn**, *The Perestroika Deception*, Edward Harle Limited, *op. cit.*

40. Sleeper, *Mesmerized by the Bear, op. cit.*

41. In addition to his positions described in Chapter 2, Sejna was a member of the sensitive deception review and planning committee for three Party Congresses and in respect of the development of the long-range plan.

42. A detailed discussion with examples of the Soviet strategy of **offensive denial** is presented in Joseph D. Douglass, Jr., *Why The Soviets Violate Arms Control Treaties* (Washington, D.C.: Pergamon-Brassey's, 1988), pages 63-83.

43. V. Ovchinnikov, 'The Drug Dealers', *Pravda*, September 13, 1964, translation by Rachel Douglas.

44. B. Bulatov, 'How the Maoists Conduct Contraband Trade in Opium', *Literaturnaya Gazeta*, March 19, 1969, page 12, translation by Rachel Douglas.

45. *Drugs and Terrorism*, 1984, *op. cit.*

46. *Ibid.*, pages 67, 68.

47. 'Among other traffickers associated with KINTEX are Syrian nationals Henri Arsan and Sallah Wakkas. Both Wakkas and Arsan, the latter having died in an Italian prison, were key figures in the movement of morphine base to Italian and French laboratories during the 'French Connection' era'. Drug Enforcement Administration, Strategic Intelligence Section, 'The Involvement of the People's Republic of Bulgaria in International Narcotics Trafficking', *Ibid.*, page 61.

48. *Ibid.*, page 65.

49. *Ibid.*

50. It seems especially curious that it is precisely when there emerges a mass of data on the official involvement of Bulgaria in drug-trafficking that US officials decide to approach Bulgaria and suggest joint operations to stop drug-trafficking through Bulgaria. Why *Bulgaria*? Who in the US Government proposed this approach? Is there a parallel between this situation and the events in the 1980s when, all of a sudden, more suggestions for 'joint' anti-drug-trafficking efforts and intelligence-sharing emerged following increased publicity surrounding the involvement of Communist countries?

51. It is also interesting that in 1986 two flattering biographies of Fidel Castro were published: Tad Szulc, *Fidel: A Critical Portrait* (New York: William Morrow and Company, Inc., 1986); and Peter G. Bourne, *Fidel: A Biography of Fidel Castro* (New York: Dodd, Mead & Company, 1986).

52. James A. Inciardi, 'Drug Abuse in the Georgian S.S.R.', *Journal of Psycho-active Drugs*, October-December 1987.

53. This was one of the principal ingredients of the **New Economic Policy** [NEP] adopted by Lenin in 1921 (see Anatoliy Golitsyn, *New Lies for Old*, New York: Dodd Mead, 1984, pages 10-52) and of the **'peaceful coexistence' deception** adopted by Khrushchev in 1954 (see Jan Sejna, *We Will Bury You* (London: Sidgwick & Jackson, 1982), pages 22-36; and Joseph D. Douglass, Jr., 'Soviet Strategic Deception', in Raymond S. Sleeper editor, *Mesmerized by the Bear* (New York: Dodd Mead, 1987)).

54. Brian Crozier, 'Drogue: la Filière Sovietique', *L'Express*, December 25, 1986.

55. Joseph D. Douglass, Jr. and Jan Sejna, 'International Narcotics Trafficking: The Soviet Connection', *Journal of Defence and Diplomacy*, December, 1986.

56. '$20 Million in Heroin Arrived on Soviet Ship', *Washington Times*, August 19, 1986, page 7A. 'Soviet Rôle in Dope Smuggling Exposed in European Press', *New Solidarity*, August 29, 1986, page 5. 'Italy Seizes Hashish from Soviet Ship', *Washington Post*, April 5, 1987, A 19.

57. The Soviets do, upon occasion, pull in their reins., in accordance with the 'one step forward, two steps back' strategy. However such operations always remain *controlled: **control is not severed***. Moreover a diminution of operational activity would also be apparent, but this is nowhere evident.

58. George Lardner, Jr., 'CIA Director: E. European Spies at Work', *Washington Post*, February 21, 1990, page A15. Earlier, Senator William Cohen (R-ME), Vice Chairman of the Senate Intelligence Committee at the time, had said: 'The intelligence services of Poland, East Germany, Czechoslovakia, Bulgaria, Hungary and Cuba continue to conduct intelligence operations in this country, not only to serve their own national interests, but also as surrogates for Soviet intelligence'. Bill Gertz, 'Despite Reform, East Bloc Spies on US', *Washington Times*, November 20, 1989, page A3.

59. US Department of State, *Soviet Influence Activities: A Report on Active Measures and Propaganda, 1987-1988* (Washington, D.C.: US Government Printing Office, August 1989).

60. Promoting the concept of reform as a mechanism to gain economic and technical assistance from the West has been a traditional (and most successful) Soviet deception strategy. In evaluating the recent Soviet 'reforms' called *perestroika* and *glasnost*, there are two especially compelling historical references to keep in mind. The first is Lenin's enormously successful deception, the **New Economic Policy** [NEP] in which Communism was portrayed as changing and embracing capitalism, but only in order to secure economic and technical assistance from the West. This eminently successful strategy, as analysed in KGB studies, is described by the former KGB officer Anatoliy Golitsyn in *New Lies for Old* (New York: Dodd, Mead & Company, 1984) [and also in his more recent work, *The Perestroika Deception*, Edward Harle Limited, 1985 and 1998, *op. cit. – Ed*]. The second is the strategic deception of **'peaceful coexistence'**, which was launched by Khrushchev in 1955 to procure economic and technical assistance from the West and to hasten the West's defeat [*see also Note 53, above*]. This strategy is described by Jan Sejna, the former Secretary of the Czechoslovak Defence Council, in *We Will Bury You, op. cit.* In both cases the Leninist tactics, strategy, and underlying motivations bear an uncanny resemblance to the events which took place under Mikhail Gorbachëv. See especially **Anatoliy Golitsyn**, *The Perestroika Deception, op. cit.*

61. *Editor's Note:* Do Western intelligence communities in fact employ **no** Russian-speaking students of Lenin who could have enlightened their superiors concerning the true Leninist revolutionary meaning of *perestroika* – reformation, as in '*military* formation'? Certainly, there is evidence of a perverse official determination to accept the Soviet Leninists' 'break with the past' lie as genuine, irrespective of the consequences. For instance, the British Ministry of Defence discarded its copies of the indispensable three-volume *Documents of the Communist International, 1919-1943*, edited by Jane Degras [Oxford University Press, 1956], since these volumes, complete with MOD Library Services stamp, were acquired by this writer. The British Foreign Office also sold off much of its Library of materials on Communism in 1990-91. So it is hardly surprising that Western policymakers remain blind. As a consequence, 'convergence' on the East's terms is already far advanced.

GRIM OUTLOOK FOR THE 21ST CENTURY

Since *Red Cocaine* first went to press ten years ago, the drug problem has continued to grow. Drugs are more widely available than ever before, prices are lower, and drug potency has increased. For example, heroin is now available that is 90 percent pure. Following a temporary decline from 1988 until 1992, teenage usage has been proliferating[1]. This is especially disturbing because of the grave implications for society's future.

From a global perspective, America is no longer the sole 'primary' target of the deliberate drugs offensive to destabilise the West and destroy Western society and democracy. Illegal drugs are flowing into Europe at record rates and into the various republics of the former Soviet Union. With them, crime and high-level corruption, which typically accompany illegal drugs, are growing everywhere. The size of the global criminal gross take is now estimated to be in excess of $2 trillion *per annum*. Health problems, which are also tied to illegal drug use, are proliferating.

Meanwhile the costs associated with measures to 'combat' the drugs scourge continue to escalate. The United States alone currently spends over $15 billion *per annum* on anti-drug operations. Apart from the spiralling expenditures and overheads, however, not much has changed. Responsive measures remain focused on:

○ Interdiction;
○ Attempts to gain the cooperation of drug-producing countries;
○ Law enforcement, and:
○ Education.

These measures remain as conspicuously ineffective today as they were 25 years ago – as is only too apparent from the ready availability of drugs, their decreased street prices, their heightened potency, and the associated increases in consumption among adolescents. Yet notwithstanding the severity of the illegal drug scourge and its consequences, there is no evident determination to address the challenge it presents in a serious manner. Moreover the official diagnosis of the crisis in the United States remains naïve and inadequate.

One reason the drugs crisis receives much less serious attention (in the United States, as well as elsewhere) than it should be receiving, is that estimates of what illegal drugs cost people everywhere – not just in monetary terms but also in respect of their impact on political and social structures, and on families and individuals' lives – are woefully incomplete and grossly understated. This appears to be because the US authorities, and some other

Western Governments as well, do not relish having to face the severity of the offensive against Western societies, and do not want to advertise the gravity of the crisis.

In America, drug use and cost estimates are based mainly upon so-called 'Household Use' statistics. These statistics are so inadequate and misleading that they may well be worse than none at all. There are two monumental problems with the 'Household Use' statistics. First, they assume that people will voluntarily tell the truth about their use of drugs. Secondly, they do not address the heaviest group of drug users – people who are not 'found in households' but rather are homeless or in various institutions such as jails, shelters, hospitals, and treatment facilities.

Important insights into the value of 'self-reports' were brought to light in 1991 when the Emory School of Medicine ran a covert test of drug user 'truthfulness' at a walk-in clinic in Atlanta[2]. Their researchers asked patients if they had used any drugs in the preceding three days. What the researchers did not tell the patients was that they intended to test their urine for cocaine drug residue. What they determined was that seventy-two percent of the men who claimed they had used no drugs during the preceding three days tested positive for cocaine use alone. If they had been tested for the use of other drugs as well – for example, marijuana, heroin, PCP, LSD, ecstacy, methamphetamines and so forth – the percentage would probably have exceeded ninety percent. Their conclusion was clear: *self-reports of drug use are unreliable*. The drug-use statistics that they calculated for the segments of the population they dealt with were three times higher than one would estimate based on the 'Household Use' statistics.

In addition, there have been no good estimates of US hard-core users, and the costs associated with drug usage by this group probably exceed all those of the non-hard core users that form the backbone of the 'Household Use' statistics. For over ten years, the number of chronic users has been assumed to be around three to five million. To its credit, the US Office of National Drug Control Policy has initiated a study to try to establish how many hard-core addicts there are in the United States[3]. Their first attempt focused on Cook County, Illinois. There, they studied the jails, homeless shelters, and institutions and used drug-use tests – both urine and hair tests – to verify reports. While their survey still yielded an underestimate, the results were alarming. The Office of National Drug Control Policy estimated that there were 330,000 chronic users in Cook County alone. Their findings were still labelled 'preliminary' and carried the warning, 'do not extrapolate'. But, if one nevertheless extrapolates these findings, the corresponding national hard-core total would be in the 15 to 20 million range, which is three to five times higher than the conventional wisdom – and, as predicted, considerably higher than the usage rates one might be tempted to employ, based on the 'Household Use' statistics.

A realistic estimate of what the drug plague costs the United States each year, using conservative figures and Government statistics where they exist, is also eye-opening. It is three to five times higher than the $50 to $60 billion numbers quoted by President Clinton and Vice President Gore a few years ago. To place these 'competing' estimates in perspective, they show the drug plague each year costing the United States more than the entire ten-year Vietnam War, with the number of illegal drug casualties each year also exceeding the total Vietnam War data[4]. Moreover, annual deaths attributable to illegal drugs are actually over four times higher than the total fatalities in the worst of the Vietnam War years.

These cost estimates do not and cannot put a dollar figure on the damage being done due to the corruption of drugs and drug money on people's lives. Brains, bodies, spirituality, and life courses are destroyed. Families, the basic building blocks of society, are burdened to the point, sometimes, of total disruption. Almost everyone one meets in the United States these days has direct personal experience of the damage inflicted by the drugs offensive on a family member or a close relative.

The Drug Enforcement Administration's estimate of US domestic marijuana production in 1992 – and that department (the DEA) rarely, if ever, overestimates the size of the supply – multiplied by the average street value of 'good' marijuana, yields an annual cash crop value of $30 billion, twice the size of any legal farm crop. All such transactions and profits are illegal and have to be laundered. How much is laundered into stocks, bonds, and real estate? **Has the endless and escalating flood of drug money sustained and bolstered the stock and commodity markets, and also the strength of the US dollar on the foreign exchange markets?** How much drug money goes into political campaigns, or shows up in election contributions? How much influence and corruption does just the home-grown marijuana proportion of the drug trade in America, buy? Add imported marijuana, heroin, cocaine, LSD and methamphetamines – and the total rises sharply. Influence-peddling and election-financing are the natural associates of drug funds: so democracy is being undermined *directly* through interference with the democratic process and by ensuring that political candidates are beholden to evil money from the outset. This makes for corrupt government, as events in 1998 confirmed.

The implications are inescapable: growing, widespread, all-encompassing drug-money corruption, including corruption of the political, judicial, police, legal, accounting, finance, and even the business communities throughout the United States. And of course the same fate awaits the other leading Western countries which are prime targets for the drug offensive. In Europe, the European Union's structures, already notorious for nomenklaturist corruption and inefficiency, are prime targets for the drug offensive.

Police corruption has featured on the font pages of the newspapers in most of the leading American cities: for example, New York, Philadelphia, Miami, Los Angeles, Cleveland, Detroit, Chicago, New Orleans, and in Washington, DC. Extensive corruption in Federal agencies responsible for combating the flow of drugs has also been reported – affecting, in particular, the Drug Enforcement Administration, the US Customs Service, and the Immigration, Justice, and Border Patrol communities. The domestic and international banking communities are heavily compromised, of course, by the drug scourge.

Everyone understands that it is usually the so-called 'small fry' who get caught. These people are the most expendable and least sophisticated. Nor does it take a rocket scientist to recognise that the same corruption that has been exposed within the law enforcement agencies also permeates the higher levels in the judicial, financial, political and political influence communities throughout the United States. It is also clearly present, as noted, in the financing of elections; but neither US political party wants to discuss this phenomenon, if it can be avoided. It must be assumed, on the basis of the evidence, that the reputations of *both* the main US political parties are equally at risk.

In addition to a general lack of serious attention, assisted by an often complacent media approach to the issue, the 'war on drugs' in America remains ineffective because the illegal drug issue is *still* not understood historically, financially, politically, or strategically. Conventional beliefs and assumptions concerning the origins of the drug plague and the reasons it has proliferated so alarmingly, contain serious gaps and mis- or disinformation. According to the 'conventional wisdom', it is *the people themselves* who are at fault; that is, it is *the people themselves* who who bear primary responsibility for the drug plague. If the people did not use drugs, there would be no scourge. This, by the way, has always been the standard argument used by Colombians when the issue is raised by visiting Americans or Europeans: in Bogotá, it is the preferred analysis – for only too obvious reasons. Moreover, US officials and the media foster the image that drug-traffickers are little more than common criminals, people who live in fear of the law and who are, in effect, renegades whose only ideology is the pursuit of profit. These same purveyors of the news would also have us believe that the US Federal Government is doing its best to curb drug production and trafficking. As is demonstrated in the preceding material, nothing could be further from the truth. The army of apologists for the drugs crisis and its consequences, together with the 'liberalisers', have powerful and influential organisations behind them – and, of course, unlimited financial resources.

But the drug crisis, as we have seen, is not home grown – the result of some deficiency in US and other Western societies. **It emerged because it was forced upon the West as an act of long-term low-level warfare by very sophisticated intelligence operations orchestrated by the Chinese and by the Soviets and their various surrogates and satellites.** When Nikita Khrushchev was reported to have informed the West that 'we will bury you', he was misquoted. What Khrushchev actually said was: **'we will be present at your funeral'**. And, as anyone who has lost a family member, relative or loved one knows at first-hand, there have been many funerals since the drugs offensive began.

In this respect, note again the data in *Figure 5* on page 135, which show the growth in the first use by addicts of heroin recorded in the Haight-Ashbury section of San Francisco and the numbers of drug dependent deaths in New York City (*Figure 4*, page 133). These data reveal a significant jump in drug abuse in 1949-50, precisely when the Chinese narcotics trafficking operation began, and an exponential rise beginning in 1960-61 – which was when the Soviet narcotics trafficking operation was launched and the Chinese Communist operation was expanded.

The message is clear to anyone interested in learning what is *really* happening – which is to say, to anyone prepared to discard the rose-tinted spectacles and 'politically correct' misapprehensions favoured in baffled US and other official circles these days. *First*, the dramatic change in the usage statistics is the result of **increased supply**; and *secondly*, **the sources of the supply are foreign intelligence operations designed specifically to attack the youth of targeted countries with illegal drugs**.

In the course of 1998, yet more data emerged which, once again, showed the same phenomenon with respect to cocaine. In 1992, during the 'Household Survey' in the United States, people were asked *when* they began using cocaine for the first time. The data from the answers received were placed on the Internet. They are plotted in *Figure 7* on page 157. What stands out clearly is a significant change in usage statistics, starting in 1967, at which time the rate of first use of cocaine starts rising. Why? **What happened in 1967?**

The potential of cocaine as the most important drug of the future was first communicated to the Czechs in 1962. Operations to construct cocaine networks had already begun and were expanded with effect from that year. Between 1962 and 1965, the relevant production techniques were modernised by the East Germans. They developed brand new processes which turned out to be far superior to the old techniques. **One plant using the new German process could produce three times more cocaine than the entire then-existing production of Colombia, Peru and Bolivia**. These techniques were introduced, and the production and distribution networks were put in place, during 1965-66.

As General Sejna explained the position in detail, 1967 was the year when the

Soviets' cocaine production and distribution operations, centred indeed in Colombia, Peru and Bolivia, came on stream – which was *precisely* when the first use of cocaine data began rising steadily: *see Figure 7*. The increase in drug usage was **the result of a substantial increase in** *supply* and associated marketing strategies, and the source of those supplies and strategies was the Soviet foreign intelligence operation – the code name of which was **'Pink Epidemic'** (*see page 33 et seq*) alluding to the blending of the **white** (cocaine) with the **red** (Communism).

The chart below also provides significant insights into the means which need to be adopted in order to achieve an effective solution to the illegal drug scourge.

First, of course, there are two sides to the crisis – supply and 'demand'. *Both* sides have to be attacked, particularly since, *uniquely* in the case of drugs, *demand is* **created** *by supply*. Any proposed ' solution' which does not attack the *availability* of the drugs in question is **not** a solution because it does **not** address the fundamental source of the crisis – **the supply. It is the** *supply* (and this includes its marketing and support networks) **which creates addicts in the first place**. If the supply is not attacked, there will be a constant increase in the number of addicts as each new generation of young people for various reasons decides to ' experiment' and gets hooked.

In all honesty, the demand side, which is dominantly the demand generated by addicts, will **ultimately solve itself as the addicts die out**. Many users may languish and may never be cured. Proposals that make it safe for users to do drugs or that provide them with cheap drugs under the assumption that this will *reduce* crime are of course intended to

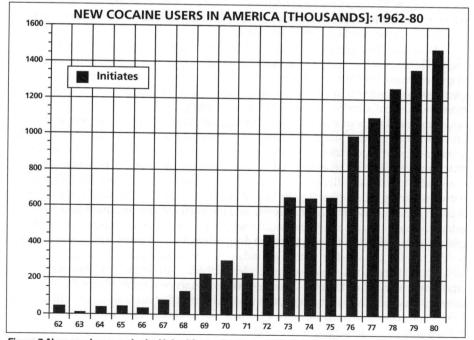

Figure 7: New cocaine users in the United States [in thousands], showing conclusively the correlation with the commencement of Soviet involvement in 1967, and thus with supply. *Data source:* Rouse, B.A., *Ed.*, 1995, *Substance Abuse and Mental Health Statistics Sourcebook*. DHHS Publication No. (SMA) 95-3064, Government Printing Office. Washington DC. Chart prepared from published official data selected by the Author.

enable addicts to 'do their thing' until they die. These fancy and false notions will not solve the crisis, or indeed contribute to its remediation, because they do not attack the supply; and as the data in *Figure 7* confirm, it is indeed the **supply** that creates the drugs crisis in the first place. The objective of this supply is to **generate addicts** so that the supply can be consumed – that is to say, **to foster demand**. There is *no equivalence* between such *addiction* demand and normal *commercial* demand, as is always deceitfully implied.

Secondly, the preceding material shows that the illegal drug question is not going to be solved by attacking it as a ' law and order' or a 'law enforcement' or even a diplomatic challenge. The accuracy of this conclusion can be seen in the fact that the prevailing 'war on drugs' has been shown to have been totally ineffective – precisely because it has been approached as a law and order, law enforcement, and diplomatic challenge since it emerged in 1950. The 'results' achieved during the Reagan Administration provide a further demonstration of this fallacy. The drugs scourge was then approached as a law enforcement matter. As a consequence, US jails went from being three-quarters full to far over capacity; yet during that period, drugs became *more* plentiful, *more* potent, and *more* easily accessible, than ever before. The policy was a total waste of money.

Treating the drug plague as a law enforcement or a diplomatic problem will not succeed because those responsible are *not* **common criminals** and because **they operate with the protection of the local law and order communities, the domestic and international banks, and** *under diplomatic immunity*. The only way to approach the illegal drug plague is to recognise it for what it is – *an intentional attack* on the United States and the West generally. This concerted and relentless assault amounts to **an undeclared war in which all available means are employed** – overt, covert, illegal, and indigenous – in the pursuit of the enemy, which remains the West.

As for the US Government's supposed determination to decapitate the producers and traffickers, another comparison provides the needed perspective. Since the drug plague emerged, the United States has undertaken numerous military adventures, at great risk, cost, and without the invitation of those who were attacked. Consider, for example, Vietnam, Cambodia, Grenada, Panama, Iraq and Libya. We have even attacked, unilaterally and without anyone's concurrence, pharmaceutical plants suspected of producing nerve agents and the training and supply depôts of individuals who evidently sponsored terrorist activities. In none of these adventures was the United States under attack, or even directly threatened. Yet, in sharp contrast, there has not been **one** instance of a similar US military attack on a foreign drug producing or drug-trafficking régime, notwithstanding the fact that it is the United States (and of course the West generally) that is under *direct* attack, is *directly* threatened, and **has suffered and continues to suffer** extensive casualties, economic and social disruption, and individual fatalities as a consequence of this offensive. Indeed, **since the drug offensive is an act of war**, those countries which encourage or sanction or turn a blind eye to it should be placed on notice once and for all that if they do not cease their malevolent activities forthwith, the United States (and, if necessary, other targeted countries) will no longer be responsible for the destructive consequences. In short, such régimes should be regarded as *enemy régimes*. In this connection, it is worth recalling that the 'former' Soviet Union respected the West *only* when it stood up to its Bolshevik bullying.

If, then, 'conventional wisdom' is set aside, and along with it all the various explanations of the drug scourge which flow so glibly from the official and unofficial talking heads in Western capitals, a sharply divergent image emerges. Specifically, the illegal drug plague will be seen to be an international criminal 'business' which, due to the corruption it engenders, enjoys the support and protection of many countries and of many powerful people, some of whom are well-known personalities. And the scourge can be seen to have grown for five primary reasons.

First, the drug plague is **not** the brainchild of 'common or garden' crooks and criminals. It is **the result of long-term strategic intelligence operations undertaken by countries with the largest and most capable intelligence services in the world:** China and the Soviet Union and its satellites, and their successors. This means that unlike an independent criminal operation, the drug-traffickers who built the business have and continue to have at their disposal the assets and resources of various states and governments, together with the benefit of open and unlimited sanctuaries in which to hide, plan, finance, organise, recruit, and train for the next phases of their collective offensive.

Secondly, the plague has been able to flourish because it has been politically protected. The protection that the US Government, for instance, has provided – free of charge – has been well documented in the cases of China, Russia, Bulgaria, Cuba, Mexico, Colombia and the former Czechoslovakia, to name a few of the countries involved. Moreover, the corruption of drug money is so pervasive that it has truly become a serious question to ask whom one can trust any more – and not just in foreign countries, but, for Americans, in the Federal Departments and agencies, and in Congress as well. Why have no Government records on the drug-trafficking and money-laundering activities run out of Mena, Arkansas, been released or *even investigated* by Congress or by the Office of the so-called 'Independent Counsel', and why have US election financing links to drug money-launderers, to the Palestinian Authority and to Chinese interests, not surfaced properly?

Thirdly, the drug plague has been free to develop without constraint because the money-laundering dimension of drug-trafficking has been organised – not just tolerated or enabled, but *organised* – by the international financial community, and by national (US) banks as well†. There is no way such a multi-trillion dollar financial stream could exist without the active and knowing assistance of banks and financial institutions, the laundering and 'investment' profits of which represent an estimated 15 to 20 percent of their aggregate annual profits. And by 'international financial community', I do not just mean banks and bankers. Of equal importance, and functioning as integral elements of the international financial community, are associated investment advisers and companies, accountancy firms and specialists, and – most importantly of all – the associated **lawyers and legal firms** upon whom the banks are **critically dependent.**

† *Editor's Note:* A case in point was highlighted in a report published by the US General Accounting Office [GAO], the accounting and investigative arm of Congress, on 4th December 1998. In a vivid example of how banks allegedly flout the law while maintaining deniability and appearing to uphold it, Citibank was reported by the GAO to have secretly transferred between $90 million and $100 million of alleged drugs money for a Mexican client without examining the source of the funds, or the client's financial background. The GAO concluded *inter alia* that Citibank, now part of Citigroup, failed to follow its own procedures against money-laundering, and 'facilitated a money managing system that disguised the origin, destination and beneficial owner of the funds'. The GAO had responded to a request by Senator John Glenn, the astronaut, to look into reports that up to $100 million was laundered out of Mexico to Citibank accounts in London and Switzerland. A separate investigation was being carried out by the US Justice Department. The GAO report revealed that Citibank's private banking unit had established an offshore private company to hold its client's assets, had waived bank references, had allowed the client to use a different name to transfer funds from Mexico, and had failed to prepare a financial profile on the prominent client in question. The bank earned about $1.1 million in fees associated with its running of the relevant accounts. A spokesman for Citigroup, cited by *The Daily Telegraph* of London [5th December 1998], insisted that the report 'contained errors of fact and interpretation', adding that 'we have looked into the matter ourselves and have found that neither the company nor any employee has violated the law. We're cooperating fully with law enforcement authorities'.

Such lawyers hide behind their protection of respectability and the 'rule of law': but they are whited sepulchres, hypocrites and active participants in this evil business. For this reason, it was encouraging to be able to read in the British press[5] in late November 1998 that Detective Chief Inspector Simon Goddard, the head of the organised and economic crime unit at the National Criminal Investigation Service [NCIS] in London had revealed that lawyers from at least six large law firms were in the process of being investigated for alleged money-laundering on behalf of drug-traffickers and other organised criminals. Reporting the essence of an interview given by this top British law enforcement officer in *The Lawyer* magazine, Mr Goddard explained that several law enforcement agencies, including a number of UK police forces, were investigating the handling of profits from drugs, gun-running and violent gangster-style activities. 'These firms are actively working on behalf of organised crime. We know who they are [the lawyers concerned]. We are aware of some of their activities, and we are at varying stages of our investigations. We certainly have lawyers who perform the rôle like an old *consigliere* in the mafia films. They know who their clients are and they know how their clients make their money, and they know it isn't from a legitimate activity'.

Sources at the NCIS further confirmed that the lawyers and the firms concerned were located in the City of London, and elsewhere in the British capital. In one case, the whole of a small firm had been identified as a front for money-laundering. In other cases, it was suspected that lawyers in some large firms were accepting illicit funds and using their positions in respectable concerns to hide their activities. Typically, the funds are co-mingled with other funds in the firms' clients' accounts, and then transferred as instructed by their drug-linked 'clients'. But of course any suspicious money transactions must by law, in the United Kingdom, be reported to NCIS. Out of 14,500 reports filed under the relevant UK legislation in 1997, precisely 240 were from solicitors (attorneys); and NCIS told *The Guardian* newspaper that many British lawyers were 'failing in their legal and moral obligations'[6]. The newspaper also confirmed that it had been told by a spokesman for NCIS that 'we have intelligence on at least six law firms we believe to be involved in money-laundering'. Police believed that 'the money is wired to solicitors, who put it in clients' accounts in London. It is then transferred to offshore accounts or trusts'.

As General Sejna described the position while he was alive, the money-laundering contacts in the various banks selected to provide 'banking services' were set up by the bankers themselves. Background security checks on the individuals who were to handle drug money transactions in the banks were run not only by Soviet counter-intelligence, but also by one of the Israeli intelligence services, Mossad, as well. **The bankers were so integrated into the operations that secret meetings took place in Prague between the Soviets and the international financiers concerned, every week. General Sejna knew this because secret villas under his control were used as the locations for most of the Soviets' meetings with the bankers involved. In other words, Western bankers have knowingly participated in this destructive, Leninist revolutionary activity from the outset of the drug offensive launched by Soviet and Chinese intelligence to destroy the West.**

In the fourth place, the explosion of the drug scourge has been facilitated by the encouragement and complicity of confused intellectuals of the Left, whose power base also controls, or has achieved mind-hegemony within, the marketplace for ideas[7]. This is no accident, of course, since it has been a consequence of the parallel revolutionary drive to destroy values, religion and morality throughout the targeted West, to which brief references have been made. The drug plague expanded between 1965 and 1980, when drug usage in the West first became rampant, to a significant degree because drug use was popularised by intellectuals in academic settings and because these people published books promoting drug use via permissive messages and a perverse and wilful insistence that there were no bad drugs, only ill-informed drug *users* – and because such permissive works outnumbered those stressing the biological and social dangers by a ratio of 50 to 1[8].

In the fifth place, people have been mesmerised – brainwashed by politicians, governments, news media, and academia – into thinking, as noted earlier, that it is *they themselves* who are the cause of the crisis [*see page 155*]; that if people did not use drugs, there would be no drug scourge, that their governments have all along been hard at work fighting the plague, and that the public should not become involved at all, since it is all so horribly dangerous. Depend on us, we have the task covered, and all we need is more time and money, US officials routinely tell Congress. Certainly, drug users and abusers are not without fault, and are themselves in danger of perdition; but they would have been far less vulnerable if they had enjoyed the benefit of principled responses and retaliation by their governments – and had not the enemy been working overtime to destroy Western culture, beliefs and values, and to subvert education.

Today, with the further intent of continuing the charade and to avoid reality (and responsibility), people ask: 'But are they – the Russians, Chinese, Cubans, and their many surrogates, still involved?'

Certainly, there have been significant changes. However, there is not *one* identifiable change that suggests any diminished Soviet, Chinese, or Cuban involvement. What has happened is that production and trafficking have entered an even more aggressive phase aimed at expanding drug usage and corruption on a world-wide scale, without restriction. Drug-trafficking is more open, in a real sense paralleling the sudden 'emergence' of Russian organised crime as a 'new' phenomenon in industrialised countries [9].

Indeed, it is hard to imagine a reasonable hypothesis as to why the Russians,the Chinese or Cubans, would not be as active today as ever – indeed more so. Consider:

First: The KGB/GRU is as alive and as 'well' as ever, and enjoys greater power than before the implementation of 'collapsible Communism'. Why on earth would they walk away from the most profitable business and the most effective political compromise, blackmail, and influence operation the world has ever seen? What bureaucracy ever went out of business without being *forced* out of business, when the parent organisation is alive and healthy and so powerful that it has become a 'state within the state' [*see page 162*] (although that in itself is nothing new at all)?

After all, the drug-trafficking operation, *'Druzhba Narodov'*, produced scores of billions of dollars in secret revenues each year. **These revenues were controlled by the KGB and never went near the official government budget. This converted the KGB/GRU into a fiscal powerhouse independent of the state.** There is no way these revenues would have been discarded, and there was no-one on the outside with the knowledge and power who could ever question or challenge their provenance.

Secondly, **the political blackmail and compromise dossiers on people holding positions of power around the world, which became crucial components of the narcotics trafficking products were – and still are – exceedingly valuable assets for use in support of Russian foreign and financial policy.** Such files and operations were so valuable that prior to the controlled geopolitical 'changes' which the KGB/GRU itself orchestrated, control of global drug operations was shifted to Moscow and the key files were moved to Russia. *Asset preservation* was a hallmark of KGB/GRU activities on the eve of the controlled disintegration of the Stalinist model ('collapsible Communism').

Thirdly, nor has the manner in which secrecy has been preserved in critical areas, been significantly changed since 1989-91. Much information has emerged, but next to nothing has been revealed of strategic importance. Where important strategic information has been identified, the means used to safeguard any leakage have remained as strong-armed and as ruthless as was always the case under 'overt Communism' prior to 1989-91.

In the fourth place, there is no coherent reason for the managers of the global drugs offensive to cease and desist – since Western Governments, having protected the drug trade for thirty years and more, are not about to change their attitudes. It is still contrary to the policies of most Western Governments to say *anything* negative about, or to embarrass, the Soviets or the Chinese. Britain has leant over backwards to placate the Chinese, even though it has handed them the world's primary drug entrepôt, Hong Kong, with its stupendous power and infrastructure, on a plate. And, in an unbelievable repeat of misjudged joint US-Bulgarian operations to help the Bulgarians curb drug-trafficking across their borders in the 1970s, an initiative that would have been ludicrous had it not been so tragic [see Chapter 9], the US intelligence communities (FBI and CIA) have opened offices in Moscow so that they can work jointly with the KGB in 'fighting organised crime, drug-trafficking, and international terrorism' – with no apparent understanding of the extent of KGB and GRU involvement in each of these three activities.

The net result of this folly is as follows: *first*, the Soviets/Russians have been well briefed on Western crime-fighting methodology, attitudes and responses. *Secondly*, they have been kept well-informed about initiatives considered and mounted by US intelligence to 'combat crime', enabling the Russians to ensure that their criminalist operatives have been able to remain *several steps ahead* of Western intelligence at all times. To keep US and Western intelligence agencies 'on side' whenever doubts may appear to have arisen in Western minds about the integrity and/or the sincerity of Russian activities and intentions, snippets of otherwise unobtainable, but usually expendable, intelligence, have been vouchsafed from time to time for the benefit of Western intelligence, so as to make sure that this ill-advised 'cooperative' crime-fighting activity could continue to be justified in Western capitals. Again, such behaviour is nothing new at all: *it is standard Leninist deception practice.*

Since 1990-91, Lenin's 'criminal state' has been exported as a model for the whole world. Drug-trafficking is more aggressive, widespread and open than at any time in human history. Russia itself has become a hotbed of crime and corruption. Organised crime controls over forty percent of private businesses, sixty percent of state-owned companies, over half of Russia's commercial banks (a large number of which were to have been closed down in late 1998, having outlived their 'usefulness'), and eighty percent of the shops, hotels and service industries in Moscow. The KGB is widely credited with being at the centre of these criminal operations, and their primary benefactor – a development which led one Russian writer, Yevgenia Albats, to be the first to label the KGB a 'state within a state'[10]. Russian organised crime has also experienced phenomenal growth in the United States and in Latin America.

The Russians also forged with the speed of light, ties and alliances with the mafia, Japanese *yukaza*, Chinese triads, Jamaican 'Yardies' (some leaders of which group were seized in a dramatic police drug-bust in central London on 30th November 1998: *see also page 164*), and other drug-trafficking organisations around the world. The KGB/GRU's political influence operations must also remain of global scope – as an inevitable and natural consequence of the tens of thousands of dossiers they hold on people of power and influence in the West and elsewhere, who have been corrupted by the drug trade.

In 1991, the Russian central banking system began printing roubles as fast as it could. Naturally, the value of the rouble tumbled. Suddenly, the law was changed. Early in 1992 it ceased to be illegal any longer to hold dollars in Russia. Overnight, US dollars became the preferred currency throughout the 'former' Soviet Union. One newspaper reported as early as mid-1993 that there were more paper dollars in circulation in Russia than in the United States – up to $100 billion in dollar bills.

Where did all the dollars circulating in the 'former' Soviet Union come from? Certainly, they did not originate among tourists or businessmen. Since US dollars became the preferred currency in Russia, between $1.0 and $3.0 billion in dollar bills have also been leaving Russia every month (at least $50 million a day), destined for foreign banks. Russian crooks now own Cyprus[11] and are moving into Malta. Their preferred money-laundering and sequestering locations these days are indeed Cyprus, Lebanon, the Cayman Islands (especially via certain Canadian banks), and to a lesser extent, Switzerland and Liechtenstein. Yet notwithstanding this immense outward flow, there are still thought to be more paper dollars in circulation in Russia than in the United States.

While all this unconstrained criminal activity has been developing and maturing over the past decade, the West (and East, but mainly the West – and within the West, primarily Europe) has been pouring massive financial and technical assistance into Russia. The socialist European Union has been particularly conscientious in this regard. All of which brings to mind the manner in which the drunken sailor spends his wages. Why would *anyone*, knowing the situation in Russia and the nature of the Russian leadership and culture, provide 'economic' assistance, or even think they could do clean and profitable business, in accordance with Western standards and norms, with the Russians – especially recognising that Western businessmen and financiers are generally not naive in pursuing their normal activities? Clearly, *there must be a dimension which is not widely understood*. Perhaps the long-term background and nature of Soviet-Western financial cooperation may have some connection with the compromise dossiers mentioned above. We have seen that Western bankers were 'integrated' into the Soviet drug infrastructure from the beginning. Given the predominant participation of Soviet/Russian and Chinese intelligence in these nefarious activities, it would be incredible if the dossiers were not in active use today, and if their use of blackmail and other methods of compromising Western and European Union politicians, bankers, bureaucrats, policymakers and agents of influence were not as commonplace and routine as in the past.

The worst is yet to come. We have observed the growth of an immense international narcotics business since the early 1960s. This business represented an outward manifestation of two state-run intelligence operations, those developed by the Chinese and the Soviets, in collaboration with their East European satellite surrogate services. The operations concerned were fully integrated from the outset, with international finance, law and politics. In parallel, the world experienced the headlong growth of what is now referred to as global criminal capitalism ('criminalism')[12].

This embraces narcotics trafficking, organised crime, illegal arms sales, the theft of national resources, income tax evasion, and pornography. And as explained above, almost the instant the Soviet Union 'disintegrated', Russian banks, managed and staffed in large measure by former KGB and GRU personnel, began proliferating, while sizeable Russian crime syndicates surfaced all over the world – forging, as noted, almost instanta-

neous ties with mafia networks (which the KGB/GRU knew well, of old), with drug-traffickers and with other organised criminal groups everywhere. Indeed, the links between
the Soviets and Italian mafia groups had long historical roots: for instance, Soviet Georgia
had traditionally provided Moscow's mafia connections in Italy with hunting privileges –
so that when the time came for Eduard Shevardnadze to seek help from Western sources
to cement his brutal régime, it was to Italian mafia-linked allies that his government
turned for special expedited deliveries of rubber truncheons (the Italians make excellent
rubber truncheons used for 'crowd control' purposes). Is all this just mere coincidence?

   In 1996, annual revenues derived from global criminalist activities were estimated
by the World Bank's experts at $1.2 trillion, of which $500 billion were thought to represent profits. These were and remain highly conservative estimates. The narcotics trade
alone is in the $500 billion or more range. A more realistic estimate today would probab-
ly be of the order $2 trillion per year, as already noted – with $1 trillion, more or less, by
way of straight profit; and some experts would raise these estimates further, towards
$3.0 trillion annually in turnover. That is to say, governments, banks and the global crimi-
nalists are arranging the transfer of at least $1.0 trillion every year of national and private
wealth into the bank accounts of the global criminal fraternity – a massive transfer of
wealth for which there has been no historical parallel. **This scandalous state of affairs
has been continuing for several decades on an ever expanding scale, and the power
conferred as a consequence threatens to destroy governments, democracy and the
international banking system itself.** Drug money also weakens and corrodes competition by favouring some economic agents at the expense of others.

   Two trillion+ dollars a year (a conservative figure, as noted) over the past two
decades, excluding interest, would imply that more than $40 trillion will have been added
to the wealth of the global criminal classes, including the managers and representatives of
Lenin's continuing world socialist revolution. Most of this money has been invested in
property, bonds and stocks, and each year a further trillion or more dollars is added to the
pool. Given that even these data are believed by some experts to understate the position,
the probable value of accrued drug money lodged in the international financial system
worldwide probably now exceeds this $40 trillion estimate by a considerable margin†.
The associated corruption among financial institutions, investment advisory services
(including stock brokerage houses and mutual funds), prestigious law firms, and among
the political classes, has by now long since reached epidemic proportions. And this transformation has been accompanied by minimal publicity, with the exception of extensively
publicised, but intermittent, 'drug busts', such as the sizeable operation mounted by
British law enforcement agents on 30th November 1998 against Jamaican 'Yardie' operatives [*see page 162*], which resulted in the seizure of hard drugs and weapons [13].

   In December 1996, *Business Week* gave some exposure to what it termed the 'tip of
the iceberg', in a feature about drug money corruption on Wall Street, entitled 'The Mob
on the Street'. The article explained:

   'In the canyons of lower Manhattan, one can find members of organised crime,
their friends and associates. How large a presence? No-one – least of all regulators and
law enforcement – seems to know. The Street's reputed ranking underworld chieftain,
Abramo, is described by sources familiar with his activities as controlling at least four

† *Author's Note:* One of the principal hidden motivations behind the contemporary drug legalisation drive
is to procure the instantaneous legalisation of drug profits and to eliminate the potential risks of disclosure
and exposure – that is, to legitimise accumulated illegal drug-derived fortunes.

brokerages through front men, and exerting influence upon still more firms'[14].

This glimpse of the obvious, if we stop to think what must be happening, will also be applicable, for instance, in banking, among the leading US law firms (as in London), and within the policymaking community, as well. Moreover few areas of US life today can be described as dependably honest any more. The decadence is pervasive, the money involved is colossal, those who control it are excessively corrupt and lacking in conscience, and minimal attention is paid to the reality that the corrupting influence of drug-related activities and money must, by now, have progressed so far that few areas of economic activity can be assumed to be immune. In some countries – Japan, for instance – corruption is an openly acknowledged way of life: indeed, there, the entire Establishment and the corporate and financial systems appear to have been tainted almost to the point of no return.

In Switzerland, the Federal Prosecutor, Carla del Ponte, has said that the value of just the Russian criminal 'profit' money lodged with Swiss banks exceeds $40 billion[15]. The $40 billion is of course just the proverbial tip of the iceberg. How large is the *total* amount of illegal booty in Swiss banks? Probably well over ten times as much, perhaps as high as 100 times as much. And this is just Switzerland. The same conditions, greater by an order of magnitude, prevail in the banking systems of Liechtenstein, Luxembourg, Great Britain, Germany, Spain, all manner of tax-free havens and offshore islands, and the United States. That is, the $40 billion officially identified as being lodged in Switzerland is merely a small proportion of the total value of tens of trillions of dollars accumulated by the global criminalists, and sequestered with commercial and private banks all over the world.

At the end of November 1998, Sr del Ponte said that he was 'convinced that Russian organised crime is a threat for Switzerland. It is enough just to look at at the main criminal investigations being carried out by our [cantons] … and these investigations are only the tip of the iceberg'. He was speaking in the context of the commencement of legal proceedings against Sergei Mikhailov in Geneva. Mikhailov was suspected of heading Moscow's *Solntsvo* criminal network, linked to another network run by the Russian mobster Vyacheslav Ivankov, who was sentenced to 115 months in jail in New York in mid-1997. These facts, though, are nothing to be surprised about: for Soviet/Russian intelligence has been integrated with the 'mafia' classes in the 'former' Soviet Union for decades: the simplistic Western notion that the Russian 'mafia' is 'stand-alone', is disinformation. Russian organised crime <u>is</u> the KGB/GRU, and its financial assets are handled and moved by the **KGB** (or its successors: but the KGB has been relabelled many times since 1917 and all knowledgeable experts these days refer generically to the 'post'-Soviet intelligence community as the KGB or KGB/GRU).

Switzerland has historically been used by the Russians primarily to corrupt Swiss banking and to obtain information on others who use Swiss banks. The Russians (Soviets) themselves have historically preferred to use banking facilities provided in countries which are less obvious than Switzerland – such as Sweden, where Lenin is reported to have stopped to draw $50 million out of a Swiss bank to help finance his takeover of the fledgling Kerensky government and to line his own pockets at the same time. Incidentally, **all** the original Soviet revolutionaries lined their own pockets: when Stalin ordered his police chief, Genrikh Yagoda, to provide him with a list of their secret numbered bank accounts in Switzerland, Yagoda made the elementary mistake of assuming that he was Stalin's *only* source of information, and duly excluded the details of his own secret bank account in Switzerland. So, after insisting that he, Yagoda, must also comply, Stalin rewarded him also with a bullet through the head. The only senior figure he spared was Lenin's widow, Krupskaya, who was nevertheless compelled, on pain of a similar fate, to repatriate the 'assets of the revolution' which Lenin, its primary author, had himself salted away 'corruptly' in Swiss bank accounts.

It was not by accident that sizeable Soviet deception activity was directed at 'keeping the [spot]light of publicity away from our friends, the banks', as Jan Sejna explained to me on several occasions. And he should have known. For not only was Sejna firmly coupled to Soviet drug-trafficking and organised crime transactions, but he was also a member of a special deception committee which specialised in reviewing past deception operations and in formulating guidelines for the forthcoming five-year deception plans which had to be prepared for each successive Party Congress, building on prevailing State strategy and policy.

Those who have constructed this global criminalist empire with its integrated influence and corruption potential are not nice people to know. They are, self-evidently, quite ruthless, and typically make prospective or actual collaborators a type of offer that few can refuse: **'Which do you prefer, gold or lead?'** They are extremely well informed, thanks to a reliable and integrated global intelligence network; and those with whom they do business – financial institutions, investment houses, accountants and lawyers – are *careful to keep them well informed*. Privacy, ethics, and not passing on insider information, are practices that *do not apply to them* – only to normal investors; and these people are far from normal: *they do not fancy losing*, and they have no qualms about taking such steps as they may deem necessary to ensure and guarantee their 'success'. Bank records, secret decisions, State decisions, private legal matters, and so forth, are **open book to the international criminal élites** – of which a significant fraction consists, in reality, as we have seen, of representatives of sophisticated, cut-throat, foreign intelligence services.

It is **critical** for the survival of Western civilisation, and in order to slow down its rapid descent into pervasive, corrosive globalised criminality and corruption, which is the grim outlook for the 21st century, that Western countries begin, *even at this late hour*, to understand the true nature of the illegal drug crisis – which means **correctly analysing its sources, especially its political origins, its enabling mechanisms, and its related criminal dimensions.** Unless the nature and provenance of the challenge is finally understood, the appropriate strategy and tactics to address it will **never** be formulated. The drugs scourge continues to escalate because the measures so far developed to counter it do not take account of the geopolitical dimension – that is to say, of the malevolent, revolutionary intent which drives it.

As a consequence, the measures taken, in the United States, Britain and elsewhere, to address the scourge, have remained essentially irrelevant and ineffective, although law enforcement developments in Britain in late 1998 were decidedly encouraging. **The plague continues to spread because the West is the victim of a deliberate, sustained and relentless offensive planned and directed by enemy intelligence which Western policymakers appear not to begin, or care, to understand. Some Western leaders even share the ideological objectives of the perpetrators of the drugs offensive.** To make matters much worse, the *values* of many policymakers have been fatally eroded; and if one has no real values, one is not emboldened to defend anything at all, let alone with conviction and vigour. Policymakers too often stand for nothing and fall for everything – for every false assessment, for every piece of fashionable disinformation and for every diversionary tactic which is intended to add to the confusion and which clouds the truth: namely, that **the West has been targeted as an act of war, and is the victim of a sustained offensive**.

Obviously, the longer this perversity and blindness continue, the more powerful and insuperable will the forces which help to perpetuate this blanket offensive, become. Soon, they will wield almost total power in some Western countries. The European Union's collectivist structures, with their pork-barrel traditions and inclinations, are conspicuously vulnerable to drug-related corruption. Politicians and policymakers will continue to be blackmailed. Bankers will continue to enjoy the proceeds of laundered money and to turn a blind eye to what is happening. Many regulators and investigators will persevere fruitlessly with their narrow, legalistic perspectives. Much of the media will continue its inexcusable *de facto* conspiracy of silence, while some newspapers, such as *The Independent* in London, will continue perversely to promote drug liberalisation. A detailed search of the distasteful documents arising from the 'work' of the Office of the Independent Counsel, Kenneth W. Starr, in connection with the degraded behaviour of President Clinton and others in the White House, has revealed that two single-word mentions of drug-taking there, to which initial reference was made in a CNN broadcast, have been erased from it[16]. This suggests a perverse collusion – as though the drug dimension, like the parallel, and glaring, security issues arising from that hideous scandal, was somehow taboo.

Is this sort of official denial simply to be expected of a society which either openly or subconsciously recognises that it has been subverted, fleeced and duped – not least by those in whom our trust has had to be placed?

Corruption associated with drugs is *so corrosive* that, short of the targeted societies acquiring and wielding powers from which democracies, however inept and degraded, must naturally flinch, it will, sooner, rather than later, destroy democracy itself. Indeed, the very means which may now be needed to purge the West of the accumulated consequences of the drug offensive which has been waged against it for several decades, could themselves be considered a threat to democracy and freedom. No doubt the evil architects of the drug offensive understood **that** potential of their strategy only too well from the beginning. They recognised that democracies would never be able to summon the backbone to purge themselves of this evil, let alone that it originated as an act of warfare.

The war on drugs has not failed: it has never existed. **There has been no war on drugs in the United States.** And look at what has happened in countries like the Netherlands, where a permissive approach has proved a total, filthy and embarrassing failure – and in Switzerland, where a sudden deterioration in social conditions occurred in response to the introduction of more 'liberal' attitudes and provisions from late 1994 onwards. Like Cyprus, which Russian criminalists have colonised following the sudden arrival there in the late 1980s of the son of the former Soviet Foreign Minister, Andrei Gromyko[17], Switzerland remains a prime money-laundering centre for Soviet/Russian intelligence community-linked criminals.

Recalling what happened to Lenin's colleagues after Stalin had demanded the repatriation of the 'assets of the revolution' which they had salted away in Swiss bank accounts [*see pages 165-166*] a similar (perhaps, but not necessarily, less drastic?) fate may well have awaited (in late 1998) the so-called 'oligarchs' (KGB/GRU officers and top Communist Party officials and nomenklaturists), who had been given temporary custody of the 'assets of the state', as part of the façade of 'post'-Communism presented to the West in 1990-91. This represented a truly novel form of Lenin's model of 'state-controlled capitalism'; and at the time of going to press, that model was in the process of being rolled up or substantially 'modified', just like its predecessors – Lenin's notorious 'New Economic Policy' [NEP], or Khrushchev's 'peaceful coexistence', or Brezhnev's *détente* scams.

In Switzerland, though, at least the population has had more sense than its bewildered political and policymaking élites. On 29th November 1998, Swiss voters decisively rejected a dangerous and misguided proposal for the legalisation of marijuana, heroin and cocaine – turning aside arguments that an officially-managed narcotics network would help to curb drug-related crime. Swiss voters saw through these false arguments, which would promote drug use, wholesale corruption, scandal and decay – as has happened so conspicuously in Amsterdam, once a jewel of mediaeval architecture that has descended into an abyss of filth and decadence. Almost 74% of Swiss voters rejected the proposals in a referendum – in the face of Federal claims that cannabis was regularly consumed by some 500,000 people in the country. Provocatively, François Reusser, the spokesman for a committee which had sponsored the initiative 'for a sensible drug policy', argued not only that Swiss voters had 'reacted emotionally to the heroin aspect', but also that the outcome might have been different if marijuana smokers had gone to the polls[18].

That statement showed that these drug-pushers are not merely misguided: **they are also stupid:** anyone who knows anything about the effect of cannabis on the body, on the brain and on attitudes, would be aware that smokers who are half-stoned out of their minds, do not cooperate if they can avoid doing so. There is, however, no end to the perversity and folly of the drug liberalisation lobby: the committee, supported by Socialists, permissive doctors, lawyers [*see above*] and drug 'experts', insisted that it would embark forthwith upon a fresh campaign to soften-up Switzerland's voters and to collect the necessary number of signatures under the Swiss referendum system to be able to force yet another ballot on the legalisation of cannabis. For the standard *modus operandi* of the revolution is to try, try, and try again until the referendum system delivers the 'correct' answer.

Why, one is entitled to wonder, are such people *so anxious* to achieve this diabolical objective? Not, we may be sure, because they care a damn about the victims of drug abuse, or about their physical, mental and spiritual welfare. But rather because the revolution never, ever, surrenders its perverse agenda. And because those promoting this scourge are themselves corrupted beyond perdition, they wish to bring the whole world to perdition along with them. It is the solemn duty of those who know and understand this, to resist their nefarious activities with all determination and might – and for political and policymaking leaderships to cast aside all hesitation and to throw the resources of the state into this prospectively final battle for the survival of civilisation[19]. ∎

References to Chapter 12:

1. 'Student Use of Most Drugs Reaches Highest Level in Nine Years', Pride Press Release, 25 September 1996.

2. 'High Prevalence of Recent Cocaine Use and the Unreliability of Patient Self-report in an Inner-city Walk-in Clinic', Sally E. McNagny, MD, and Ruth M. Parker, MD, *JAMA*, February 26, 1992.

3. Office of National Drug Control Policy, *A Plan For Estimating the Number of 'Hardcore' Drug Users in the United States, Preliminary Findings,* Fall 1997.

4. Joseph D. Douglass Jr., 'Assessing Progress in the 'War on Drugs'', *Journal of Social, Political, and Economic Studies,* Spring, 1992.

5. See 'Lawyers 'launder drugs cash'', *The Daily Telegraph,* London, 24 November 1998; and 'Gangland money-laundering inquiry into City law firms', *The Guardian,* London, 24 November 1998.

6. 'Gangland money-laundering inquiry into City law firms', *The Guardian,* London, 24 November 1998, *op. cit.*

7. See U.S. Congress, House of Representatives, *Report of the Special Committee to Investigate*

Tax-exempt Foundations and Comparable Organisations (Washington, D.C.: U.S. Government Printing Office, December 16, 1954); René Wormser, *Foundations: Their Power and Influence* (New York: Devin-Adair Company, 1958; reprinted by Covenant House Books, Sevierville, TN, 1993); and William H. McIlhany II, *The Tax Exempt Foundations* (Westport, CN, Arlington House, 1980).

8. Gabriel G. Nahas, M.D., *Cocaine:The Great White Plague*, Ericksson, 1989.

9. That there has been no strategic revolutionary discontinuity (as opposed to a *Leninist* discontinuity) has been carefully explained by the genuine Soviet defector, **Anatoliy Golitsyn**, in his two famous books *New Lies for Old* [Dodd, Mead, New York,1984], and *The Perestroika Deception* [Edward Harle Limited, London and New York, 1995 and 1998]: see the leaflet enclosed at the back of this volume: and page VI. Contact the publishers of this book for details.

10. See, for instance, Yevgenia Albats, *The State Within a State*, Farrar, Straus and Giroux, New York, 1994.

Editor's Note: Care must nevertheless be exercised when considering the work of this author, who was granted privileged access to Soviet/Russian intelligence files and sources. Her work formed part of an extensive *corpus* of materials which served the purpose of 'explaining' the continued existence of the powerful KGB/GRU ('successors') in the context of the subsequently exposed deception that the Communist Party of the Soviet Union [CPSU] no longer existed. See *Soviet Analyst, passim*, and the CPUSA journal *Political Affairs*, for refutations of that lie, which is a central component of the strategic deception surrounding 'collapsible Communism'.

11. See *Note 17* below.

12. 'Criminalism', a word coined by the Editor for use in *Soviet Analyst*, means 'the use of organised criminality in the interests of strategy'.

13. Various UK press reports, 1st December 1998.

14. Gary Weill, 'The Mob on the Street', *Business Week*, 16th December 1996, page 93.

15. 'Swiss begin fraud trial of Russian mafia suspect', *The Washington Times*, 1 December 1998.

16. *Editor's Note:* The transcripts of Grand Jury testimony and related documents, contained in seven separate volumes published for the Office of the Independent Counsel, Kenneth W. Starr, in connection with the Clinton-Lewinsky scandal, were intensively examined for two known references to the taking of drugs in the White House. These had been explicitly referred to in a CNN broadcast monitored by Rachel Ehrenfeld, the respected drug and money-laundering expert. The Editor found that these references had been expunged from the formal printed record.

17. *Editor's Note:* Gromyko Jr, who opened up Cyprus as a leading Russian money-laundering centre for Russian criminalist funds in the late 1980s, has remained in Cyprus. His name is found in the Limassol telephone directory. Before surfacing in Cyprus, he served as head of the Soviet Academy of Sciences under Gorbachëv, a post from which he mysteriously resigned 'for health reasons'. This intelligence offers two insights of exceptional importance which support the analysis contained in the present work. *First*, it provides yet further confirmation of the lack of any true discontinuity between the Soviet régime and its 'successor' – to be added to the immense volume of evidence that the discontinuity was Leninist (i.e., deceptive, dialectical) in character, as explained by Anatoliy Golitsyn in *'The Perestroika Deception'* [*op. cit.*]; and *secondly*, it reinforces an impression which emerges from *Red Cocaine* – given that the KGB/GRU maintained its own budget financed in part by drug proceeds, thus becoming a 'state within a state' – that the sheer scale of drug operations had become so immense that they provided *their own justification* for discarding the rigid Stalinist model as a prerequisite for enabling criminalism to achieve its full potential as a mechanism for global revolution. This is not to say that this was the primary justification, but merely to argue that a proper understanding of the Soviet-Chinese drugs offensive is a necessary precondition for forming a coherent assessment of continuing Leninist world revolutionary strategy today.

18. 'Swiss voters turn down legalization of narcotics', *International Herald Tribune*, 30 November 1998.

19. See also Joseph D. Douglass Jr., *'KGB Alumni, Terrorism and Drug-trafficking'*, Conservative Review, August 1992, and 'Organised Crime in Russia: Who's Taking Whom to the Cleaners?', *Conservative Review*, May/June 1995.

INDEX

FURTHER READING SUGGESTIONS.

As the years have passed, more and more evidence has accumulated that the global drugs scourge is a *primary* instrument of the continuing Leninist World Revolution. No genuine discontinuity occurred in 1989-91 – merely a *Leninist* discontinuity, stage-managed by Soviet intelligence under a strategic collective fronted by Gorbachëv, whose long political pedigree stretches back to the 20th Congress of the Communist Party of the Soviet Union [CPSU] held in 1956, and the 22nd Congress of October 1961 at which the revitalised long-range strategy was approved ready for presentation to the Congress of 81 Communist Parties (6th December 1961). Nor has Western intelligence monitored changes in the general directions to the KGB/GRU from the continuing Communist Party of the Soviet Union [CPSU]†. Just about the only matter of substance which remains to be resolved is whether the Cubans were correct in their assessment, reported in this book, that targeted Western countries could be 'softened-up' with drugs for takeover from within, over a period of 35 years – or whether the Soviet opinion view that 50 or 60 years (two generations) would be necessary, was nearer the mark.

Red Cocaine provides the essential background information upon which the serious student of the continuing, relentless Leninist Revolution – which seeks fulfilment of the demented idea of World (Communist) Government, a sure recipe for global dictatorship – can profitably build a coherent understanding of the diabolical intentions of Lenin's heirs, whether operating overtly or, as Lenin himself advocated, 'working by other means' (i.e., covertly, as is more extensively the case today). One means of continuing a study perhaps begun with this book is advertised on the final page, where we provide owners of *Red Cocaine* with the opportunity to subscribe, at a specially reduced rate, to *Soviet Analyst* – the *only* journal which specialises exclusively in revealing and explaining the essence of the Soviet-Chinese strategic deception and long-term intelligence offensive against the West. In the pages of *Soviet Analyst*, you will find no 'politically correct' ideas whatsoever – not least because the origins of 'political correctness' have been definitively traced – in the pages of *Soviet Analyst* itself – to the bowels of the Soviet Communist Party apparatus.

For an essential perspective on the strategic deception offensive – the essence of which is *convergence* of the West with the East, but on the *East's* terms, not ours – the reader's attention is directed to *The Perestroika Deception: The World's Slide towards the 'Second October Revolution'* ['*Weltoktober*'], by the genuine Soviet defector, **Anatoliy Golitsyn** – famous author of the prophetic work, *New Lies for Old*. Mr Golitsyn's second book, originally published by Edward Harle Limited in 1995, and republished in 1998, is as prophetic as his first remarkable volume. *For details, see the reverse of the Soviet Analyst leaflet insert at the back.* ∎

† Among the sources to which any sceptic is directed for confirmation of the continuing existence of the Communist Party of the Soviet Union long after the alleged 'collapse of Communism' and of the USSR in 1991, are the October-November **1994** and April **1995** issues of the CPUSA's theoretical journal *Political Affairs*, which contain explicit references to the continuing existence and central importance of the CPSU. It 'coordinates' the operations of the fake 'post'-Soviet political parties. Western Governments, led by the British Foreign Office and the US State Department, chose prematurely to accept the demise of Communism and its associated pyramid of lies, including the new 'democratic' structures, at face value.

EDWARD HARLE LIMITED

STATEMENT OF POLICY OBJECTIVES.

The well-known Irish-American author, Dr Malachi Martin, a friend of the publisher of the present work, has described it as **'a Luciferian fog'**. We were discussing the remarkable inability of intelligent, well-informed people, especially among the policymaking and media communities, to understand the *Leninist* significance of the 'changes' which overwhelmed the world in 1989-91, and which have permeated everything that has happened on the political, cultural, institutional and religious stages ever since. Malachi's term is appropriate indeed. He was referring, of course, to the ever more apparently supernatural dimension of the evils the world faces today, of which the global drug scourge and the relentless attack on morality and society's institutions are the most pernicious symptoms.

The Luciferian fog that has enveloped the minds of many Western observers, politicians, bureaucrats and pressmen has, since 1989-91, all but obliterated objective reality, which has been replaced – by the intent of Soviet intelligence – with a structure of false images and lies. Communism collapsed all of a sudden. Soviet military power is no threat. (Did not the 'former' Soviet Union and its Warsaw Pact allies sign a document on 19th November 1990 entitled the 'Joint Declaration of Twenty-Two States' which pronounced that the signatories – the NATO countries and those of the 'former' Soviet Bloc – were 'no longer adversaries'?). The CPSU ceased to exist. The mafia in the 'former USSR' is 'stand-alone'. Free enterprise has 'taken root'. The 'former' Soviet Republics are truly independent. **All these assertions are either wholly false or, at best, deliberately misleading.**

What in fact happened should have been as clearly evident to scholars of the Russian language as to the few Western students of Lenin who remained appropriately sceptical that the sudden, orchestrated 'changes' could have been anything but manifestations of intelligence operations designed to deceive the West. For the true Leninist, dialectical meaning of *'perestroika'* is of course **'reformation'**, as in *'military* formation'. The whole world is now paying the price for its leaders' millennial failure to discern the deceptive revolutionary meaning of Gorbachëv's *'perestroika'*; and the destabilising consequences of this strategic failure will be a millstone round the necks of future generations.

Edward Harle Limited was established to publish books which address this failure and its evil legacy for Western civilisation. Its remit is to disregard 'political correctness' in all its insidious manifestations and to cut through the lies, the mis- and disinformation and the fantasies which bedevil our understanding of what is happening to our civilisation, and to explain *why* it is happening. For the only effective weapon of defence is **exposure**. ∎

CHRISTOPHER EDWARD HARLE STORY, London, January 1999.

SOVIET ANALYST

A REVIEW OF CONTINUING GLOBAL REVOLUTIONARY STRATEGY

Soviet Analyst, a strategic intelligence newsletter, provides a necessary antidote to fashionable, 'politically correct' and therefore confused thinking about revolutionary developments in the so-called 'former' Soviet Bloc countries, and their consequences for the whole world. Applying the analytical methodology explained by **Anatoliy Golitsyn** in *New Lies for Old* and *The Perestroika Deception*, this publication, established in 1972, reviews the activities of the continuing Leninist policymakers from the perspective of the implementation of their long-range strategy. It focuses on the rapid progress they are making, in the context of the false discontinuity of 1989-91 and the lie that Communism was 'abandoned', towards the realisation by stealth of Lenin's unchanged global revolutionary control objectives. For Lenin's heirs seek nothing less than the progressive weakening, decapitation and integration of nation states and their piecemeal replacement by intricate 'cooperative' cross-border and regional structures which are intended as part of the framework for World Government.

This 'New World *Social* Order' will, by definition, be **a global socialist dictatorship**. Those in the West – especially policymakers, bankers, churchmen and opinion-formers – who are collaborating *de facto* with the continuing revolutionaries in the furtherance of their continuing strategy of 'cooperation-blackmail' – whether *knowingly* as agents of influence, or *unwittingly* as what Lenin called 'useful idiots' – recklessly imperil the future of civilisation. They are providing a 'Red Carpet' for the revolutionaries who masquerade as their comrades-in-arms, but who secretly seek their downfall. Such collaborators disregard the evil reality of the contemporary 'war called peace'.

It was President George Bush who mindlessly recycled Gorbachëv's Leninist phrase 'New World Order'. Other purveyors of this revolutionary slogan include Karl Marx and Henry Kissinger, who has remarked: 'NAFTA is a major stepping-stone to the New World Order'. And speaking at a United Nations Ambassadors' Dinner on 14 September 1994, Mr David Rockefeller observed: 'This present "window of opportunity" during which a truly peaceful and interdependent world order might be built, will not be open for long. Already there are powerful forces at work that threaten to destroy all our hopes and efforts to erect an enduring structure of global cooperation'. Whether Mr Rockefeller and similar *de facto* collaborators *understand* where their 'Red Carpet' policy is leading, is open to legitimate debate; what is clear is that 'global cooperation' in practice means, *and is intended to mean*, 'global **collectivisation**' – the very *essence* of Communism.

In 1932, William Z. Foster, then leader of the Communist Party USA, wrote in his book *Toward Soviet America* that the objective of Communism was the establishment of a 'New World *Social* Order'. In 1985, two Soviet *apparatchiks*, F. Petrenko and V. Popov, explained [in *Soviet Foreign Policy, Objectives and Principles*, Progress Publishers, Moscow] that 'the transition step to the "New World Order" involves merging the newly captive nations into regional governments'. In 1942, Stalin wrote: **'As growing numbers of nations fall to the revolution, it becomes possible to reunite them under a Communist world régime'** [International Publishers, New York]. Lenin wrote that the Communists' aim was **'a future union of all nations in a single world... system'**. This objective remains unchanged. **'The point is'**, says Yelena Bonner, the widow of Andrei Sakharov, **'that the Communist goal is fixed and changeless – it never varies one iota from their objective of world domination, but if we judge them only by the direction in which they** *seem* **to be going,** *we shall be deceived'*.

Soviet Analyst, directed by **Christopher Story**, publisher of this book, circulates world-wide among official agencies, embassies and, professional analysts, the diplomatic profession, intelligence communities and informed observers. It is published on a prepaid annual subscription basis [for ten issues per Volume/series] by **World Reports Limited**, London and New York. **To subscribe at the specially reduced rate for owners of *Red Cocaine*, complete the enclosed order form and mail it in the reply envelope.** *To fax your order, dial:* +44 [0]20-7233 0185 [London]; 212-679 1094 [New York]. ∎